Getting to Lean

Transformational Change Management

Lawrence M. Miller

LAWRENCE M. MILLER

MILLER MANAGEMENT PRESS, LLC

ANNAPOLIS, MARYLAND, 2013
LMMILLER@LMMILLER.COM
WWW.MANAGEMENTMEDITATIONS.COM

ISBN # 978-0-578-12181-9

Printed in the United States of America

1. Organizational Change Management

2. Leadership

3. Industrial Organization

4. Health Care Management

Version 2.0

TABLE OF CONTENTS

ACKNOWLEDGEMENT

Those most deserving of acknowledgement are my many wonderful clients who trusted me enough to allow me to co-create transformational change in their organizations. My most important learning is from those opportunities in which I could see what worked, and what did not, in creating transformational change.

Before I sold my previous firm I had a wonderful partner, Jennifer Howard, and dozens of incredible consultants who all participated in our shared learning. Together we explored both team-based continuous improvement and socio-technical systems design, what we called *Whole-System Architecture*, as a methodology to build high performing organizations. In particular I would like to thank Duane Cross, Alan Wilgus, Helene Uhlfelder, and Will Jones among others who helped think through the whole-system methodology and demonstrate its power to create large scale and sustainable change.

Many authors and friends have helped me formulate the method presented in this book. I must especially thank Norman Bodek who introduced me to several of the architects of the Toyota system and to the writing on socio-technical systems. Those two bodies of knowledge set me on a path that leads to this book. My exposure to Honda America Manufacturing, largely thanks to Mr. Yoshino, President, the then Executive Vice President, Scott Whitlock, gave me an opportunity to understand the workings of a very different system than those common at the time.

INTRODUCTION

No theory or method of management has had the impact that the Toyota Production System, or lean management, has had over the past fifty years. Norman Bodek first brought its architects, Taiichi Ohno and Shigeo Shingo, to the United States and translated their books to English. It was then popularized by James Womack[1], Jeffery Liker[2] and others as lean management or lean culture. Lean management has become today's standard of management for most organizations whether in manufacturing, healthcare or other sectors of the economy. Lean management has repeatedly proven its effectiveness to improve both efficiency and customer satisfaction. But the implementation of lean management has proven to be problematic for many companies. Managers understand the idea of lean, but too often don't recognize the significance of the transformation required in both behavior and organizational system, and too often change is not sustained. What is often missing is a method of change that engages managers and employees and makes it their own. This book presents a method for transforming the entire system of the organization - its architecture and culture. It is a process of co-creation that instills ownership and commitment.

When many companies begin their lean journey they may not realize that both Honda and Toyota started their operations in the United States and other countries outside of Japan with a green-field site where they designed the plant layout, organized the equipment, aligned their suppliers, hired all of the managers and associates and trained them in their way. They created a unified *whole-system* whose parts were all aligned to the same philosophy. They were not changing a culture, overcoming resistance, or redesigning

---

[1] Womack, James P., Jones, Daniel T., Roos, Daniel. *The Machine that Changed the World.* New York, Free Press, 1990

[2] Liker, Jeffrey K. *The Toyota Way.* New York, McGraw Hill, 2004.

existing facilities. However, this is entirely different than the challenge facing most companies. Toyota and Honda succeeded because they had a unified, whole-system, which they built over time and for which they had common understanding and commitment at every level of the organization. In that sense, they had it easy.

Most companies implementing lean today are focused on tools and techniques. Too often they have disaggregated the whole-system and have focused on small pieces of it. They have implemented 5S, just-in-time, work teams or PDCA problem-solving groups. But the old culture is firmly embedded in the systems, structure and symbols that remain untouched and guarantee resistance to change. The most common cause of failure is the failure of the leadership to address the need to align the systems, structure and symbols to the desired culture.

***

> About twenty years ago I was invited to the Merck Cherokee Pharmaceuticals plant in Danville, Pennsylvania to discuss the possibility of assisting them to create a team-based culture. I remember that first meeting very well because I drove through a blinding snow storm to get there. The meeting at the Pine Barn Inn was attended by all the senior managers of the plant as well as the union president and his senior officers. They agreed to begin a process of co-creating their future organization. The senior team, with the union, who together formed a steering team, wrote a design charter specifying the goals and boundaries. Design teams were formed and they analyzed the work flow and the social system. They then designed the teams around the work flow. But the design didn't end there. It included a competency model for team members and qualification for "star points," skills for which team members would be paid. It redefined management jobs and titles. It also included a plant wide bonus plan by which all salaried and hourly employees shared an annual bonus based on the same metrics which they tracked throughout the year. The design included training for teams at every level, including the senior management team. It included sharing of all significant information on plant performance.
>
> A couple years ago I was asked to return to Danville and assess the state of the process and help refresh the teams, particularly for managers who were new to the plant. The team process and culture had been sustained for eighteen years, and through five changes in

plant manager. The union president, Ed Vallo, enjoyed pointing out that he had to "educate" each new plant manager on the process.

The point of this story is that significant culture change can be achieved and sustained. Would this same change have been sustained over twenty years if it were merely the idea and initiative of management? Probably not. Would it have been sustained if the design had been presented by consultants and then sold to the employees, rather than facilitated and co-created by them? I suspect not. Would it have been sustained if it was only the formation of teams and systems of training, information and motivation were left unchanged? I doubt it. The managers and employees of the Cherokee Plant had co-created and developed shared ownership of the process. Together they modified the design as they experimented and learned. Most important, they understood and addressed the whole-system of the organization. They agreed on cultural values and they built the organizational system around those values. That is the process presented in this book.[3]

***

Whole-Systems

The human body is a *whole-system* comprised of separate organs or sub-systems that fit together as a brilliantly unified interdependent architecture. The heart relies on the lungs for oxygen and they both rely on the digestive system for nourishment. And, they all rely on the nervous system for information and instructions. If you remove any of these sub-systems from the whole, it will quickly die. If one organ of the body becomes damaged or sick it will quickly impact the functioning of other organs. Our national culture and economy operate by similar laws. We have principles stated in a Constitution and we have laws defining the functioning of institutions. Our education system, financial system and justice system are all sub-systems, organs, of the body of the national culture. Damage one and you damage the whole.

---

[3] A number of excellent managers nurtured and helped the system evolve over the years, particularly Mike Rocci, George Santos and Justin Noll, as well as a competent team of internal consultants, including Christine Moyer.

Organizations are similar whole-systems. The financial, communications or information systems, and all the systems affecting people, are all subsystems of the organization's culture. Lean management is also a whole-system. Components of lean management most often die like fish out of water because they depend on the other organs for their survival. You cannot implement a lean management structure, with strong teams at every level, without changing the decision process, the information flow, and the reward systems. You cannot implement just-in-time work flow without changing the information flow, the decision-making process and without redefining jobs at the first level. And, you cannot implement lean culture without changing the functions and structure of management. These are all organs of the same body.

Organizations, whether public or private, are living and changing bodies. Most will fail, sooner or later. The cause of failure is rarely the external threat, the attack of the barbarian or the fierce economic competitor. The cause is most often an act of suicide, self-inflicted by one's own hand. Civilizations most often decline when there is an internal loss of unity, of common vision and faith in the future – companies do the same. *Whole-system architecture* is designed to create unity of purpose, values and alignment of systems and structure to strategy.

Disruptive Environments Require Transformational Change

Sustainable organizations adapt to their environment and when that environment changes, they too must change. Every organization lives on a landscape, and as every architect knows, the structure must be drawn taking into account the soil and the surroundings.

Bureaucratic organizations can only survive in a world in which the external environment is slow to change. Fifty years ago that was possible. It is no longer. Most industries are affected by disruptive technologies or markets. Many of those technologies are clustered around the Internet and related marketing channels. But there are also disruptive technologies that impact how things are made and designed. Print-on-demand technology, for example, has enabled ordering a book on Amazon one day; the very book you ordered being printed that night; and shipped out the next day, to arrive at your door the following day. That has enabled a revolution in marketing channels, not to mention the impact of e-readers. Borders, Brentanos and other book chains have disappeared and the only remain chain of bookstores, Barnes & Noble, at the time of this writing appears to have a very uncertain future. In almost every industry companies are confronted by disruptive technologies. Those disruptions require dramatic changes in internal processes and organization. Most lean implementation efforts fail to account for the landscape. While they may improve efficiency, at the same time they may do little to improve the capabilities that will be needed for survival on the shifting landscape. What is required is transformative and holistic change. The whole-system architecture methodology presented in this book is exactly that.

Life-Cycles, Bureaucracy, and Transformation

All living things go through transformations from one stage of life to the next. Organizations, like people, are not robotic or predetermined in their transitions. However, just as one can predict behavioral tendencies of a two year-old or thirteen year-old, one can also predict that an organization will go through life-cycle stages. Each stage requires transformations in the design of the organization's systems and structure, just as different human life stages require different structures to our lives.

As the American automobile industry aged and grew too comfortable in the middle of the last century it developed increasingly complex structure, with increasing levels of management and increasing divisions across functions. The silos and rigidity of the walls between silos, like the hardening of the human arteries, is a natural result of aging. In *The Machine that Changed the World*[4] the authors tell the story of a door lock engineer who worked designing door locks for twenty-seven years. At the same time, across town, in the manufacturing engineering department there was an engineer who worked on door lock manufacturing process for twenty years - one designing what it is; the other designing how it will be made. How often did they meet? Never! That is how high or thick the silos were at the old GM. That is an astounding failure of organization design!

In the same book the authors describe the process by which General Motors and Honda designed similar cars, the GM10 platform and the Honda Accord. In both cases *"A number of functional departments – marketing, power train engineering, body engineering, chassis engineering, process engineering,*

---

[4] Womack, James; Jones, Daniel T; and Roos, Daniel. *The Machine that Changed the World.* Free Press, New York, 1990.

and factory operations – must collaborate intensively over an extended period of time to develop the new car successfully."[5] But how this was accomplished at GM and Honda were entirely different. In both cases a cross functional team was assembled comprised of individuals from each of the functional organizations. But there the similarity ended. In the GM case each employee was concerned with his career ladder in his functional organization. The team leader had the power of persuasion, but not the authority and decision-making power to bring the work of the functional groups in line with the needs of the design of the new car. After many delays the team leader quit in frustration. It took two more team leaders and several years to bring the car to market. During that time Honda had produced two generations of Accords and both sold well. The sales of the GM 10 were disappointing.

At Honda the team leader of the Accord design team reported directly to the CEO. It was clear to all that there was no more important executive and no more important group in the company than the team designing the new Accord. This team leader had the power of authority, to make decisions, and it was the job of the functional organizations to meet the needs of this team. At GM the team leader was a coordinator. At Honda the team leader had decision-making authority and control. The roles and the understanding of the teams were entirely different. One represented the classic problems of bureaucracy and the other the understanding of lean.

In an independent study Professor Kim Clark at Harvard did a comparative analysis of Japanese, European and American auto product development.[6] He found that a totally new Japanese car required 1.7 million hours of engineering and forty-six months on average. In contrast, U.S. and European companies required 3 million hours and sixty months.

The differences cannot simply be explained by pointing to a PDCA or continuous improvement cycle. Nor can it be loosely attributed to culture. It is more than that. It is the design of the work process, the organization around the process, and the structure of decision-making authority. In other words, it is the real stuff of organizations and that must be deliberately designed! And that is particularly true if your company has developed the normal rigidity of bureaucracy.

---

[5] Ibid. p. 106.

[6] Kim B. Clark, W. Bruce Chew and Takahiro Fujimoto, "Product Development in the World Auto Industry," Brookings Papers on Economic Activity, No.3, 1987.

The damaging effect of bureaucratic structures is not restricted to old-line manufacturing companies. The development of the iPod at Apple Computer and the lost opportunity at Sony provides a similar example. Sony had a music division and contracts with a larger number of the most popular bands and artists. They were a dominant force in the music business. They had another division that had created the Walkman, a personal device to carry and play music. They had a computer division producing personal computers. They even had software to sell music online. And, at the time, they realized that Napster and other free music download websites were destroying the profitability of their business. It was out of control. Within the Sony brand they had every piece required to solve the problem. However, the three big and powerful divisions fought among themselves and could not collaborate to develop a solution.

At Apple Computer there was a leader who understood disruptive technology. It wouldn't be unfair to call Steve Jobs the Crown Prince of disruptive technologies. At that time Apple was merely a personal computer company. They produced no personal or portable devices. But, Jobs loved music. He understood that the personal computer could be the "music hub." He personally led the charge to develop the iPod and there were no warring divisions within Apple. Jobs personally met with music royalty including Bob Dylan, Bono, the head of Universal, Sony and other music studios. He went to Japan and found the disc drive at Toshiba that could hold a thousand tunes. He developed an end-to-end solution that met the needs of the artists, the music studios, his own company, and most important, the customers who loved music! He practically lived with Jony Ive, the chief designer, whose aesthetic sense of elegant simplicity for not only the device, but even the packaging, created a unique brand image and advantage. The combination of iTunes software for your computer, the iTunes store, and the iPod, met the needs of all key stakeholders. It was a victory of seamless integration. It eliminated waste in every component of the music delivery process. It could only have been achieved by an organization devoid of silos and a leader who understood the advantage of a seamless experience by the end user.[7]

Each of these examples demonstrates the competitive advantage or disadvantage of organizational structure and systems. Lean management and culture cannot be achieved without the alignment of the whole-system of your organization.

---

[7] Isaacson, Walter. *Steve Jobs*. New York: Simon & Schuster, 2011. P. 417-433.

From Birth to Death and Revolution

It is obvious that an early entrepreneurial company has a very fluid and flexible organization, if it has any organization at all. With growth comes the requirement of specialization both in core functions such as research, engineering, manufacturing and marketing; and, with that specialization comes increasing administrative processes, accounting, human resource and information systems, with increasing definition and complexity. And, with the growth of those administrative systems comes the risk and burden of bureaucracy.[8]

Thomas Jefferson said that *"I hold that a little rebellion, now and then, is a good thing, and as necessary in the political world as storms in the physical."* What did he mean by this? He meant that from time to time we need to rethink how we do things; rethink our system and organization and question whether it meets the needs of the time in which we live. This is as true for every company as it is true for a nation. The development of rigid bureaucracy is a natural result of aging, whether in government or business.

Most entrepreneurial companies are born with the inspiration of an idea and faith in that idea. And, that idea is generally a response to a challenge, large or small. That person, like the founders of civilizations, are most often better at spreading "The Word" than they are at organizing people and processes. The entrepreneurial stage is when the organization is creatively responding to the challenges from its environment. The process of growth in companies, like in civilizations, is one of creative response, followed by a success, and then a higher level challenge requiring a higher level response.[9] Neither companies nor civilizations emerge in the absence of challenge and the failure to recognize a challenge may be the cause of collapse. As Arnold Toynbee said, *"We have rejected the view that civilizations are apt to be generated in environments – physical or human – which offer unusually easy conditions of life to Man." "We have now perhaps established decisively the truth that ease is inimical to civilization. The results of our investigation warrant the*

---

[8] I have described the process of rise and fall, integration and disintegration is more detail in *Barbarians to Bureaucrats – Corporate Life Cycle Strategies*. New York, Fawcett Columbine. 1990.

[9] Toynbee, Arnold. *A Study of History*. Cambridge University Press, London. 1934.

proposition that, the greater the ease of the environment, the weaker the stimulus towards civilization which that environment administers to Man."[10]

It is this mechanism of challenge-response that leads to successive stages of growth in organizations and each stage requires some degree of redesign of the organization's architecture.

As organizations grow, the dominance of the personality who founded the organization must give way to the dominance of principles and process. All great companies and countries are dominated by principle rather than personality. It is an immature country or company in which the personality of leaders is more important than the principles and processes that govern the behavior of its members.

The first point of failure in this life-cycle is the failure of this transition – establishing principles that will outlive the personality and form firmer ground upon which the structure of specialized functions and defined processes can be built.

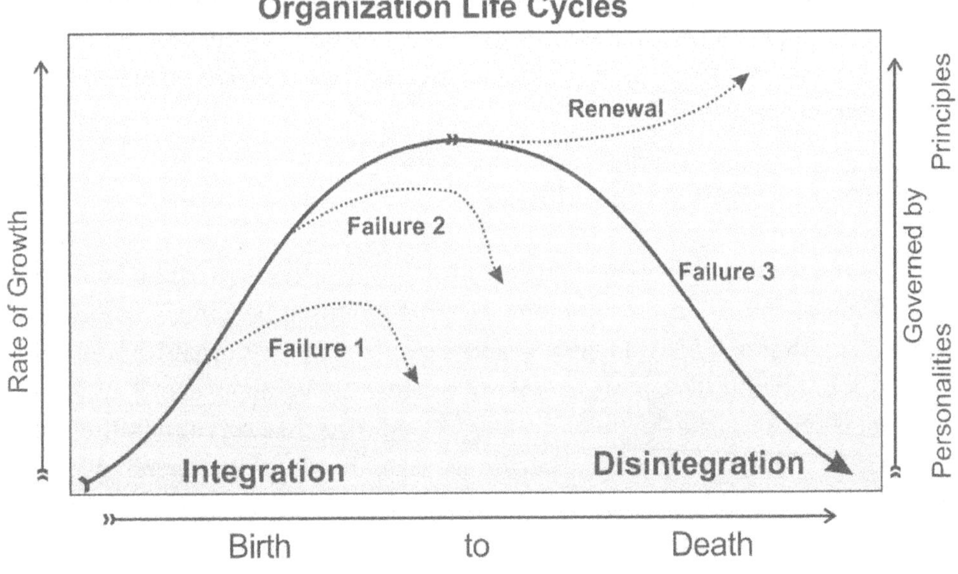

The second most common failure point is when those systems of specialization, both in core and enabling processes, become dominant in the life of the organization and its members owe their loyalty to the marketing or manufacturing organization and not to the whole. This is when the

[10] Ibid, Volume 2, page 31.

organization becomes focused on making legs, rather than making chairs and the processes of disintegration sets in prematurely.

Assuming the leadership of the organization achieves integration of these specialized functions, the organization will progress toward maturity. But, maturity has its own risks. With maturity comes security, wealth, and what Arnold Toynbee called *"a condition of ease"* or the failure of the mechanism of *"challenge and creative response"*[11] and it is then that the leaders fail to recognize new challenges on the landscape and lose their creativity, relying on yesterday's successful response but now in the presence of new challenges, and mechanically pull the same lever faster and harder but with decreasing effect. It is the failure of creativity, the worship of heroes of the past rather than the present, which signals the death of a culture and the beginning of disintegration. It is this loss of creativity and will, the internal act of suicide, which is the most frequent cause of disintegration and death.

Unlike in human life, the death of organizations is not inevitable, only likely. There is free will. The natural process of aging in organizations can only be averted by the willingness to conduct your own internal revolution from time to time. Whole-system architecture is about conducting your own controlled internal revolution. It is about instituting a creative response to the challenges of this day.

Socio-Technical Systems

When I first read an article on socio-technical systems (STS) by Lou Davis it was one of those "ah-ha" moments when something becomes obvious and useful. The theory of STS is simple and elegant. In every organization there are work or technical systems (the work process or "value-stream") and there are social systems, the "people" systems or culture that surrounds the work process. In most organizations these have been designed independently and are misaligned, producing sub-optimal performance. Socio-technical system[12] design, or what I choose to call *whole-system architecture*, is a change methodology as well as a way of looking at the nature of the organization. STS or whole-system design is based on a process of co-creation, in which the stakeholders in the process together analyze the current state and design a

---

[11] Ibid. Vol. 2, page 271.

[12] Pasmore, William A. *Designing Effective Organizations: The Sociotechnical Systems Perspective*. New York; John Wiley & Sons, 1988.

future ideal state.[13] The theory is that by having managers and employees who work in the system, customers, and suppliers engaged together, not only will the future design be more effective for all; it will also gain their ownership and commitment. That ownership and commitment will lead to successful implementation. This is the principle of co-creation and it is a key element in successful change management.

About a month after I read the Lou Davis article[14] I was presenting a consulting proposal to Moody's Investor Services in New York and I couldn't help myself. I proposed that we do an STS intervention to redesign their work system. They bought it and miraculously it worked. Over a twenty year period after that my consultants and I did more than one hundred STS or whole-system architecture projects.[15] When I became involved at Honda it was very obvious that their system was a dramatically different technical and social system than those I was used to. They did not use that language, but they didn't use "lean" language either. I simply incorporated the lessons from Honda (see Appendix: The Honda Way) into our whole-system architecture projects as a model of what an alternative system might look like.

Most things that are useful are essentially simple. Socio-technical systems are simple. The tractor, car, airplane, telephone, the cell phone, the Internet, the iPad, are all technical things that have altered the prevailing technical systems. And, they all have dramatically altered social relationships. They have altered how children learn their ABC's, how we communicate with family, how we find dates and life partners, and how we buy or sell houses and cars. People change with technology and technology changes to meet the needs of people – it is all one big socio-technical-economic system. And, every factory, office, or hospital is a socio-technical-economic system. It's that simple. But, within our organizations change often results in misaligned social and technical systems.

---

[13] Cherns, A. (1976). The principles of sociotechnical design. Human Relations, 29(8), 783-792.

[14] Davis, L.E. Evolving Alternative Organization Designs: Their Sociotechnical Bases, Human Relations, 39 (3), 261-273.

[15] To be clear, for twenty years I owned and managed a consulting firm, the Miller-Howard Consulting Group, with approximately twenty consultants. The "more than one hundred" number represents the work of the entire team of consultants and we agreed that it was a conservative estimate since each consultant did approximately one project a year.

In writing this book I am drawing on two primary strains of knowledge. The first is previous systems thinking. The second is lean management and the study of the Toyota Production System (TPS). Proponents of TPS/lean are too often focused on tools and too infrequently focused on the system. My purpose is to bring the best of these knowledge streams together to help you redesign your whole-system to lean standards.

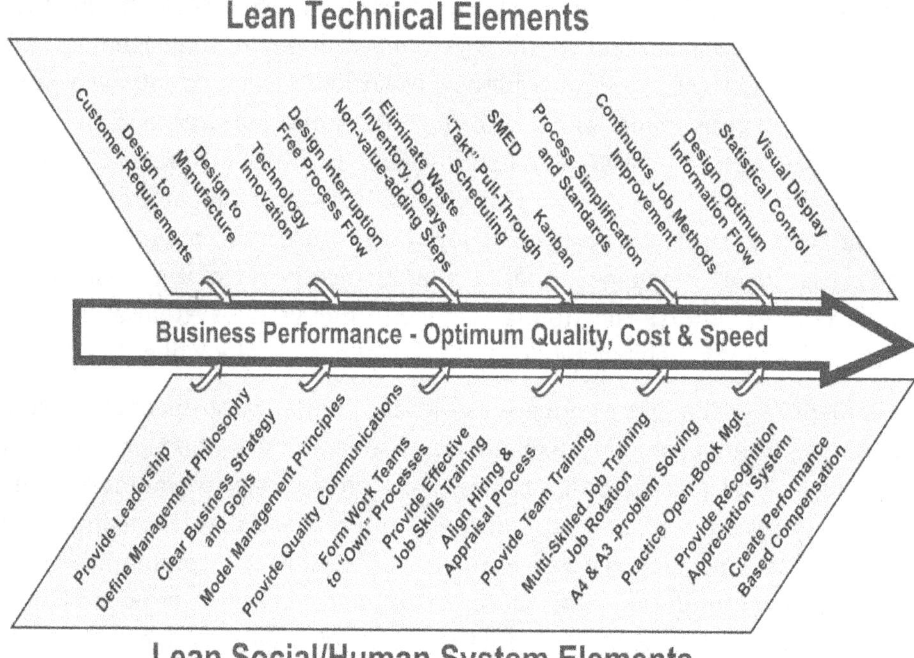

Let me be clear about the theory and method presented in this book. Every book on management is built on a stream of learning and the work of previous thinkers. This book builds methods and concepts from all of the following change management methods:

- Socio-technical system design.[16]
- Systems-thinking.[17]
- Idealized design. [18]

---

[16] Trist, E. (1981). The Evolution of Socio-Technical Systems. In A. a. Van de Ven, *Perspectives on Organizational Design and Behavior*. New York: Wiley Interscience.
[17] Senge, Peter M. *The Fifth Discipline.*, New York: Doubleday, 1990.
[18] Ackoff, R. L., Magidson, J., & Addison, H. J. *Idealized Design.* Upper Saddle River, NJ: Prentice Hall. 2006.

- Interactive planning[19]
- Re-engineering[20]
- Appreciative inquiry[21]
- High-performance organization design[22]

All of the above theories and change management models have the following in common: First, they all seek to achieve significant, transformational change in the culture and capability of an organization. Second, they all view the organization as a dynamic open-system interacting with its environment and engaged in adaptation to that environment. Third, they all view the organization not only as a mechanical system, but as a human or social system, that performs best when the psychology of humans is taken into account in the design of the system.

What I am attempting in this book is to incorporate the lessons of all of these theories into a methodology I call Whole-System Architecture (WSA) focused on creating the lean organization and system.

The First Principle of Change Management

Whole-system architecture is a change management methodology that recognizes the organization as a living, organic whole that must change in a coordinated way; and to do so in a way that will maximize the commitment and ownership of those who live within the organization. The first principle of managing change is that *we are committed to that which we help to create*. Conversely, we will not be committed to something that is imposed on or sold to us, no matter how good the sales pitch.

There is what I call the Habitat for Humanity principle. Habitat for Humanity builds homes for the disadvantaged. They learned an important lesson about sustainability. They do not just build a home and give it to a

---

[19] Ackoff, Russell L. Re-*Creating the Corporation: A Design of Organizations for the 21st century*. New York:Oxford University Press, 1999.

[20] Hammer, M. and Champy, J. A.: *Reengineering the Corporation: A Manifesto for Business Revolution*, New York: Harper Business Books, 1993.

[21] Cooperrider, David L. *Appreciative Inquiry: Rethinking Human Organization Toward a Positive Theory of Change*. Champaign, IL: Stipes Publishing, 2000.

[22] Lytle, William O. *Designing a High-Performance Organization*. Clark, NJ: Block, Petrella, Weisbord, 1998.

family. It is a requirement that members of the family must participate in the building of the house. They hammer nails, carry wood and use the paint brush. By doing this they are far more likely to care for and maintain that home. Their participation makes the home and the community more sustainable. The exact same thing is true of change within organizations. Habitats mission statement says *"We view our work as successful when it transforms lives and promotes positive and lasting social, economic and spiritual change within a community; when it is based on mutual trust and fully shared accomplishment; and when it demonstrates responsible stewardship of all resources entrusted to us."* [23] This would be a good mission statement for almost any corporate change process. It must not only move equipment around and speed a production process. It must transform the lives of those within the organization. It must promote positive and lasting social, as well as economic change. And, those who live in the house, the organization, must participate in creating that design. Then you will have commitment.

Consultants may be useful to guide the process and to ask questions that can help your people think creatively. However, it must never be the consultant's design. He or she must never own it. It must be owned by those who will then implement it. It is their house and they will live in it.

Whole-system architecture presents a useful metaphor. When you walk into a great cathedral your head goes back and you look up into the heavens of stained glass and flying buttresses. You marvel at the construction. And your first impulse is to focus on the physical thing of the structure. But, the architect had an end in mind. The architect understood that the nature of physical space, the interior structure of the cathedral, has an effect on the human spirit, emotions, and possibly behavior. You feel that effect when you walk into the cathedral, regardless of your religious views. The structure of your organization also has an effect on your spirit, emotions and behavior. But in most cases the effect is unintentional and often stifling, rather than uplifting of the human spirit. Our organizations need more than engineering; they need architecture.

STS and Lean Systems - The Missing Link

STS theory and methodology was the basis for all of the early self-directed team plants in the United States. The Gaines Topeka pet food plant

---

[23] See Habitat for Humanity web site.

was one of the first. Proctor and Gamble and Corning designed many of their plants using STS methods and the team process became the norm. For the most part these plants were successful; but, not in all cases. Similarly, many lean implementations fall far short of expectations or even completely fail. There is a common cause and it has to do with understanding the "whole-system."

As my associates and I implemented projects we increasingly recognized the complexity of organizational systems. For example, we designed Shell Oil Company's deep water operations in the Gulf of Mexico, Corning's Fiber Optics manufacturing, several airline operations, and several banks. These were not simple operations. They were complex systems that included a great deal of information processing, relationships with contractors, high levels of uncertainty and risks. We realized that they were not only social and technical systems; they were economic or financial systems. That should be obvious, but it is not always taken into account in change management. It became apparent that the failure to take into account the flow of money into and out of the system may make the design of the social or technical system fail or not be sustainable.

One of the most well-known cases of STS was Volvo's very progressive work system at their Uddevalla plant in western Sweden.[24] The plant was designed by joint union-management committees and they designed the system for small teams of eight workers to assemble an entire car. The moving assembly line that determined work speed in a traditional assembly plant was abandoned. In the Volvo system a work team controlled their own pace of work; they were all trained to do all jobs on the team and they could decide when to rotate jobs within the team. According to STS theory, this was ideal. They assembled four cars per day per work team. That amounted to a productivity rate of about twenty work hours per car. The problem was that Honda and Toyota were assembling cars in less than twelve work hours per car and every other auto company was rushing to adopt the lean model that enabled this rate of production. And, unfortunately, the Volvos being produced at that time were not of high quality. Their quality ratings were significantly below those of Honda or Toyota. After four years of operating this production system Volvo closed the plant in 1994. It is now a warehouse.

---

[24] Sandberg, Ake, Editor. Enriching Production –Perspectives on Volvo's Uddevalla Plant as an Alternative to Lean Production. Digital Edition. Avebury, Stockholm, 2007.

Enter the Economic System

Does this mean that STS is a bogus theory, or that developing a work system that is humane and provides for an enriched work experience is a bad theory? Or, that the method of high participation design is not workable? Absolutely NOT! I have done this successfully many times. What it does mean is that if you focus only on the work system and social system it is possible to design a system that is not economically viable.

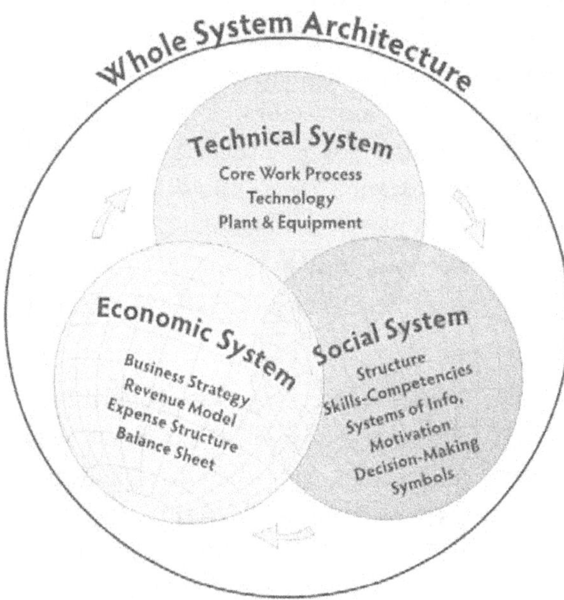

Every business enterprise is an economic system. Hospitals and non-profit organizations are also economic systems. Money comes into the system first as capital, and then revenues. Money goes out in the form of expenses and goods produced. The revenue must exceed the expenses and input value of the goods produced. In other words, the system must add value in economic terms. This is no news to anyone running a business. But it is news to some who implement both lean and STS systems. In both cases they can be designed without regard to the economics of that system.

> ***In order to design the organization one must design and align the technical, social and economic systems together. If either of the three is not aligned with the others it is not a sustainable system.***

The same model can be applied to any institution and even a country. The whole-system architecture process must begin with an analysis of the current state: work system (cycle time, eliminating waste, variances, etc.); an analysis of the culture or social system (the empowerment, decision-making, competencies, motivation, etc.); and an analysis of the money flow. Based on that analysis, design teams then design the future.

When to Use Whole-System Architecture:

We have been introduced to many problem-solving models as the solution to all ills. Whether it is Six-Sigma's DCMAIC, or the Shewart Cycle of PDCA or PDSA, or the A3 problem-solving model, they are all predicated on the idea that there is a specific problem to be solved. Why do you think there are so many problems? Could it be that there is something more fundamentally wrong?

Maybe there is something wrong with the nature of the system. In healthcare we know that if the basic diet and patterns of exercise, the basic system of managing input into the body, is deficient, solving each illness is not the real solution. It is masking the problem.

Whole-system architecture is about pro-actively creating the future organization and system. It asks, "Given the future environment, the technology, the market and social changes, what do we need to be like in the future and how do we create that future?" It is designing a fundamentally different house than the one we are living in. Yes, there is a "problem" but you won't find the problem by fixing every rash and headache. The problem is that the design of the organization and its capabilities is not suited to its current or future needs.

Paths to Lean Implementation	
Whole-System Architecture	Continuous Improvement
✓ Focused on Strategy ✓ Rethinking the Whole-System ✓ Big System Change ✓ Questioning why we do everything ✓ Changes in both work systems and social systems ✓ Involves all stakeholders including the customer ✓ Design with the changing landscape in mind ✓ Rethinking Organization Structure	✓ Focused on Problem-Solving ✓ Change within a stable system ✓ Gradual & small improvements ✓ Questioning how we can best do something. ✓ Focused on a Work Process ✓ Done by those doing the work at every level ✓ Process owners experiment and improve ✓ How to improve work within the current structure

Whole-system architecture is a process designed to create significant change in the culture and work processes of an organization and produce significant improvement in performance. If your organization has a relatively traditional culture, you need WSA to engage your people, gain understanding and commitment to change. If you only need to make small improvements, to engage people in continuous improvement, you do not need WSA. If you need to align your organization and culture to your strategy, you need WSA. If the organization creates walls and barriers to the flow of work, you need WSA. If the market place is changing significantly and your organization needs to respond to changing technologies, customer demands, or regulation, you need WSA. And, if you have had difficulty implementing change, gaining commitment from your own managers and employees, you need WSA.

WSA and CI are both good! The question is do you have a platform, the culture, structure, systems and processes upon which you can build the gradual continuous improvement process? If you do, proceed to that process.[25] If not, please keep reading.

Lean Organizational Strategy

The essence of strategy is recognizing the threats and opportunities presented by the external environment; and, then responding to those in a way that aligns the organizational systems to meet those challenges. In other words, if the future of marketing our products is going to be through the Internet and social media, with single day response and overnight delivery to customers, virtually every system in the organization needs to be aligned to achieve the success of that process. The old system will likely not have that capability. Continuous improvement will not get you there. Intentional redesign will.

There are two words that are keys to strategic thinking: these are *adaptation* and *alignment.* The failure of organizations to adapt to the dynamics of the external landscape and the failure to align internal systems and behavior both result in wasted energy. They both cause friction - friction between the organization and the environment; and, friction between members of the organization. Whether it is in a mechanical system or in a human system, friction is wasted energy.

---

[25] See *The Team Guide to Continuous Improvement*. Miller, Lawrence M. Miller Management Press, 2013.

ADAPTATION

All living things adapt or die. It matters little whether the living thing is a plant, a bug, or a company. As the environment changes they must change with it. Each living thing is a sub-system of a larger system and the larger system demands adaptation. Humans living in northern climates developed the engineering and construction skills they needed to survive in cold winters, while those close to the equator didn't waste their energy in that pursuit. As the environment changes, you will adapt or die. Too many companies are too slow to adapt.

Henry Ford's model of simplification of production started with the assumption that you could have the Model T *"in any color you want, as long as it is black."* That worked for a while. But then other companies offered cars at equal quality and cost in multiple colors. Ford's business declined until he adapted to the changing demands of the market place. Steve Jobs, in one of his numerous mistakes, believed that there was no reason for personal computers to display images in color or to have a hard drive. That worked for a while... and then he chose to adapt rather than die. The history of business is the history of companies adapting to changes in the external landscape or dying. As Dr. Deming said *"You don't have to change. Survival is not mandatory."*

The marketplace is a vast ecosystem, a jungle, if you like, in which new organisms (companies) are born every day and others die off. There are numerous reasons for the decline of companies but the most common is the failure to recognize the need for adaptation. The longer it takes for a company to adapt to external changes the more wasted energy and effort.

Too often, lean implementations are too slow to address significant issues of adaptation to customer preferences. Many lean consultants assume that using the PDCA cycle on the factory floor is the answer to becoming lean. But, often they are working on processes that should be eliminated entirely or need to be restructured, re-organized, or changed in large and rapid ways.

In the ideal system adaptation would be instantaneous. The moment a new healthcare technology or treatment was developed it would be instantaneously adopted by every healthcare provider. But, of course that doesn't happen. We suffer from the law of inertia (a property of matter by which it remains at rest or in uniform motion in the same straight line unless acted upon by some external force). The law of inertia applies to human behavior just as it does to physical objects. We tend to stay in our current place or state because it requires less energy than change. The path of least resistance is the path that we are on, even if that path ignores external realities and leads to a cliff. However, the degree to which we are on a path that diverges from the needs of our customers, that degree represents wasted energy. Every measure of energy spent diverging from the demands external realities, whether technologies or customer preferences, is wasted energy.

The purpose of WSA is to provide a process of adaptation and alignment.

The Law of Adaptation:

Organizations progress and are sustainable to the degree that they are capable of sensing shifts on the landscape and then developing those capabilities that will satisfy the market on the future landscape.

Corollaries to the Law of Adaptation:

- It is natural for organizations to remain on their current path and this inevitably leads to wasted energy and market dissatisfaction.
- The speed of changes on the landscape (technology, etc.) defines the necessary capacity to transform the internal capabilities of the organization.
- Transformation toward future capabilities requires transformational leadership, the impulse to foresee external changes and to drive internal adaptation by overcoming inertia.

Alignment

Principles or values have the power to create alignment and alignment creates unity of energy and effort and reduces friction in a system. The failure to seek alignment to principles is a failure of leadership.

Some years ago I was about to begin a project to design self-directed teams in a Corning Fiber Optics plant. As I toured the plant with the plant manager we were discussing the needs of the plant and the objectives of the design project we were about to initiate. I asked how the hourly employees were compensated. He immediately told me not to concern myself with that; he had another consultant who came in every year to adjust the hourly compensation model. They were paid on a piece work incentive. I immediately stopped him and said "So, you want us to develop great self-motivated teams, but they are paid on individual piece-work incentives?" He said, "Yes, that's right." I immediately told him that was impossible. You can't have one system of motivation pointing people in one direction, and a structure that asks people to behave in a different way. The systems and structure must be aligned. Along with the design of the team process we aligned the compensation system, information flow, job titles and every other element that would reinforce its success. The process proved to be sustainable over many years. It was sustainable because we reduced friction by aligning systems and structure.

I am confident in stating that the majority of lean implementations are crippled by the misalignment of systems, structure, symbols and skills. Lean management is a "whole-system" and each sub-system (HR, IT, etc.) must be aligned to reinforce the same behavior.

Alignment does not happen by accident. When Honda came to the United States they carefully designed all their internal systems to be aligned to the same principles. For example, one of their principles was the Unity Principle. It is not an accident that everyone wears the same uniform, indistinguishable by rank or work assignment. It is not an accident that everyone is referred to as an *Associate*. And, it is not an accident that there are no private offices. These were all intentionally designed as components of the social system of the organization to create alignment with their principles.

Friction is the result of misalignment. If you are told that the front-line team is to be an empowered, self-directed team, but the job definition and title of the supervisor hasn't changed, you have created a state of misalignment. If are asking management teams to take responsibility for business performance, but those management teams do not receive the financial and other reporting that would engage them in the business game, you have created misalignment. If the process of hiring and on-boarding are not aligned with the principle of respect for people you are most likely creating misalignment and friction.

The Law of Alignment

The degree to which all of the systems, structure, skills, style and symbols of the organization are aligned to the same principles and purpose, they are aligned with each other, and friction is minimized and sustainability is enhanced. The degree to which there is misalignment there is wasted energy and the organization is less sustainable.

Corollaries to the Law of Alignment:

- Different functions operating within their own structure tend to create processes and systems that are misaligned from those created by other functions and operations.
- Those working within a function or operation will tend to believe that other functions and operations should be aligned to their function or operation and not the reverse.
- Therefore, alignment is only created as an act of intentional leadership and system design.

These principles and laws are neither complicated; nor are they obvious to those working within organizations. Yet, a large percent of time, particularly management time, is wasted energy, a direct result of both the failure of adaptation to the external realities and the failure of internal alignment. Whole-system architecture is intended to eliminate the waste of misalignment.

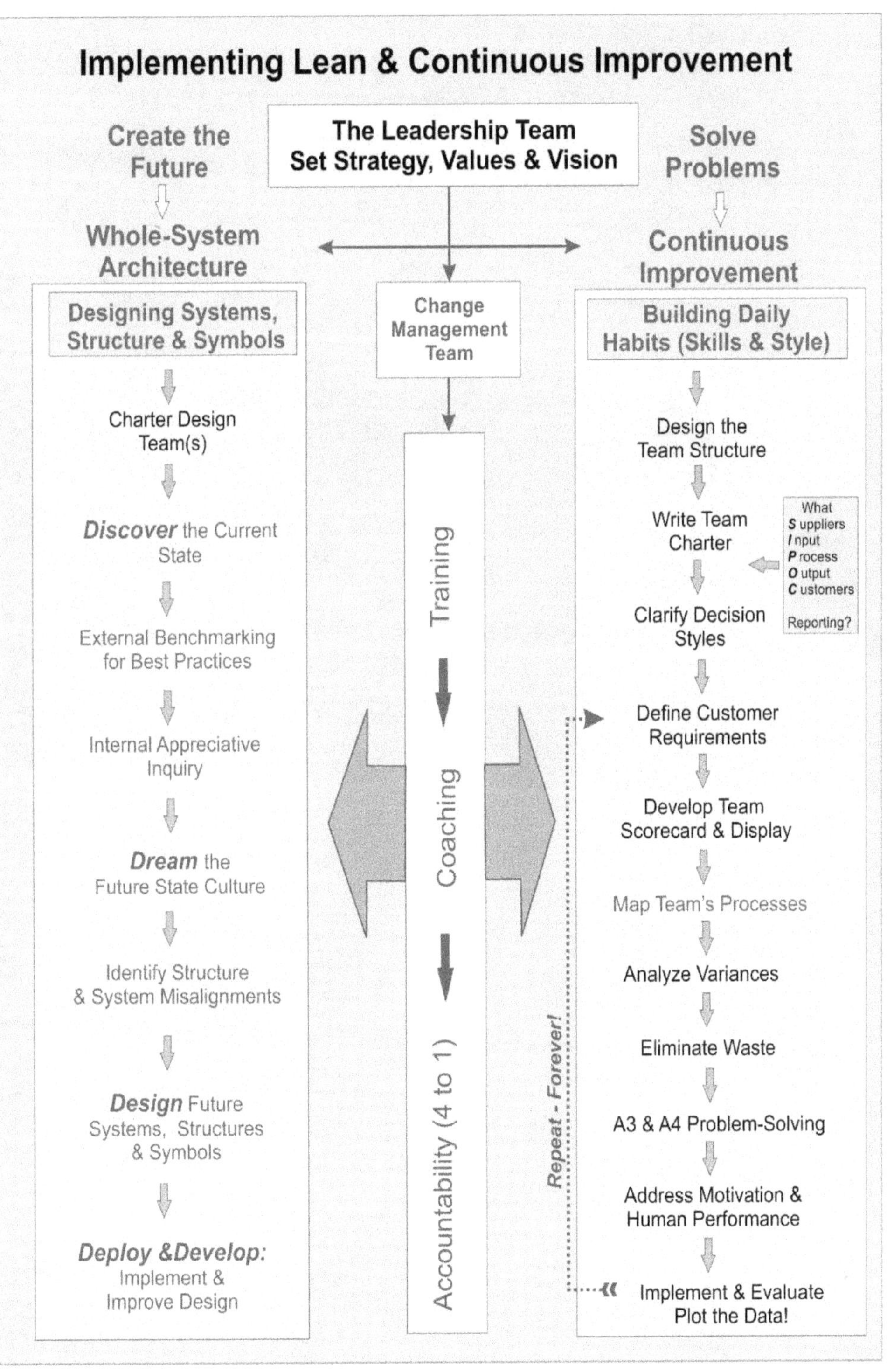
Implementing Lean & Continuous Improvement
Create the Future
Whole-System Architecture
The Leadership Team
Set Strategy, Values & Vision
Solve Problems
Continuous Improvement
Designing Systems, Structure & Symbols
Change Management Team
Building Daily Habits (Skills & Style)
Charter Design Team(s)
Discover the Current State
External Benchmarking for Best Practices
Internal Appreciative Inquiry
Dream the Future State Culture
Identify Structure & System Misalignments
Design Future Systems, Structures & Symbols
Deploy &Develop: Implement & Improve Design
Training
Coaching
Accountability (4 to 1)
Repeat - Forever!
Design the Team Structure
Write Team Charter
What
S uppliers
I nput
P rocess
O utput
C ustomers
Reporting?
Clarify Decision Styles
Define Customer Requirements
Develop Team Scorecard & Display
Map Team's Processes
Analyze Variances
Eliminate Waste
A3 & A4 Problem-Solving
Address Motivation & Human Performance
Implement & Evaluate
Plot the Data!

Part One

Overview of Whole-System Architecture

CHAPTER 1

PRINCIPLES

This chapter introduces the principles of lean and whole-system architecture. Change management must begin with an understanding of principles – both principles that will define the desired future state, and principles that will define how we will change. Remember – *how you change is the change!*

WHAT IS LEAN?

Years ago, when I would visit the Honda plant in Marysville, OH, I arranged for some of my clients to tour the plant. It was helpful, but too often they didn't get it. They would see that the plant was as clean as anyone's kitchen. They would see that they all wore the same uniforms. They would see that there was no warehouse. They could see the material results of the culture, but they couldn't see the underlying principles and behavior that define the culture. They didn't see that every newly hired manager and engineer spent six weeks working on the line. When I asked a woman, the public relations manager, how she felt about working on the line for six weeks she said, *"I worked in welding. Honestly it was frightening! I didn't like it. But, two year later I realize it was the best thing. I learned "respect." I learned to respect the world's greatest experts who are on-the-spot."*

Too often lean or Toyota Production System is understood as merely a set of tools. But it is more. It is a way of life, a culture that is embedded in the systems of the organization.

At Honda the process of hiring and educating new managers and employees is part of the architecture of lean. The plant layout is part of the whole-system. Incoming goods are delivered directly to the work station where they are assembled. The absence of private offices, with the President of Honda America Manufacturing sitting right out in the center of a large open office area, is part of the architecture. The visual posting of charts and graphs of performance, seemingly everywhere, is part of the architecture. The point system that rewards associates for suggestions, serving on quality circles, for attendance, and for other desired behavior, is part of the architecture. All of these and much more are all part of the architecture of a lean management system and organization. They all support and reinforce each other... just like the organs of the human body.

If someone tells you that "lean management is this" and not something else, if someone puts it in a box and ties a bow around it and presents it in a neat package with four walls around it, then that someone knows not of what they speak. Why? Because lean management is in motion and it is not a framed picture hanging on the wall. It is a melody, a rhythm, and not a note. Even Toyota has redesigned their own system to meet the needs of their people. Without calling it that, they have practiced whole-system architecture.

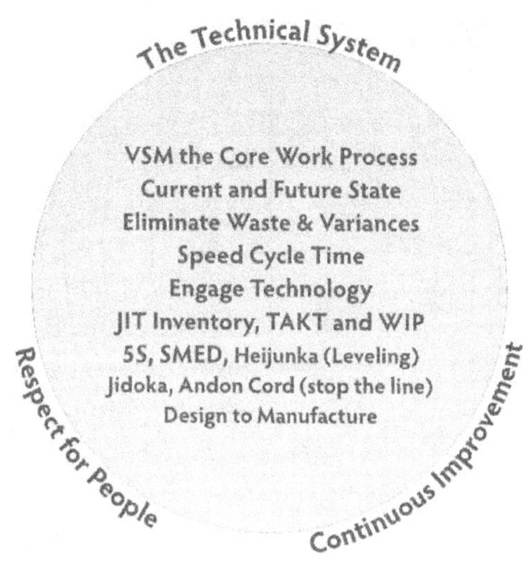

Lean management is generally derived from the Toyota Production System as developed by Taiichi Ohno, Shigeo Shingo and others over a forty year period. It began with efforts to reduce die change time on the stamping press which then allowed for a reduction of in-process inventory and this became just-in-time inventory management. This resulted in the need for less warehouse space, fewer forklifts, unnecessary space, etc. Once the flow of work can be interruption free, free of materials sitting, standing, and redo-loops, waste is eliminated. Lean is the elimination of waste. But, more importantly, lean is continuous improvement in all work processes.

In order to improve the work of the die press and reduce waste Shingo did not instruct the workers. He asked the workers to think. He challenged them to innovate and find ways to speed the process by eliminating unnecessary activities. The workers who operated the press and changed dies worked as a team and together they experimented and sought improvement. It was the front line workers, who were on-the-spot, and who were truly the world's greatest experts in their work, who experimented, watched the data, and learned from the facts.

This model of improving the die change process by those who do the work, by those who are on-the-spot, is the essence of lean management. The model of Shingo asking the work team to think, to experiment, and to learn from the data, is the model of the lean manager. It is management that is humble and not arrogant. It is management that observes, encourages, challenges, and learns. Lean culture is management that gathers the facts, encourages experimentation, and spreads best practices. It is management that practices what they preach to others.

This example illustrates the two most important principles of lean, and these are not just hollow slogans, they are profound philosophy that impacts every practice at Toyota: Respect for People and Continuous Improvement (kaizen). We will keep coming back to these and other principles because everything you do in designing your future system should incorporate these two principles, at a minimum. The process of whole-system architecture incorporates both of these principles.

This model was quickly copied by Honda and other Japanese companies and has now become the standard of world class manufacturing. And, it has become the standard for management in all types of work settings.

Lean is a moving target because, at its heart, lean is a process of learning and improvement. It cannot be defined as something that is standing still or fixed. It is not simply mimicking what happened at Toyota or anywhere else. And, most importantly, it is not a kaizen event or a project.

Quality of Work Life and the Toyota System

Books on lean management and the Toyota Production System too often present this system as if it has been a virtual heaven of production efficiency and worker satisfaction. In some author's enthusiasm, questions about stress and work life are rarely raised or they are glossed over. In Japan there have been serious issues raised about the quality of work life at Toyota plants and Toyota has openly addressed this issue itself, along with its union, and conducted its own whole-system system redesign to improve the attractiveness and reduce the stresses of working within their system. They have been aligning the technical and social systems.

In the 1990's Toyota faced its own labor crisis with 25% rate of turnover among new recruits to the workforce, an aging labor force, and a general aversion among young Japanese to working in factories. This raised serious questions within Toyota about their own system and how it impacted the quality of work life. The following paragraphs are quotes from an important study of what Toyota did in response to this crisis, a study that has been overlooked by most proponents of lean manufacturing.

> "Facing up to the labour shortage and to the exhaustion of the whole work force, the management and the union at Toyota began to question the production system and the method of managing work. They concluded that a radical resolution of the crisis of work could only be found in a reorganization of the production system to make work more attractive, for they were in agreement that the cause of the labour shortage was the nature of assembly line work and the Toyotaist method of managing work."
>
> "The management of efficiency lay in the reduction of the number of workers, which was accomplished by Kaizen activities on production tasks and procedures. This in turn was based upon the ideas of 'just-in-time' and 'autonomization' (labour saving) which had been sustained and developed by T. Ohno. But the underlying cause of the crisis of work that Toyota was experiencing was precisely this system for managing productive efficiency. Therefore the idea of 'just-in-time' was questioned. 'Just-in-time should not be applied to people', according to a section leader at the Motomachi factory. 'If the number of production workers is increased, productive efficiency will be lowered. But we should not think solely about productive efficiency', according to the personnel management department. The implication is that the reduction in the number of production workers should not be pushed too far. In other words, 'lean production' should not be applied to production workers. Otherwise, work will continue to be detested by the younger generation and will continue to tire production workers and supervisors. Hence the committee proposed to modify the management of costs."
>
> "This questioning of the production system has finished by modifying the idea of 'just-in-time' and the management of productive

efficiency: 'just-in-time should not be applied to people', and 'we should not think solely about productive efficiency'. Hence a humanization of the production system and of work was launched. By investing massively to improve working conditions, by developing a new conception of the production line, by allowing segments of the line to keep buffer stocks, by making social relations of work more equitable and rational, Toyota has changed the rules of the game. For Toyota, 'lean production' appears to be the model of the past, because it placed too much pressure on people. The new strategy at Toyota is to give a more humane dimension to its production system but without hindering productivity; even if progress remains slow, and is held back by the old Toyotaism."

"In terms of team work, four production workers form a work team which is responsible for a segment composed of a series of connected tasks (three or four tasks). The work team takes responsibility for the quality of its tasks, whereas on traditional lines, each person is responsible individually." [26]

The lesson of Toyota's experience at its own plants is that the lean system of production is not simply a technical or mechanical system in which the only goal is to improve production efficiency by eliminating waste. It is also necessary to design a system that takes into account the human factor, the social system that enriches the work and the quality of work life.

The other lesson from the above study is that the Toyota Production System, or lean, is an "open-system" able to adapt to the environment in which it lives.

---

[26] "*Humanization of the production system and work at Toyota Motor Co and Toyota Motor Kyushu.*" By Koichi Shimizu, In Enriching Production: Perspectives on Volvo's Uddevalla Plant as an Alternative to lean production. Sandberg, Ake, Editor, Digital Edition, Stockholm. 2007. P. 398.

The Philosophy of Lean

Lean is best captured as a philosophy rather than a particular method or technique. If you don't have the philosophy, you don't have it. Philosophy matters. If you were designing the culture of a country you might start with principles such as "government of the people, by the people, and for the people;" and freedom of speech, press and religion; or, the equality of men and women. Every country continuously pursues their philosophy and almost never achieves being there. But, the philosophy drives them toward the goal. Lean philosophy or principles are similar. The beginning of WSA is to decide on your principles and your philosophy. Here are several lists of principles that may help you decide on your own. Of course, there is overlap between these, just as almost every religion states the Golden Rule in slightly different language.

Lean Principles and Philosophy (End-State Principles)

Lean is where we are going. It is the "what" that we are trying to create or, the end-state. The process of getting there is something else. First, let's consider the philosophy that defines where we want to go.

Here are some ways of describing lean philosophy or a lean system:

- Lean is a culture of continuous improvement practiced at every level of the organization and by every team.
- Lean is the application of the scientific method of experimentation and study of work processes and systems to find improvements.
- Lean is respect for people. It is respect for the voice of the customer and it is respect for those who do the work, who are "on-the-spot" and are, therefore, the "world's greatest experts" in their work.
- Lean is the elimination of waste in all its forms. Lean is the ability to distinguish between work that actually adds value to your customers and work that does not. By eliminating waste, you free resources to devote to value-adding activity that serves your customers.
- Lean is a work environment that assures the quality and safety of all work for both customers and staff.

- Lean is a focus on improving the work process and not on blaming people or creating fear.
- Lean is a culture of teamwork, shared responsibility and ownership that cuts through organization walls or silos.
- Lean is a culture that returns the joy to work. Honda speaks of the three joys of buying, selling and making the product. We do our best work when we have joy in our work.
- Lean is flow. Lean is an interruption free process that flows from beginning to end without interruption.

Toyota Way Principles

Jeffrey Liker in his book The Toyota Way[27] summarises the key architectural elements of Toyota's lean system in the following fourteen points.

- Do business with a long term philosophy rather than constantly driving short term gains.
- Grow leaders from inside your organization.
- Create a "learning organization" that is continuously improving.
- Drive decisions through consensus.
- Empower employees to stop production to fix problems.
- To understand issues, go see them for yourself rather than simply getting reports from others.
- Respect your suppliers and network of supporters.
- Create continuous product flow to expose quality problems.
- Create pull systems to regulate work.
- Create visual inventory control.
- Level the work load so groups are equally balanced.
- Use reliable and stable technology.
- Employ exceptional people.

---

[27] Liker, Jeffrey K. *The Toyota Way*. New York. McGraw-Hill, 2004.

- Standardize processes and tasks.

Dr. Deming's Fourteen Points

It is also reasonable to compare these with Dr. Deming's Fourteen Points[28] upon which much of the quality movement was built. These are also a good set of principles to consider as you design your own lean system.

1. Create constancy of purpose toward improvement of product and service, with the aim to become competitive, stay in business and to provide jobs.
2. Adopt the new philosophy. We are in a new economic age. Western management must awaken to the challenge, must learn their responsibilities, and take on leadership for change.
3. Cease dependence on inspection to achieve quality. Eliminate the need for massive inspection by building quality into the product in the first place.
4. End the practice of awarding business on the basis of a price tag. Move towards a single supplier for any one item, on a long-term relationship of loyalty and trust.
5. Improve constantly and forever the system of production and service, to improve quality and productivity, and thus constantly decrease costs.
6. Institute training on the job.
7. Institute leadership. The aim of supervision should be to help people and machines and gadgets do a better job.
8. Drive out fear, so that everyone may work effectively for the company.
9. Break down barriers between departments. People in research, design, sales, and production must work as a team, in order to foresee problems of production and usage that may be encountered with the product or service.

---

[28] Deming, W. Edwards. *Out of the Crisis*. Cambridge, MA. The MIT Press, 2000.

10. Eliminate slogans, exhortations, and targets for the work force asking for zero defects and new levels of productivity..

11. a. Eliminate work standards (quotas) on the factory floor. Substitute with leaders.

    B. Eliminate management by objective. Eliminate management by numbers and numerical goals. Instead substitute with leadership.

12. Remove barriers that rob employees of their right to pride of workmanship and eliminate the annual rating system

13. Institute a vigorous program of education and self-improvement.

14. Put everybody in the company to work to accomplish the transformation. The transformation is everybody's job.

Lean Organization Architecture

Putting aside the assembly line or the specifics of work processes, is there a difference between lean and traditional organization? If you accept that lean is a culture, and not merely a mechanical process, then it is worth understanding that culture comes to be reflected in the organization's structure and systems, and these in turn, reinforce that culture. It is one reason why cultures are hard to change.

When the Internet was first appearing as a reality of life I was working in a large engineering organization. Some enterprising young engineer who knew more than most about the Internet, set up a discussion list so engineers of a particular specialty could communicate about common problems. He was setting up an internal social network, although the term "social network" didn't exist at that time. He was fired. He was fired for violating the chain of command and encouraging people to share information without first going through their manager, and their manager's manager. He violated the architecture of the organization. He violated the values upon which that architecture was built. Of course, if the managers had more sense, they would have encouraged and promoted him instead of firing him. But, that is the interplay between culture and organization architecture.

If you were forced to draw a picture of your organization you might draw something like the following organization chart on the left. It is neat, orderly, and everyone knows their place. Everyone knows who they report to and they are likely to stay in their boxes and follow the lines. The one on the right is another matter entirely. It's very confusing and appears "unmanageable." But, is that reality or, is it merely our cultural perceptions that we impose on reality? Living forms in nature look much more like the one on the right and they have worked well for millions of years. But those biological systems tend to be self-organizing, rather than responding to command. Systems that rely on self-organization tend to be highly sustainable and those that rely on imposed order tend to be unstable and unsustainable.

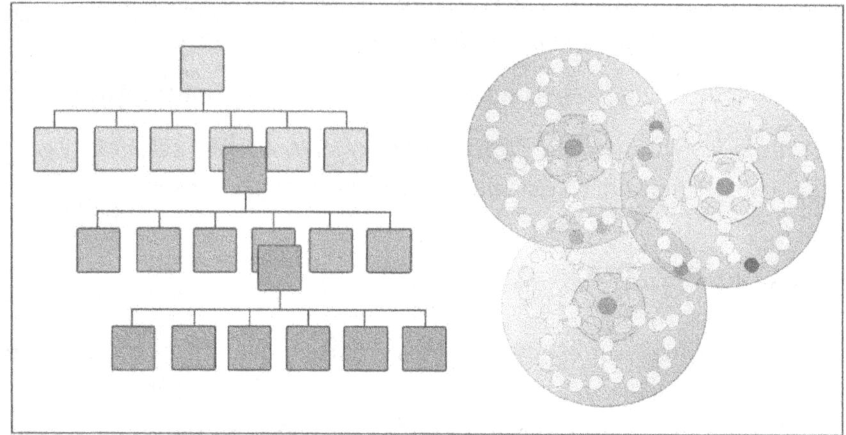

In which organization do you think learning will occur more quickly? In which organization do you think people are more likely to collaborate and self-organize groups to work on projects or to share information? The organization on the right is perfectly orderly with five teams in each of three clusters and within each cluster there is a leader and five coaches. Some of their work overlaps and some members may serve on more than one team, both within a cluster and across clusters. Why isn't that architecture just as sensible as the one on the left?

The organization on the left might be more suited to the orderly assembly line where the work flows in a linear manner and is done the same each day. But, that is not what most of our organizations do. Most of our organizations produce knowledge work where the most value-adding activity is thinking and innovating and that is much more likely to occur in the organization architecture on the right.

The architecture is more than structure. It is also systems of decision-making, information flow, training and development, reward and recognition and others. The nature of systems is an equally important part of the architecture and equally reflects cultural values and assumptions. Who sees and understands financial reports? Why doesn't everyone? Who has access to technical developments, problems or challenges? Why or why not? Who can communicate directly with customers or suppliers and how long does it take? Who do we trust? All of these questions are ones the design team will need to address. Their job will be to create the architecture that will enable the strategy of the organization.

Principles of Whole-System Architecture

Whole-system architecture is an interactive planning process that relies on a dialogue between customers, employees and managers. It asks for a team of managers and employees to create an idealized design. Change management requires principles of change. In order for any dialogue to be effective there must be a *safe space* in which dialogue to occur. Agreement on principles and process goes a long way to create that safe space. The principles that underlie whole-system architecture are derived from the best business, management, and psychological theories and are combined in a unique way. It is principle-centered design.

Principles are important to the design process for two reasons. One, the process of whole-system design is not linear or simplistic. When design choices have to be made, underlying principles can help guide people to make better decisions. Two, the principles are used throughout the design process to provide consistency and flexibility. It is through the use of principles that people can continue to modify and adapt designs, yet not lose the core purpose of the design. When you write the charter for your transformation effort you must decide on your own principles.

The following principles underlie the methodology.

1. The organization is a complex system that requires alignment of its parts to the same goals and purpose.
2. Design the organization as an open-system that adapts to its environment and aligns with the requirements of its environment.
3. The design should optimize the opportunity for its members to work as natural work teams, to learn from each other, and achieve the intrinsic satisfaction that can be derived from enriching jobs.
4. The organization design should be done by the "world's greatest experts" and those who design should implement that which they have designed. Enlarge the circle of involvement as you implement

but do not lose the understanding of those who did the analysis and design of the new system.

5. Shared principles create unity of systems, processes, and people and must be applied at all levels and across all functions.
6. How you change is the change. The process used for designing the organization should be compatible with how the organization will function in the future.
7. Design for variance control at the point closest to the origin of deviation. Immediate feedback loops enable immediate improvement or solving problems that create variances. Design in feedback loops to minimize wasteful errors.
8. The purpose of the organization is to meet the needs of its customers. Involve the customer and focus on meeting customer requirements.
9. Appreciation and understanding of human needs and values should be reflected in the design. Design for the growth of human potential including expanded multi-skilled work, job rotation, load-leveling and expanded decision-making.
10. Expect an imperfect design, with no fear of failure, but opportunity for learning and continuous improvement.
11. Design to an ideal or future state beyond your "village." Every company and every industry is a village or tribe that assumes the norms within. Look outside and beyond for models of excellence.
12. Engage in appreciative inquiry to find centers of excellence within your organization and incorporate those lessons.
13. All complex living systems contain processes of self-organization. Allow for and promote self-organizing processes within the design.

One of the first steps in the development of WSA is for the steering team, usually the senior management team to develop a charter that will guide the design teams. Part of that charter is a statement of principles that defines where we want to go and general principles of how we will get there. I recommend that you study all of the above statements of principles and then select from them or write your own statement of principles.

CHAPTER 2

WHO WILL PARTICIPATE?

Cleveland, Georgia is approximately fifty miles north of Atlanta and outside the borders of the culturally progressive metro area. The manufacturing plant produced high-tech textiles, Kevlar and other fabrics used in bullet proof vests and other high stress applications. In some ways it was high-tech; culturally it was still an old Southern textile mill. The goal was to improve quality, reduce waste and create a culture that empowered employees.

We began with the V.P. of Manufacturing and his team writing a charter for change for all the manufacturing plants. Then the senior team of the plant modified and adapted that charter to the specific realities and goals of their plant. Then they appointed a design team of hourly employees and managers who would analyze and redesign the work process and all the elements that drive the culture.

Mary had worked in the plant for about four years. She was a young woman, African-American and single mother, with all the associated stresses of her situation. She had a high school education. Her job was clean-up. She swept the floors, the most humble job in the plant. Mary spoke in a soft and uncertain voice that reflected her own humility and caution. She appeared unremarkable in every way.

The formation of the design team began with a brief explanation of the goals and process to all employees and a request for volunteers. Volunteers were to simply write their names on a slip of paper and put it in a box. The management team, the steering team for the process, then select ten employees to serve on the design team along with two managers.

Mary volunteered and she was selected. For about eight weeks Mary spent three days a week in design team meetings. At first, she was her usual quiet self, unsure of her ability to contribute; but, as the days went by something changed. All the time that Mary had been sweeping the floors she had been observing how others worked, what caused others to be stressed, motivated, or unmotivated. She observed how materials flowed from one area to another. As the design team mapped their work flow she was able to point out where things stood still and where there was waste and errors. She was also able to contribute to the discussion about motivation and how people worked together. And, gradually Mary began to change. She began to speak with more confidence. She appeared to walk more upright and with more certainty. She began to take the magic marker and write ideas on the flip charts. She invited others to give their ideas.

When the design team made their final presentation to the senior team, Mary was front and center, presenting with confidence and assuring management that "this will work!" Whether or not management understood the full implications of the new design or not is uncertain, but they did understand that Mary was different. Something had happened to her and other members of the design team. After the design was approved team coaches were selected and Mary volunteered to be a team coach. She was trained in team problem-solving and coaching skills and she successfully coached other teams in the plant. She was now a very different person than before the process began. She wasn't alone.

Ricky Wolfe was the Vice President of manufacturing and I attended the design team presentation with him. When we were leaving he said to me, "These are different people. They aren't the same people that were here before." I said to him, "They are the same people; you had just never seen what was inside them before." Ricky then told me about his mother who had worked in the weave room in a textile plant in South Carolina most of her life. She was what Ricky said were called "lint heads" because they came home with lint in their hair. He remembered the stories his mother had told him at the dinner table about how she was spoken to by managers in the plant. He had sworn that no employee in his company would ever go home and tell their children similar stories. He could see the change and he remembered his Mom.

This story has been repeated over and over again. When humble employees are shown respect and are genuinely allowed to have their voices heard, they change. The system changes the behavior of people. And, that change begins with the process of change. Again – *How you change is the change!*

INTERACTIVE PLANNING

Whole-system architecture is an interactive planning process. The interaction begins with clear communication from the senior managers of the organization, the steering team. The purpose, underlying principles, strategy, boundaries, and objectives of the process are clearly spelled out in the *charter.* The design charter is the formal statement of the leadership's direction, their vision of the future. This charter is given to an appointed design team, or teams, that redesign the work system and human systems, while seeking to optimize the economic system of the organization. These designs are then presented back to the steering team for approval and an implementation plan is developed.

Whole-system architecture is much like Hoshin Kanri, or policy deployment in the language of Toyota. The charter may be viewed as the policy to be deployed. One component of Hoshin Kanri is what they call "catch-ball" which refers to interactions like a game of catch between two people. The ideas and experiences go back and forth and with each exchange there is learning. This is what we expect to happen between design teams and the steering team, and with customers and employees. It is all one big game of catch-ball with the intention of designing the ideal future system of work and organization.

Interactive planning was promoted and written about by Russell Ackoff[29] of the Wharton Business School some years ago. His research showed that when planning was linear, or non-interactive, it produced less change in performance, less results, than when the planning was interactive. An interactive planning model is like a discussion in which one person says, "I'd like you to do X." And, the second person says, "In other words you want me to do x." And, the first person again says, "Well, not exactly, I would rather it be a bit more like a big X rather than a little x." In a conversation, or in interactive planning, both parties are thinking, contributing, and stimulating thoughts in the other. In linear planning the interaction is much more like, "Yes, sir, I'll do

---

[29] Ackoff, Russell L. *Re-creating the corporation: A design of organizations for the 21st century*. New York. Oxford University Press, 1999.

it in the morning." And the person may or may not understand what is to be done and makes little contribution to the creative process of decision-making

Whole-system architecture, when it is done best, involves a series of interactions, beginning with the steering team presenting the charter to the design team; questions and suggestions from the design team back to the steering team; a second response, etc. It will also involve a series of interactions with the customers, employees, and suppliers. This interactive planning process is nonlinear and may appear chaotic at times. It will, however, produce a result that is far more intelligent, with far greater commitment and support from those who must carry out the plan to achieve results.

Who Participates in Co-Creating the Future?

Whole-system architecture is conducted by those with hands on knowledge of how things actually work in the organization. The members of the design team and the steering team will both participate in implementing the design. The more members of the organization can be engaged in the process of designing the change, the easier and quicker will be the implementation. Ask yourself ***who knows, who cares, who must act*** as a guide to who should be involved.

As with all good management practices, you begin by gathering and understanding the facts. Facts are both internal and external. What do the numbers tell us about our business? Is quality improving or declining? Is customer satisfaction increasing or decreasing? Are costs of production increasing or decreasing? And, how do our own employees perceive the culture of the organization? It is helpful to know the answers to these questions, and many more, before the process begins. The facts define what some like to call "the burning platform" or the general need for change.

The steering team must be comprised of those who can approve the design. Think of the steering team as the owners of the house and the design team as the architects they are going to hire. The charter they will write will define boundaries within which the design team must work. In other words, can they redesign the building itself? Can they move equipment around or change offices? Can they change titles and levels of management? All of these must be within the steering team's span of control if they are going to ask the design to develop a design that may include changes in these elements of the organization's architecture. Generally speaking, the broader the scope of the design process, the more creative the design.

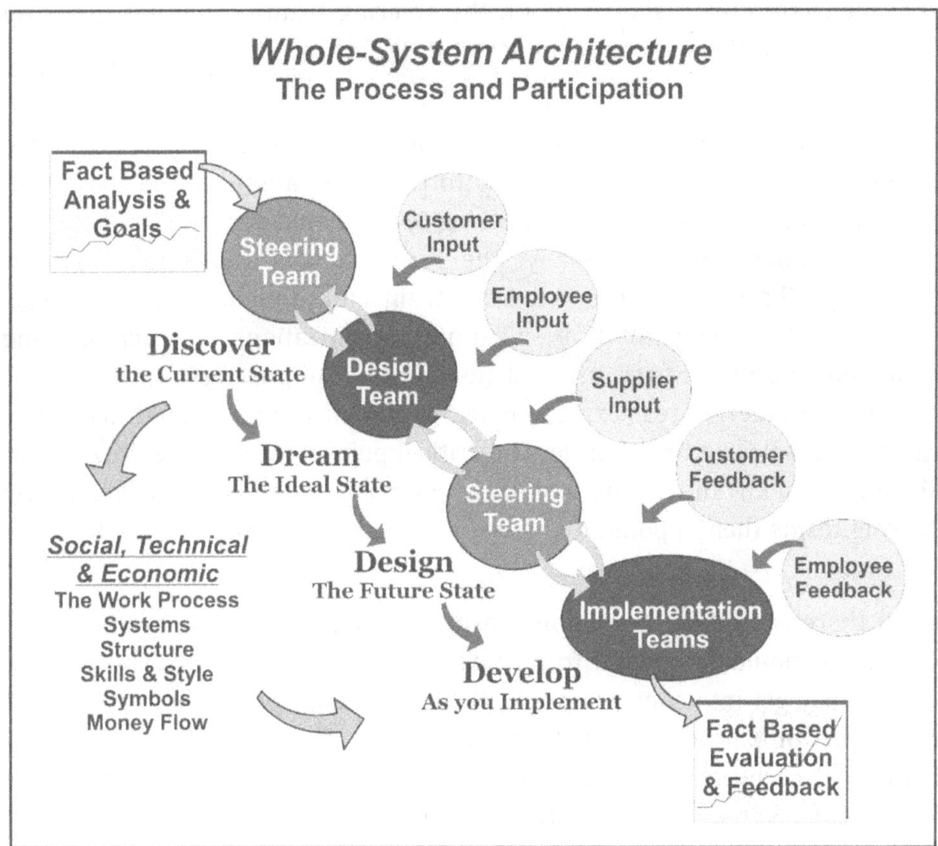

The design team will do the hard work of analyzing the current state and designing the future state. They will then present their design back to the steering team who will approve or modify the design. It is normal for a steering team to suggest that more work be done on some aspect of the design and this "interaction" should be viewed as a positive contribution to the work, not as a failure.

The Steering Team: Roles, and Responsibilities

"Who should be on the steering team?" is usually one of the first questions asked. Before we can answer that question, one must answer, "What is the scope of the transformation process?" Is it for a department? A division? A plant? An entire corporation? Once you know the scope and boundaries of the system, you can decide who is on the steering team. The senior management team of the organization that will be redesigned should form the steering team. If you are working on one manufacturing plant, the plant leadership team should be on the steering team. If you are doing an entire company, the senior executives of the company should be the steering team.

There can be more than one steering team at different levels of the organization. At one time I was asked to redesign an entire pharmaceutical company. There was a corporate steering team, then a steering for the three major functions of the company: the research labs, manufacturing, and marketing. There were other steering teams for human resources, legal, information technology, and other support organizations. On each steering team were executives from internal customer or supplier organizations. For example, the steering team for the research organization included the senior executive of sales and marketing. The critical point was to create linkage and alignment among the teams and their members. Each of these high-level steering teams then appointed and wrote charters for design teams for their processes.

If there is a union, the union president should be on the steering team. The union should be invited to participate at this level because the design process may get into contractual issues and working conditions that concern the union. Our experience is that the union can be a valuable ally and an asset if involved early in the process. If they are ignored and surprised by the design they will understandably become an obstacle. Remember that at Toyota the union participated in leading the redesign of their system.

The following are the specific functions of the steering team:

1. Become educated champions. Develop knowledge of lean management and culture so you can be a model and know it when you see it.
2. Develop and communicate the business strategy and financial results.
3. Write and communicate the charter.
4. Meet as a team, practice team skills, and improve your own work.
5. Meet regularly with design team(s).
6. Serve as boundary managers for the transformation process with the rest of the organization.

7. Accept, reject, or modify recommendations from design teams.
8. Provide support, resources, and guidance throughout the WSA process.
9. Appoint implementation teams to carry out the implementation of the design.
10. Communicate regularly with the organization.
11. Provide positive reinforcement for positive efforts.

Design Team: Membership, Roles, and Responsibilities

"How many design teams should we have?" "Who should be on the design team?" "Is it a full-time job?" These are a few of the questions often asked. The answers to these questions depend on the scope and boundaries of the change process. After the steering team writes the charter, they decide if one design team is enough and who should be on it.

The detailed work of WSA is best done by a dedicated design team. They might meet every week for three days, or every day each week. The amount of time they spend on the task depends on the scope of work and how quickly the design must be completed. Even when they are not in meetings they may be collecting data, meeting with other employees, or doing benchmarking trips. A design team functions best when they have a room in which to work, store materials, and leave things hanging on the wall.

A design team is typically eight to fourteen people. At least half are typically first-level employees who are "hands-on" and are expert in the work. The other half is managers and staff supporters from human resources, quality, finance, etc. It is important that design team members are representatives of the process. In other words you can't have all employees from Department A and none from B or C. They should represent the diversity in age or other demographic factors in the plant. You want them to be trusted by all.

It is useful to have one member of the steering team serve as a primary "champion" of the process and a liaison between the design team and steering team. A competent and experienced facilitator is also critical to this process.

Criteria for Design Team Members

Design team members should have certain characteristics or qualities to be successful. Here is a list of characteristics to consider when selecting the design team members:

- Respected by others
- Open-minded, flexible, and creative
- Assertive
- Good communication skills
- Team player
- Can handle ambiguity
- Willingness to learn
- Knowledgeable about one or more parts of the company and/or processes

The quality of the design team members is critical to the overall transformation process. If bright, creative people are not on the team, people will not have confidence in the final design. If the design team members are not respected by the employees of the organization, then the final design will lack credibility. You can use a nominating process where employees make recommendations for design team members. However, the steering team ultimately decides who is on the design team. They must make sure the team is balanced and that the team understands the total picture, organization, and systems.

Design teams need to be trained and facilitated in their work. If a design team does not have sufficient training and facilitation, it will likely stumble and take unnecessary detours. We have heard stories about design teams working for two years just to redesign the work processes and not completing the task. This usually happens when there is not a facilitator who has experience leading a design team through the WSA process.

There may be times when you need more than one design team (multiple plants, separate businesses within the operation, or operations in different countries). If you have more than one design team, you need to create a linking mechanism among the various teams. This can be accomplished by having an integrated design team with members from each of the separate design teams. Or, you could have several design teams working separately on the work processes who later work together on integrating them and completing the human design.

Design Team Roles and Responsibilities

- Be an active, responsible member of the team.
- Do benchmarking.
- Communicate with other employees.
- Define current state work and human systems.
- Analyze variances and data.
- Define the future or ideal state for work and human systems.
- Consider the economic consequences of their design and decisions.
- Make presentations.
- Be a change champion.

Engaging Other Stakeholders

The design team should not go into a room, lock the door, and then come out with a design. On the contrary, they should "go-and-see" how the work is actually done. They should engage any stakeholders in the organization that may have insight into the nature of the current system or ideas for the future. They should listen to their customers who know better than anyone how they feel about the product or services they receive from the current system. Only customers are expert in their requirements and they are best at communicating those requirements.

We tend to create walls that are more imagined than real and those walls need to be knocked down. Some years ago I was working with Inland Steel at their large plant in East Chicago on Lake Michigan. They made rolled sheet metal for the auto industry. As U.S. auto companies were in decline and as the Japanese car companies established operations in the U.S. they sought contracts with them. They agreed to a contract with Honda to supply sheet metal.

Inland Steel had been very controlling in communications between their operations and their customers. There was one guy, whose job it was to communicate with Chrysler. He was the account manager. It was strictly forbidden that any other employee communicate with Chrysler in any way. He was a tall, good looking guy, with French cuffs, starched shirt and a tie pin under his well-formed Windsor knotted tie. He was well spoken, a good joke teller, and very good at golf. He played a lot of golf. I think that was his core competence.

Buried somewhere in the newly signed contract with Honda was a provision that Honda managers and engineers were free to visit that plant at any time, 24/7, and speak directly with those making steel. Desiring the contract, Inland management paid no attention to this, assuming business would be as usual. And, then it happened. At three o'clock in the morning a Honda Accord with four Japanese engineers inside pulled up to the guarded gate. The befuddled guard had never encountered anything like this. He told them that none of the managers were here, but would be at eight o'clock in the morning if they would come back then. But, the Honda engineers made clear that they had no interest in talking to the managers. They wanted to talk with those who were making steel for them. The guard then suggested that there was a good hotel a mile or two away. That didn't work either.

This was a cultural shock. It was a shock to those who have true faith in the imagined notion of corporate walls, boundaries that interrupt the flow of work and have some perceived sacredness to them. Honda doesn't believe in them or care about them. They only care about the actual quality of steel, how it is made and how it is delivered. Inland soon realized that these engineers had only one motive. That was to improve and assure the quality of materials they were purchasing. They were not there to catch anyone doing anything wrong. They were there to help and to learn. And, they were certainly not interested in talking to someone whose core competence was golf! And, this is the relationship with all Honda suppliers.

Customers want to be engaged in improvement. They can only do their jobs well if they receive good input from their suppliers. The design team should listen to the voice of the customer directly. Ask them questions. And, let them express any anger, frustration, or other emotions they may have. This is the "real stuff" of customer relations and they should not be shielded from it.

In the Appendix you will find a case study on the conference method of design by one of my associates, Alan Wilgus (who, it happens, was employed at Inland Steel before I hired him). This is a way of engaging a lot of people at the same time. My associates and I have done these with a number of clients and there is a dramatic effect. I have seen a conference in a large hotel ballroom with three hundred managers and employees all in attendance. These are working sessions in which they give input on the nature of the work system and the social system; and, participate in designing the future. It is normal for customers to be invited to attend these sessions and "tell it like it is" directly to those who do the work and manage the work. I have seen a customer point his finger at the audience and virtually yelling in frustration "Why don't you people listen to us. I have told you over and over again..." This gets everyone's attention and the entire audience is eager to understand the cause of the customer's frustration.

The wonderful thing about design conferences is that they can involve getting input from a large number of employees. Those employees can review a proposed future state design and give their feedback and approval. This participation almost assures successful implementation. Remember, we are committed to implementing that which we helped design and build. That is the magic of co-creation.

CHAPTER 3

OVERVIEW OF THE PROCESS

Essentially there are four major stages of the design process: *Discover, Dream, Design,* and *Deploy & Develop.* The design team will *discover* the current reality of the technical, social and economic system. They will scan both the internal and external environment. They will assess the organization's assets and liabilities – not just financial, but social and human assets. This will include interviews, value stream mapping of the process, surveys and analyzing all relevant data. While doing this they will be obtaining the voice of the customer, associates and the market place. They will then *dream* about an ideal state - what could be. Dreaming sounds "not like work" but it is actually a critical activity in getting to a significantly improved future state. Then the design team will *design* the details of how the technical system will work, how the social system will be aligned with that work system, and how the economic system will be improved. They will then present this design to the steering team who will either approve it or provide feedback to improve the design. Design team members will then participate on implementation teams, expanded groups, who will *deploy* and *develop* the design. Deploy and develop are concurrent and lead to sustainability. As you deploy your new work process, teams, job functions, etc., you will be learning how to modify and improve them at each step.

These four stages of the WSA process are not of equal length. They are also not linear. As the design team is going through the discovery process they can't help but dream about how things could be done in a better way. Discovering, dreaming and designing are all, to some extent, overlapping in the minds of the members of the design team. Human beings don't think in separate isolated boxes. As the design team is discovering together someone will say "Yeah, and we should have the primary care teams make those decisions themselves." And, the facilitator will say, "That's a good point for us to consider when we are designing those teams. Let's put that on a parking lot to come back to." So, the mind wandering from discovery to dream to design is a good thing if you capture ideas to incorporate later.

It is typical that the most amount of time is spent during the discovery process. If this is done well, the dream and design stages flow easily. Dreaming may just be a few hours in which the design team members consolidate and articulate a consensus view of their ideal design for the social, technical and economic systems of the organization. Design will take longer because in this stage they will develop a future state process map in some detail and go through all the issues around job descriptions, teams, motivation, communication, etc. Deploying and developing the new design may go on for a year or more as they begin to standardize the things that have proven to work well and revise things that can be done better.

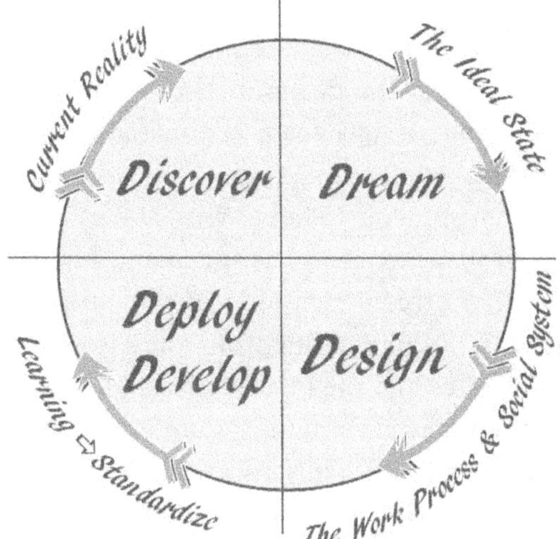

Of course, each whole-system architecture process is unique because every organization is unique. But at a high level these four D's provide a proven road map.

You can compare the 4D process with the well-known Shewart cycle, Plan-Do-Check-Act, that has been used as the basis for quality improvement and continuous improvement for many years. One of the great advantages of the PDCA cycle is that it is elegantly simple and easy to remember.

Stage 1: Discover

Many different activities can be employed during the discovery phase, but you can generally divide them into *external* and *internal* discovery. External would include anything happening outside the organization that may impact the organization or that may generate ideas for a better future. Some call this an *environmental scan*, which has nothing to do with the weather! The environment includes the business marketplace, the technology environment, social environment and other factors that are external; as well as customers, suppliers and partners which all create requirements and opportunities for the organization.

The internal environment begins with clarification of the guiding values, mission, vision and strategy. These principles and ideas should give direction to all of the work of the design process. It is the responsibility of the steering team to provide this guidance.

The next step is mapping the core work process. The design team may spend a good bit of time developing this graphic depiction of the work of the organization. As they discover this map they will want to ask questions about the organizations strengths and discover stories about how individuals or teams have done heroic things to serve their customers and improve the product or service. These stories will be important in developing the dream of the future organization.

The design team will then identify all of the enabling processes, those that support and make the core process successful, such as human resource processes, financial, or quality management. Depending on the scope of their effort, they may want to map these processes and follow the same steps they did for the core process or make a list of process requirements for later consideration.

Discovery activities may include individual interviews, small focus groups, web based surveys, or large scale conferences. It will also include studying all available data on the organization's performance. The design team members may develop a series of interview questions focusing first on the strengths and positive performance of the organization and then on wishes, desires, or needs. They may split up into pairs to go interview customers and suppliers, or they may schedule focus groups. This is all part of the process of discovery.

Stage 2: Dream

To dream is to imagine a better future. To dream is to image what could be versus what is. All significant change is based on a dream of a significantly better future. This is what distinguishes whole-system architecture from a problem-solving approach.

There are three questions that can help develop the dream of their future:

- Considering our mission as an organization, what would be the ideal future service or product for our customers? What would this look like and how would it make our customers feel?
- What would the ideal work process look like, that would have the least amount of wasted activity, space, time, materials, and the fewest possible quality variances.
- What would make this the world's best place to work while we accomplish our mission? What would it feel like? What about the work setting would provide the most encouragement and development for the members of our organization?

Around each of these four big questions it will not be hard to image many other questions. There are numerous exercises and fun ways to explore the dream. For example you can ask individuals or small groups to write an article for the Wall Street Journal that is doing a story on your company ten years from now. The WSJ is writing an article about your company as a success story that will inspires others. The story should reflect everything you want the company to be, what you hope you will be able to say about the company. You can also call upon the creative imagination of members of your organization by asking them to develop and act out skits that reflect the dream of your future company. These skits, for example, could be at a cocktail party. The President of the United States, ten years from now, is having a dinner and cocktail party for winners of the National Quality Award. As a member of the team who helped make this happen, you have been invited. Now write a script and act out the conversation where you are explaining to others at the cocktail party what you did that made your company worthy to win this award.

These are just examples of some of the fun things you can do to encourage the development of the dream. Remember that people dream in groups. In other words, one person's story stimulates ideas in another. It is a brainstorming process. Have you ever watched a group sitting around and imagining what could happen together? They feed on each other, laugh with each other, and from the dialogue comes a collective dream that none of them alone would have imagined.

Out of the discovery and dream stage you will form a "consensus dream."

STAGE 3: DESIGN

Based on the discovery and the dream, it is now time to begin the design process. While the dream phase put practical concerns and all forms of skepticism aside; now is the time to begin to get practical. Now is the time to say, "Ok, what can we actually do that will make that dream come true?"

During the Discovery and Dream process you have generated a long list of things you would like to change. Now you have to organize those and start designing in some logical manner. The beginning point should be the core work process. It is best if they start with a clean sheet of paper and ask themselves the question "if we were starting a new company and had no restraint, what would we design to be the ideal process to meet the needs of our customer?"

Since the organization exists for the purpose of creating the output of the core process, the enabling processes (human resources, information systems, etc.) should be designed to support and optimize the core work process. At this stage the design team may create process requirements for the enabling processes.

Once the core work process is designed into its ideal desired state, the design team begins to address the structure and systems around the process. There is one BIG rule as they begin to do this. Design the organization from the bottom up! In other words, first design the organization of groups or teams at the first level, where the work is done. This is where the organization adds value to customers.

This is the beginning of structure. The structure of society begins with the structure of the family. The beginning of organization structure should be the design of the small work teams who will manage and improve their work on a day-to-day basis. After the first level groups are formed, the question is then asked "What help do they need to do their work in the best possible way?" Think about how this question is different than asking "How many managers are needed?" If you ask what help is needed you will get a very different answer, and it will be a more "lean" answer. If the right training, information, tools, decision authority, and coaching are provided, you will find that far less management is needed. Like zero-base budgeting, you are doing zero-base organization design. This is how you eliminate bureaucracy.

Similar questions are then asked about all of the systems in the organization. For example:

- How can the information systems most help those who do the work?
- What method of presentation and delivery of information would be most helpful to the teams?
- What training systems would most enable teams and individuals to do their job in the ideal way?
- What methods and patterns of communication would be most helpful and encouraging to employees?

The design team will identify all of the relevant systems that support the core work, and will then develop a list of questions and issues to be addressed in their design work.

From the point of the work teams the rest of the organization structure is designed to support those teams and to eliminate any walls that interrupt the flow of the work. The design team will consider all forms of motivation, how decisions are made, how communication occurs, how skills are developed and all other systems that impact the culture of the organization.

Stage 4: Deploy & Develop

Rather than think of any design as complete, or finished, it is best to acknowledge the inevitable reality that you have only done the best you could do at this time. In short order, as groups set about implementing the new design, they will quickly find ways to improve it. Rather than create any resistance to this, it is best to plan for it, encourage it and hope that the process of implementation is one of on-going development and learning.

It is important that everyone involved has an attitude of continuous improvement when implementing the new process, systems or structure. It will never be 100% right! It will be your best shot at this point in time. However, once you start implementing the new design you will start learning. You will find that some of the pieces don't fit together perfectly; or, you may find you have not thought of some element of the process that also needs to be aligned.. If you view these discoveries as mistakes or failures, you will stifle the learning process. It is much better to understand that these are inevitable and the natural process of learning that occurs during implementation.

Chapter 4 Case Study: Implementing Lean in Home Health Care

Case studies are generally presented as quick examples or in the back of a book as a reference. However, this author thought it would be most helpful to present a complete case study of lean implementation using whole-system architecture early in the book so the reader has a context for the more detailed description of the methodology that follows.

The name HomeCare is a fictitious name but all the details and data in the case are very accurate and have been reviewed or provided by the client.

***

HomeCare is a large and well established and community based health care service delivery organization. It is a Canadian charitable organization. In 2011 it was apparent that poor service delivery to both funders and clients required a major redesign of its care delivery process and a significant change in the culture of HomeCare. The leadership team of HomeCare decided to employ lean methodology to engage their employees in a process of significant change in the system of service delivery and the organizational processes that support service delivery. Results reported by funding agencies demonstrate dramatic improvement in satisfaction; time required for scheduling a nurse had dropped from an average of five hours to less than five minutes; productivity has improved by an average of twenty-five percent; while the satisfaction level of service providers and managers has also improved substantially.

Background

The primary service of HomeCare is providing in-home nursing care and home support services.

Prior to 2004 HomeCare's organization could be characterized as a loose association of relatively independently managed district organizations with their own Boards, fund raising and management. However, with the increasing role of the national government in setting health care policy and funding, with the growing need to employ information technology, and with the recognition that there was a lack of quality control, it was decided to bring more central control and standardization to the service delivery process.

HomeCare's primary home care services are funded by local government Community Care Access Centers (CCAC's) that are notified by hospitals and doctors when a patient requires home support or nursing. The local funding agency contacts HomeCare to schedule a nurse or home support worker who then provides the services and submits a report of service that results in payment to HomeCare.

The centralization process included developing organization wide financial, human resource, and information technology processes. It also included the development of a centralized planning and scheduling center that required all funders to call into this regional center to initiate the scheduling of service to a patient. While the management of nurses and home support workers was the responsibility of local district managers, the scheduling was being done through this regional service center. There were a number of problems associated with this process.

- It denied control and responsibility to the local managers who were not scheduling their own staff.
- The central planning office was located in one city of a large province. Those doing the scheduling were often not familiar with the geography, the nurses, or the clients. This resulted in nurses being scheduled with unnecessary travel, poor continuity of service (the same nurse providing the care each day), and frustration on the part of the funding agency case managers.
- Funding agency staffs were often put into a queue when they called into the planning center, never knew which planner they would be

speaking with, and had to repeat their need or restate their problem several times. When surveyed, 9 of 14 funding agencies expressed dissatisfaction with service, particularly the planning and scheduling function. More than 50% of funding agency staff reported that they were either dissatisfied or very dissatisfied with HomeCare's service in a baseline satisfaction survey. Sixty percent reported dissatisfaction with HomeCare's scheduling function.

- HomeCare's Care and Service Managers reported that they spent half of their time in what they regarded as "waste," time required to fix errors, miscommunications, and rework in the planning and scheduling process. This was time taken away from their primary job of assuring quality of nursing and home care work, training and supporting the nursing staff. This lack of clinical supervision was regarded as creating a significant risk to patient care, dissatisfaction among care providers and frustration by care managers.
- And, although it is a very subjective condition, it is profoundly important that the culture of HomeCare had become very contentious with a great deal of blaming and fear. For managers, in particular, it was not a happy place to work.

In 2011 the CEO asked the Vice President of Quality and Risk to take on the task of analyzing the Home Care Service Delivery Process and developing a path to improvement. To assist her she engaged this author as her consultant. Together they conducted interviews, surveyed staff and funders, and developed a path forward. The essential and simple analysis was that the

Current State
The Core Work Process

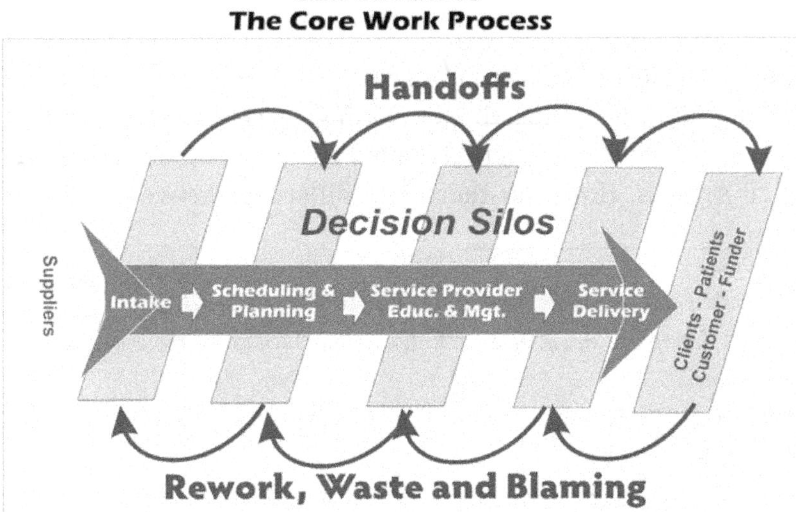

organization was siloed, particularly between the planning and scheduling function, the district management of nurses, and the communication with funders. It was recommended that the entire process, from beginning to end, had to be significantly redesigned. The problem was both the formal arrangement of the work process, but also the social system of organization, communication, decision-making and culture.

It was recommended that the initial design involve two districts, Toronto Area Nursing and Trenton Home Support. The lessons learned from these pilots would then lead to the design of the remaining districts in the Central Region and then the remainder of the national organization. The first two pilot districts were implemented following the redesign process in April of 2012. The success of these two pilots was so dramatic and swift that the design proceeded in five more districts and these were implemented in July and August of 2012. Six more districts were designed and implemented in September of that year.

METHODOLOGY

There were already improvement initiatives underway at HomeCare utilizing lean problem-solving methods ("rapid improvement events" following the PDCA cycle). However, these were focused on small improvement and were not looking at the larger system of work and organization. They were seeking small improvements within the existing structure (silos) or process of work. Small improvements would never have solved HomeCare's problem because the poor service was causing the loss of contracts and financial losses were mounting. A more holistic approach was required.

Lean management has proven successful, not only in manufacturing but in increasing numbers of health care settings.[30] ThedaCare[31] [32] and Virginia Mason Medical Center[33] have provided models of successful implementation in hospital settings. However, there is a difference between hospitals and

---

[30] Graban, Mark. *Lean Hospitals*. New York: Productivity Press, 2011.

[31] Toussaint, J., Gerard, R. A., & Adams, E. *On the Mend.* Cambridge, MA: Lean Enterprise Institute. 2010.

[32] Tousaint, J. S. (2013, January). The Promise of Lean in Health Care. Mayo Clinic Proceeding, pp. 88(1):74-82.

[33] Kenney, C. *Transforming Health Care.* Boca Raton: CRC Press. 2011.

home care service delivery. Hospitals, like factories, have processes that are in a fixed location, are generally visible and repeatable. In hospitals it is relatively easy to have team meetings, visual display of performance, shared problem-solving groups, and for managers to observe and reinforce work practices. Home care nurses and home support workers most frequently leave from their homes to drive to their client's home, provide services independently, and report the results of their service electronically. Most often, they work alone and without direct supervision. Their individual skill and motivation, their discretionary effort, is a major determinant of their effectiveness. Therefore, the application of lean management at HomeCare required some innovative thinking and design.

Traditional methods of implementing lean management are also likely to fail to take into account the potential and influence of information systems and technology. In the Toyota factory you can see the stamping press stamping out the shape of the fenders and bumpers, and you can see the workers installing the dashboard or seats. You can measure the time and motions involved. But, the value-adding work in many of our organizations today is less visible and more complex.[34] Complexity theory[35] recognizes the rapid, often invisible, interactions between those creating and using information. It is also an important understanding of the work of health care organizations.[36] While in the patient's home, a nurse may observe a patient's wound that is not healing as expected. Her decision process at that time is absolutely critical. How her decision process is enabled by current or potential technologies is one of the most important elements of the home care service process. It will be simple if she knows what to do. But, she may be uncertain and her ability to consult with peers on patient care decisions, and in real time when in remote locations may be one of the most important steps in the work process. That ability can be lifesaving. The design process at HomeCare had to take into consideration the non-linear knowledge based interactions that are very different than those common in a manufacturing setting or in a hospital.

---

[34] Rowe, A. a. (Volume 51, Issue 4, 2005). Use of complex adaptive systems metaphor to achieve professional and organizational change. Journal of Advanced Nursing, 395-405.

[35] Wheatley, M. *Leadership and the New Science.* San Francisco: Berrett-Koehler. 1999.

[36] Reddy, M. P. (2003). Sociotechnical Requirements Analysis for Clinical Systems. Methods of Information in Medicine, 437-44.

Co-Creation: Gaining Ownership

HomeCare had lived through a number of previous change efforts. By their own admission they were "terrible" at managing change and implementing improvement projects. One of the primary causes of these failures was the reliance on outside experts who prescribed a solution, handed that solution off to managers and employees, and then departed.

The consultant was very clear about his role: he was to provide a structured process and to facilitate that process, but all the analysis and decisions would be made by the two design teams. They were comprised of those who worked in the current system and they would be engaged in implementing the new system. The design teams would present their solution to the steering team which was comprised of the senior management team of HomeCare. They would then approve the design. It was of paramount importance that the design team took complete ownership for the new design, participated in implementation, and were then willing to learn from that implementation and make changes.

The senior management team appointed the design teams and wrote a "Charter" that stated the objectives, the principles, and the boundaries of the design process. There was a design team for the Trenton area home support process; and a design team for one CCAC in the Toronto Area Nursing. On the design team were two district managers, a manager from the central planning center, two care and service managers who managed nurses and home support workers, two nurses and two home support workers, two administrative personnel from the two sites, and four employees from the central planning center.

The design teams met for three days a week over a twelve week period. Much of their time was spent in the two separate teams, defining the home support and the nursing work flow, but also sharing their design work, and learning from each other.

The dynamics of the group changed dramatically from the first week to the last. When they started, the four young women who did planning and scheduling in the central planning center sat in the back of the room and were very quiet. They knew that there had been a lot of anger directed at the planning center and as they reviewed the feedback on the current state they felt guilty and blamed for "the mess." However, the consultant repeatedly emphasized that "The problem is in the process, not the person. Don't blame the person, fix the process!" These dynamics would change dramatically as the team members became comfortable and confident in their assignment.

There was also a disbelief that the senior managers would actually listen to a complete redesign the system that they had created. This fear would prove to be unfounded.

The Process of Whole-System Architecture can generally be divided into four stages of work: *Discover, Dream, Design*, and *Develop*.

The Charter

This is an important document that defines the objectives and boundaries for the design team. It is written by the senior management team that served as the steering team. The HomeCare senior management team had two meetings during which they wrote each component of the charter. It was important that the Charter represented a consensus among the senior management who had differing views about the cause of their current performance.

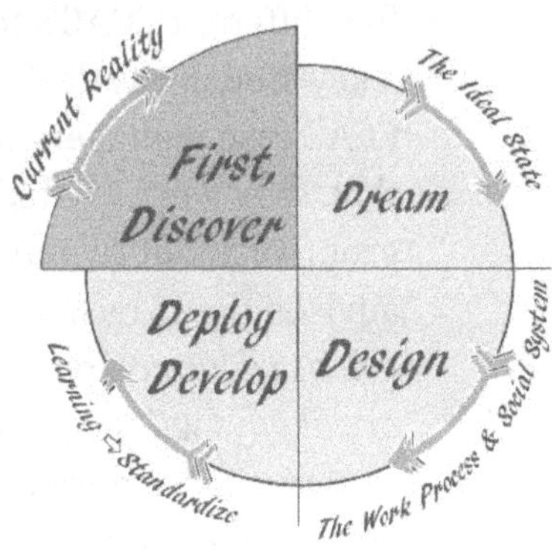

The Charter becomes the authoritative document for the design team and the more than once when design team members would ask "Well, can we do…." the consultant would simple refer them to the charter and say "If it is within the boundaries of the Charter you can design it and propose it."

The complete Charter is presented as an example in Chapter 6. Please go to page 115 to review the HomeCare Design Charter.

Stage 1: Discovery

The purpose of the discovery phase is to learn from the current state – both within the organization and from the external environment. An important reality of the discovery by these two design teams was that all of the design team members had experienced the frustration of the current system, the anger of customers, and the internal conflict that the system was creating. However, different members had very different understanding of the cause. If you worked in the planning center where nurses where scheduled you might view the problem in terms of the nurses failing to listen to their voice mail or read their faxes. If you were a nurse you might view the problem as the schedulers not getting you the needed information in a timely manner. Both perspectives were true and both were the result of the current system design.

Prior to the work of the design teams the Vice President of Quality and Risk and this author conducted interview of HomeCare staff and managers and CCAC case managers. They also administered web-based surveys to the funding agency case managers and HomeCare staff. They also had prepared all the data on key performance indicators to present to the design teams. However, the direct discovery work of the design teams was critically important.

- The design teams conducted interviews with the representatives of five different CCAC's to gain their direct and personal input. This was a key step in the design teams gaining confidence. They knew that the CCAC case managers were frustrated and angry at HomeCare. Despite that, they were invited into the room to be interviewed by the entire group of about twenty design team members. The consultant had advised them, based on prior experience that *"It never fails that when you ask your customer to help you improve how you serve them, they are always willing to help."* When the CCAC managers came for their interviews the design team learned that some of them had even worked for HomeCare in the past and had a very sincere desire to see them succeed.
- The design teams reviewed the surveys of both internal managers and external funders.
- The design teams reviewed employee satisfaction surveys of all the groups involved.
- They also compiled and reviewed the key performance data on service visits per day for service providers, missed visits, referral acceptance, and other key measures. These were all graphed so they could see trends and variability.
- The design teams discussed competitive intelligence – how and why competitors were achieving higher levels of customer satisfaction.

- And, most importantly, the design teams spent considerable time mapping and studying their own work processes, the cycle-time through the process, and the quality variances that occur at each step of the process. For each step, they asked whether it was "waste" or "value-adding." From the time a CCAC contacted HomeCare with a request for service, to the time service was completed, there were 176 steps in the process. By mapping the process the design team could see why there was so much frustration and opportunity for errors.

Stage II: Dream

Dreaming may sound like it has no place in a work setting. However, spending some time to brainstorm the "ideal state," the possibility of a dramatically different condition, is often a key phase of significant improvement. It is an opportunity to step outside of the current culture, current technology, and current process, to imagine an ideal future.

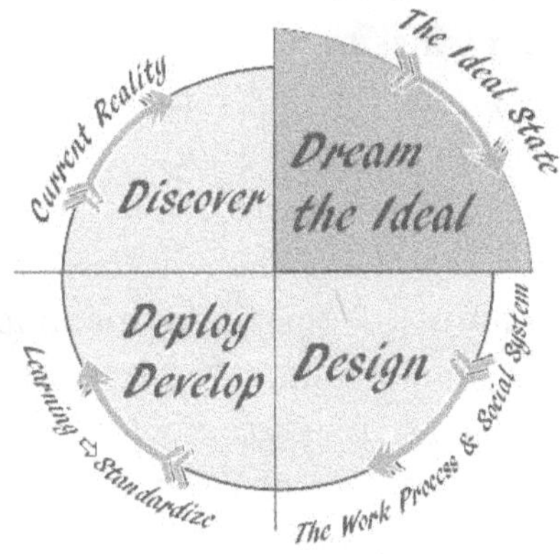

The two design teams were organized into five groups to develop the dream of the future state. The teams were:

- Representing the views of the CCAC's and Clients
- Representing the views of a Communication Team representing all of those who transfer information from one person or group to another.
- From the perspective of the home care nursing providers.
- From the perspective of the home support teams.
- And, from the perspective of all of those other groups within HomeCare who support the frontline work of the organization.

The dream included things such as "one person and one number for a CCAC manager to call who can answer and solve problems immediately." It included forming small client centered Primary Care Teams that would include the person doing scheduling, the care manager, and service providers.

These Primary Care Teams would be able to use technology to communicate every day in daily "huddles," request help from one another, access clinical resources and education, and perform administrative functions such as completing time sheets.

When the dream of the ideal state was compared between what was desired by the funder, the clients, the service providers and the managers, they all essentially imagined the same future ideal state. The design teams consolidated these into a consensus dream. Now, it just had to be designed.

Stage III: Design

The change methodology asks the design teams to first design the future ideal flow of the work from beginning to end. Then they design the social system to enable and support that work flow. The two design teams completed their initial work process flow for both home support and for nursing. It was understood that these designs would be modified based on any feedback from the Senior Management Team, from consultation with CCAC's, and from gaining more input from additional groups of employees. They will also be modified as they are implemented. In other words, this newly designed workflow is a starting point for continuous improvement.

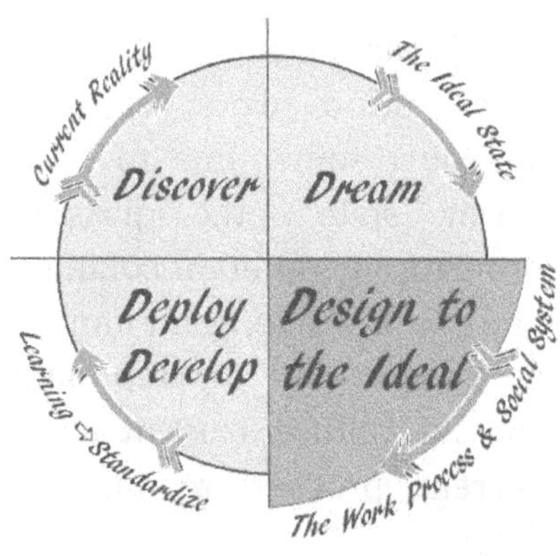

The teams then designed the social system. This included the

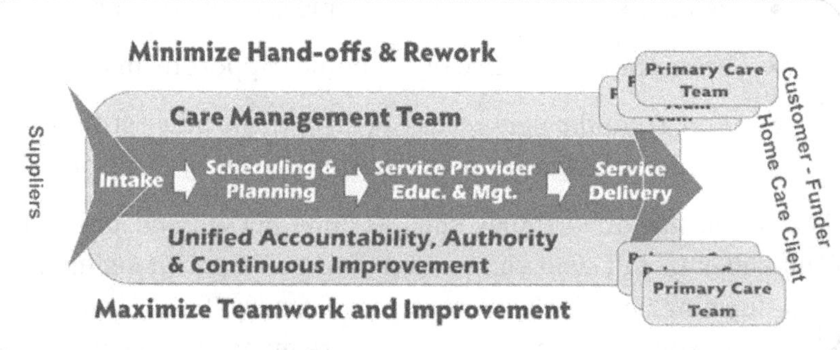

organization of people (team structure), job descriptions and the competencies required for each job, an analysis of the desired decision processes, and proposals regarding the motivation of staff.

While the consultant provided some training in both lean thinking and the design process at the beginning, most of his training occurred as each step in the design process was followed and specific issues were encountered.

There were two presentations to the senior management team: first to present the new work process, the second to present the proposed social systems. How the presentation was done was important. The two teams were to present their designs and include as many of their members as possible. The consultant sat in the back of the room and was to only interject if there were questions or concerns for which he was needed. It belonged to the members of the design team.

While practicing and preparing for the presentation several of the members voiced the belief that there was no way that the senior management team would accept their proposal. It was too radical, required too dramatic a change in the way the business was conducted. By the time the presentation was over, the senior management team stood up and applauded the design teams. They accepted the proposed design with virtually no changes.

The Work Process

The proposed future work process reduced the number of steps involve from 176 to 58. It eliminated the role of the central planning center (which has now been closed down) and created local planning and scheduling conducted by Client Service Associates who are part of the Care Manager's team who provides service to a CCAC. Along with the nurses or home support workers they form primary care teams responsible for all the service within a relatively small geographic area. These teams are closely aligned with the work of funding agencies and provide for much greater "customer intimacy," personal relationships between all of

those working to serve clients who are served.

The following graphic loosely illustrates the new work flow in which the Care Management Team takes complete ownership for the quality and efficiency of service delivery to one CCAC. There are no silos and blaming is replaced with continual problem-solving and improvement at each level.

The communication process is at the heart of the new design. Every nurse and home support worker now carries a Blackberry. They participate in a morning team huddle every day to discuss the schedule for that day and to solve any immediate problems, particularly scheduling problems.

In their report, the design team pointed out that it takes five hours from the CCAC making an offer of service to the scheduling of the first visit by the nurse. They projected that this would take forty-five minutes in the new system. They were wrong. It now takes five minutes!

The Social System

It has been said that "culture eats process for breakfast." It may be more accurate to state that culture and process are equally dependent and rely upon each other. The design teams recognized that they had to begin designing the elements of the culture with principles in mind. Just as national cultures are grounded in principles such as "freedom of speech, press and religion," the new HomeCare would have to be grounded in new principles. They agreed on the following principles that would guide their design of the culture:

1. We will have a unity of vision and values.
2. Decision-making will be transparent and perceived as fair: We will know who makes what decisions and how they are made.
3. We will treat others as we would want to be treated.
4. We will always demonstrate respect for our colleagues, clients and customers.
5. We will enhance individual and team responsibility.
6. We will develop a culture of recognition for good performance.
7. We will become a learning organization by effective listening and the appreciation of diverse points of view.

8. We will develop patterns of behavior, celebration, and unity that are rhythmic and reinforce our cultural values.
9. We will focus on improving processes rather than blaming individuals within the culture.
10. We will make opportunities for learning, development and advancement available on an equitable basis.

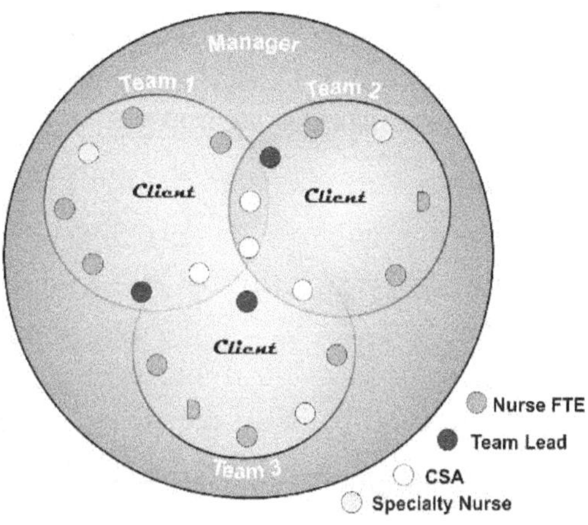

At the heart of the proposed social system was the team structure. The staffs were organized into teams around the new process both at the primary care level and the management levels. The following diagrams illustrate the new organization structure. Many readers may at first be confused. These don't look like "normal" illustrations of organization structure, with the senior person in a box at top, straight lines leading to more individual boxes of subordinates, etc. There are no squares, no straight lines, only circles, which symbolically represent the wholeness of jobs, the unity of teams and their shared responsibility. Each circle is a primary care team and the larger circle is the larger team serving one CCAC and their clients. The Client Service Associate, who does the scheduling, is a member of the primary care team. The design teams computed exactly how many service providers were needed in each geographic area. In the case of home support workers, an RPN serves as the team lead and can provide health care advice and coordinate with other health care professionals when needed.

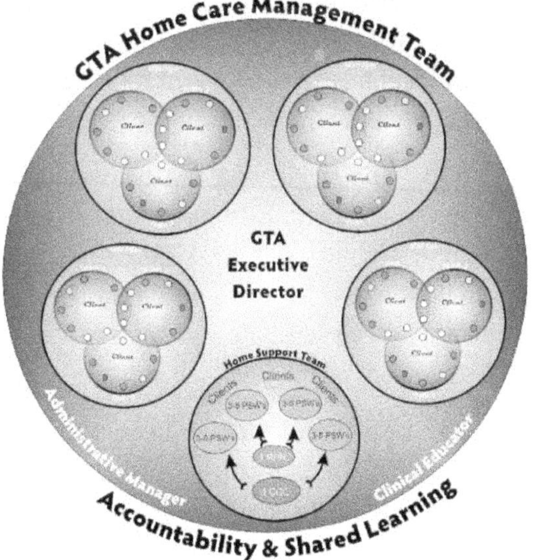

The design team also proposed larger circles that

would encompass all of the CCAC's served in the Toronto District and how corporate services such as human resources, finance and information systems would work with these teams. They were illustrated with overlapping circles intended to illustrate the breakdown of walls, the fluid flow of information between groups, which was not previously the case. The organizational principle illustrated in these diagrams is one of flexibility and fluidity, rather than rigidity. It is an attempt to adapt to the realities of the natural environment and to illustrate the desired change in the HomeCare culture.

In addition to the team structure the design team did a lot of work identifying all of the specific competencies required of each position in their design. They also wrote job descriptions and defined the decision-making process.

Decision-making is particularly important in the culture of any organization. Who will be involved in which decisions? And will these decisions be made in a *command, consultative* or *consensus* style? This was developed for each position. Here is an example of the decision matrix for nurses who are members of primary care teams.

In addition, the design teams analyzed the flow of information and identified exactly what types of information would be provided to individuals and to teams; where that information would come from; and how it would be delivered. This created the basis for common scorecards for each primary care team, care manager and district manager. There were eight key metrics, most of them required by the funding agency and used in their evaluation.

They also identified possible forms of reward and recognition that would be provided to teams as they improved their performance. Eight key measures of performance where agreed to and each team now tracks these on a weekly basis.

Following the approval of the design by the senior management team a detailed implementation plan was developed and implementation teams were assigned. The District Executive Director in each district and the Care and Service Manager for each area had the key responsibility for implementation. They had all served on the design teams and fully understood both the details and the intent of the design.

The implementation plan included moving from the design phase to a phase of continuous improvement. This phase included the assignment of internal coaches to each team and following a development process laid out in the consultant's team manual which was customized as the *Home Care Team Guide.*

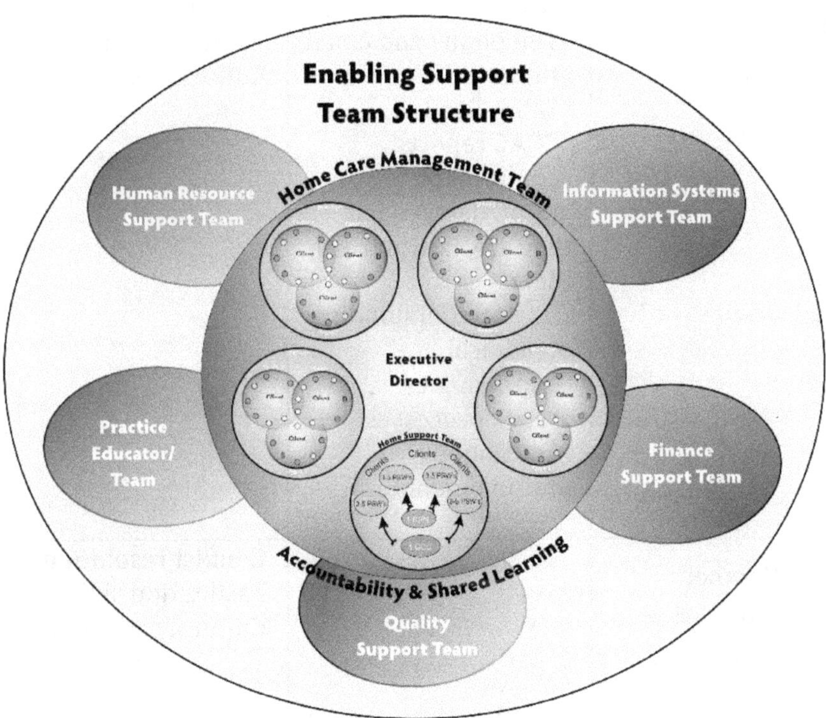

Following are two of the competency models developed by the design team for primary care team members and team leads. Also, following the competency models you will see an example of the decision worksheet. There was a similar sheet for every position. These defined not only what decisions the individual was had responsibility for, but also the style in which they would be made.

TEAM MEMBER COMPETENCY CHART – ALL MEMBERS		
Priority	**Technical Skills**	**People Skills**
A. Required for Team Membership	Computer skills – i.e. email, sending attachments, saving files, searching for files Telephone and email etiquette Self reflection CCAC report requirements CCAC data – what they are, how to read them Basic understanding of medical terminologies Work processes Continuous improvement	Customer/client service Team dynamics and roles Effective communication Cultural awareness
B. All Members Should Work Toward Developing		Conflict resolution Facilitation skills Cultural sensitivity
C. Most Member Should Develop These Skills		
D. Some Members Should Develop		
E. Would be Beneficial but Not Necessary		Diverse language skills

Team Member Competency Chart – Team Lead – ALL ABOVE PLUS BELOW:		
Priority	**Technical Skills**	**People Skills**
A. Required for Team Membership	Understand CCAC contracts Working knowledge of team dynamics RN designation Use and action data Scheduling principles Clinical experience Collective agreement	Desire to be Team lead (motivation/initiative) Know when to escalate to management Advanced customer/client service, conflict resolution, problem-solving and communication skills
A. All Members Should Work Toward Developing		
B. Most Member Should Develop These Skills		
C. Some Members Should Develop		
D. Would be Beneficial but Not Necessary		

Decision-Making Worksheet - Nurses

Command Decisions

Command decisions are those decisions that are made by one individual with authority on the spot. Best when the priority is speed and conformity to the decision such as in a fire drill or crisis mode.

1. Clinical care decisions – within scope of practice
2. Decisions about reporting to CCAC
3. Identifying and reporting Risk
4. Case load planning and visit schedule
5. Delegation of care to unregulated caregiver
6. Assessing appropriate level of service provider

Consultative Decisions

Those controlled by one person who consults with others who have knowledge or who must be committed to the decision. Use when time is important and when the decision is not sufficiently important to justify an entire team meeting.

1. Assignment of new referrals
2. Coaching/mentoring
3. Workload
4. Team huddles

Consensus Decisions

Decisions made by the entire team as a group. Use for those decisions that are important to all team members, need the commitment of entire team, and provide important learning for team members.

1. Schedule – goal of team member is to reach consensus. In the absence of consensus the team lead will make a consultative decision with the nurses – if that fails the decision will be made by the manager
2. Quality feedback – what to do as a team to improve
3. Unplanned absent coverage

Stage IV: Develop & Deploy

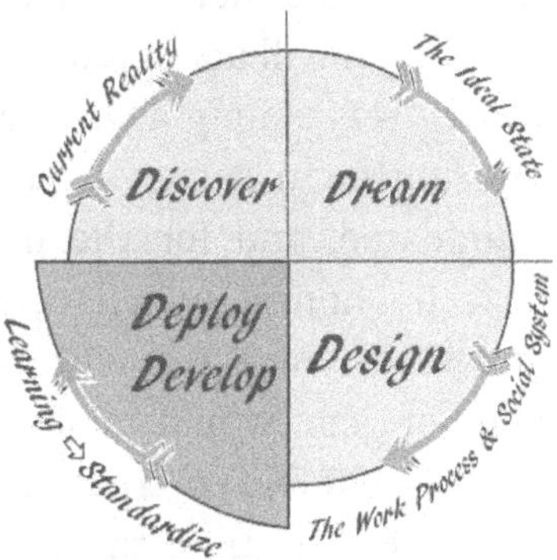

Once the work flow and the social system had been approved by the senior management team the design teams developed an implementation plan. This implementation planning involved additional members of the organization, particularly from IT, and Human Resources. A project manager was assigned to each site at which the new design was being implemented. These were in addition to the line manager responsible for that site. The project manager role proved invaluable because of all the coordination that was need involving IT/IS functions, human resource changes, and training.

As was expected, following approval from the senior management team, and initial implementation, many lessons were learned and modifications made during the implementation of the process in the remaining districts. At no time was it ever considered a "failure" to learn that the time needed for training for certain positions was inadequate, or that the exact number of people required for a jobs had been underestimated. The design teams and the organization had adopted an attitude of science, an acceptance of experimentation and learning, as an essential aspect of the culture.

For approximately six months the Senior Vice President led a Wednesday morning Lean Implementation Steering Team meeting over WebEx. These were attended by all District Managers who were implementing the new design, the project managers, key corporate staff members, and the consultant. Initially these meetings focused on who needed to do what to achieve the implementation. They gradually changed into a meeting where each district shared their key performance data and improvements in the data were discussed. There was an atmosphere of open sharing that was essential to the learning process.

Outcomes

There are both objective and subjective outcomes of this process. There is an outcome that might be overlooked in the desire for empirical proof of the validity of the new design. And, that outcome has to do with the psychology and development of human potential. You will remember the four young women from the planning center. One of them, the youngest, was there by accident. A planner who had been selected and scheduled to be on the design team became ill and a quick replacement had to be found. This young woman, Brandi, was simply available. Who is available is usually a terrible selection criterion for a design team member. But, there she was – a bit confused, intimidated, and for the first several weeks she contributed little. To be perfectly honest, when this author spoke to her, she spoke in a rather adolescent voice and with that adolescent sarcasm that made one question whether she would make any useful contribution. But, the process of involvement and co-creation transforms people – or, at least the perception of people. By the time the design work was completed Brandi and the other three were all facilitating break out groups and demonstrating the essential value of their knowledge of the scheduling process and the workings of the software that was used, and would be used, in the new design. In a few months Brandi become an extremely effective team leader of the team of GTA Client Service Associates. She was leading meetings, developing standard work, training new Associates, and tracking performance data. She was a new person. The other three young women all became trainers and coaches of the Client Service Associates in the subsequent Districts as the design was rolled out. By traditional thinking, one might have asked "what can they contribute to the redesign of the organization and culture" because of their low rank and inexperience. In fact, they each became true heroines of the new design. They were easily among the most important players in the process.

The other subjective outcome of this process is the dramatic change in the culture of problem-solving and decision-making in the organization. In the past there was a high level of distrust and blaming. Today, there are regular team meetings in which the focus is on the data, the key measures of performance, and the processes that result in that performance. The absence of blaming has become the new normal.

Productivity of Service Providers

From an internal and financial standpoint the most critical number is the number of visits made per day or week by service providers. This measure is expressed as "visits per FTE" (full time equivalents). In all Districts where the process has been implemented these measures have improved. The reason for this is primarily the effect of the primary care teams who, in their morning huddles every day, discuss their service levels, their targets, and who can handle additional visits. The waste created by walls between functions and the unnecessary steps in the process have been eliminated. The team now knows exactly what their level of productivity is, as well as missed visits, continuity, referral acceptance and other KPI's. The Client Service Associate is now part of that team and is intimately familiar with the team members' schedules and is in frequent communication with the funders. This intimacy, transparency and teamwork have resulted in across the board increases in productivity and significant improvement in the financial performance of the organization.

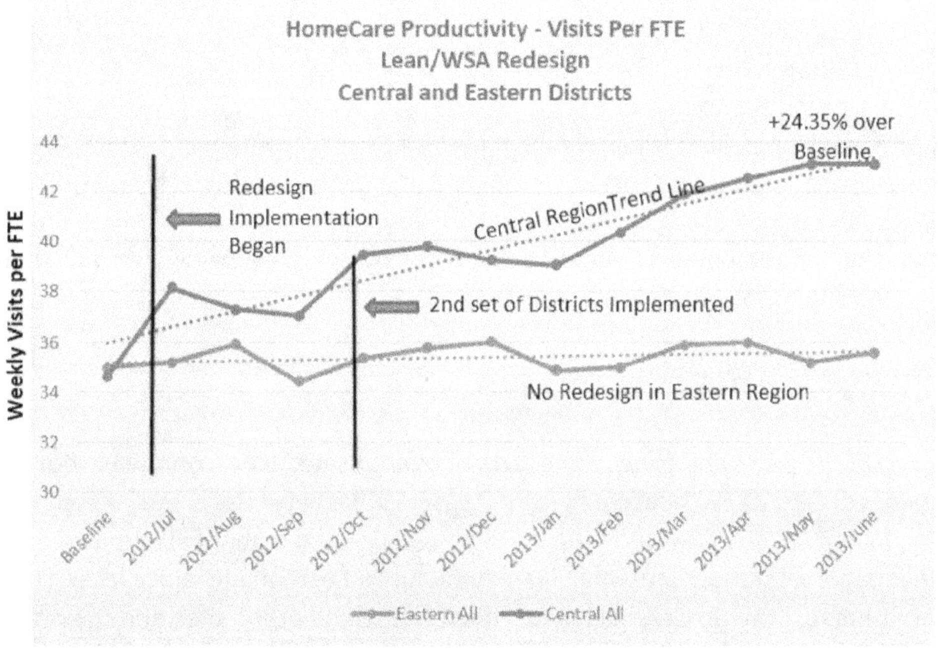

The above graph illustrates the impact of the redesigned process compared to baseline and a control group. This case study is being written eighteen months after the first two pilot sites were implemented. Many of the sites have been in implementation less than six months and the trend line continues to point upward. Note the baseline data prior to July 2012. This baseline was reasonably stable over the previous year.

It is unusual to have a control group when implementing a change management process. The Eastern District of Canada was not included in the redesign for a number of reasons. You will see that the performance of the Eastern District remained relatively stable while the Central District has experienced a 24.35 percent improvement in productivity. This obviously represents a major improvement in financial performance.

One might ask "If productivity improved this much, was it achieved to the detriment of quality measures?" The short answer is no. The quality measures, and these are monitored by the CCAC funding agencies, are missed visits, continuity (not a different nurse every day), and complaints by clients. For most districts each of these measures improved over the course of implementation. Again, this can be attributed to increased control by the care providers and their constant monitoring of their teams data.

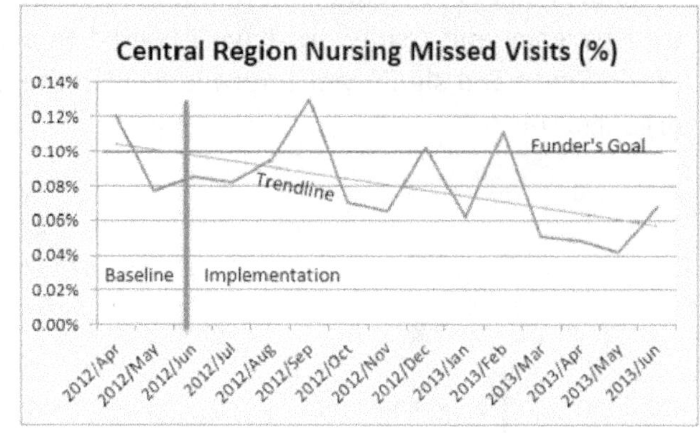

Customer Satisfaction:

On the following pages are charts of overall satisfaction on the part of the funding agency's managers and case managers for the first two implementations. The follow-up survey was completed about six months after the implementation and improvements have been made since that time. Additionally, the process has been rolled out to the other sites and they have experienced similar improvements in customer satisfaction.

In the following charts, it may be hard to read the options, but the first two columns two the left are "Very Dissatisfied" and "Somewhat Dissatisfied." You will see in the Trenton Home Support survey before implementation more than fifty percent of the respondents were either very or somewhat dissatisfied with the level of service they were receiving from HomeCare. Six months after implementation no respondents reported being either very or somewhat dissatisfied. In the pre-survey none reported being "Very Satisfied" and in the post survey 40% reported being very satisfied with the level of service.

In the Greater Toronto Area the funding agencies rated their level of dissatisfaction, with more than fifty-percent responding that they were either Very Dissatisfied or Somewhat Dissatisfied. In the post redesign implementation survey, also administered about six months after implementation, only eighteen percent reported being very or somewhat dissatisfied.

In conversations with HomeCare managers and funding agency managers it was generally agreed that this dramatic improvement had saved major contracts from cancellation. The key factors that resulted in the change in their satisfaction levels was the ability to communicate quickly and easily, to have problems solved by a knowledgeable person, and to have a consistent point of contact.

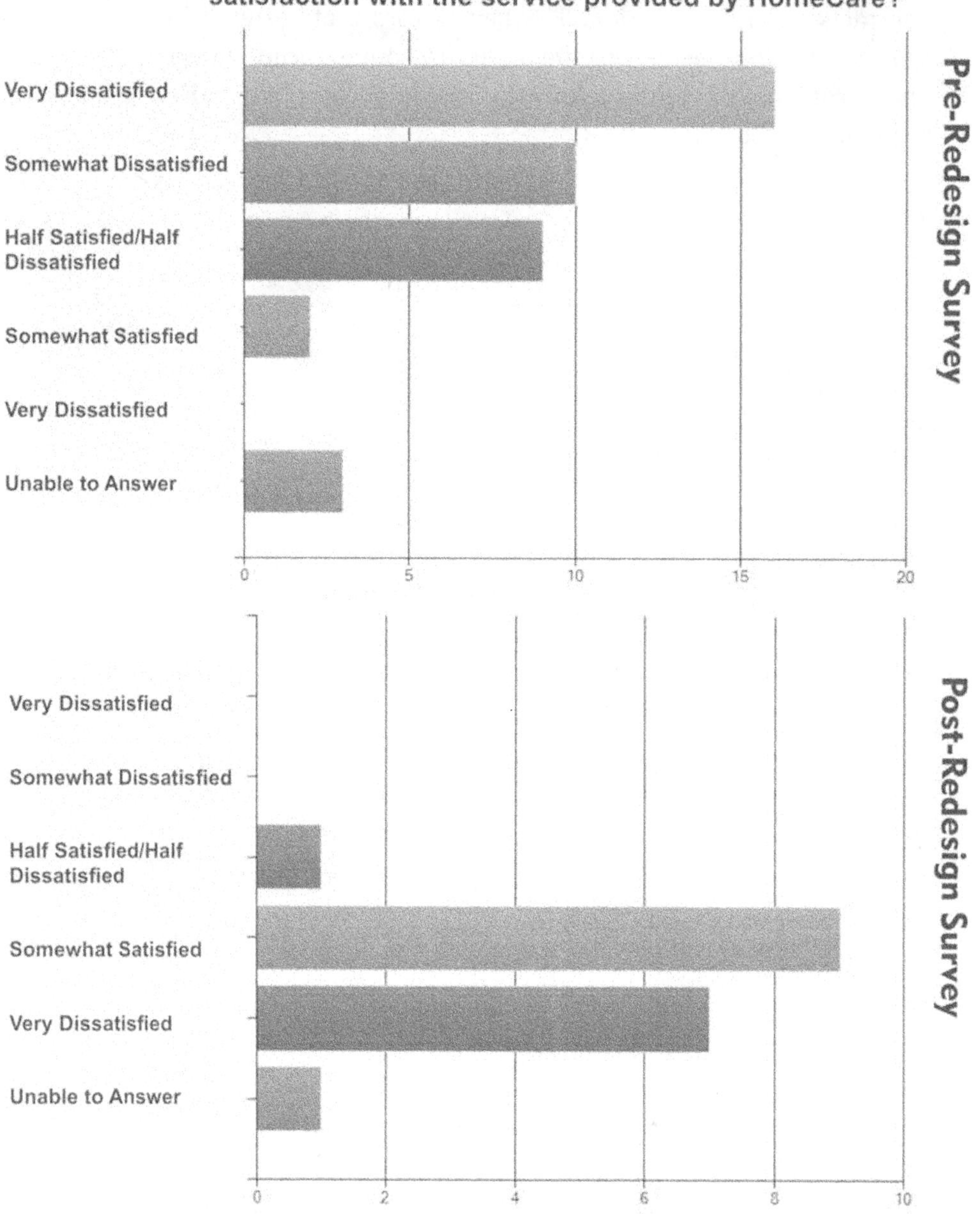
Trenton Home Support
From your personal experience, how would you rate your satisfaction with the service provided by HomeCare?
Very Dissatisfied
Somewhat Dissatisfied
Half Satisfied/Half Dissatisfied
Somewhat Satisfied
Very Dissatisfied
Unable to Answer
0
5
10
15
20
Pre-Redesign Survey
Very Dissatisfied
Somewhat Dissatisfied
Half Satisfied/Half Dissatisfied
Somewhat Satisfied
Very Dissatisfied
Unable to Answer
0
2
4
6
8
10
Post-Redesign Survey

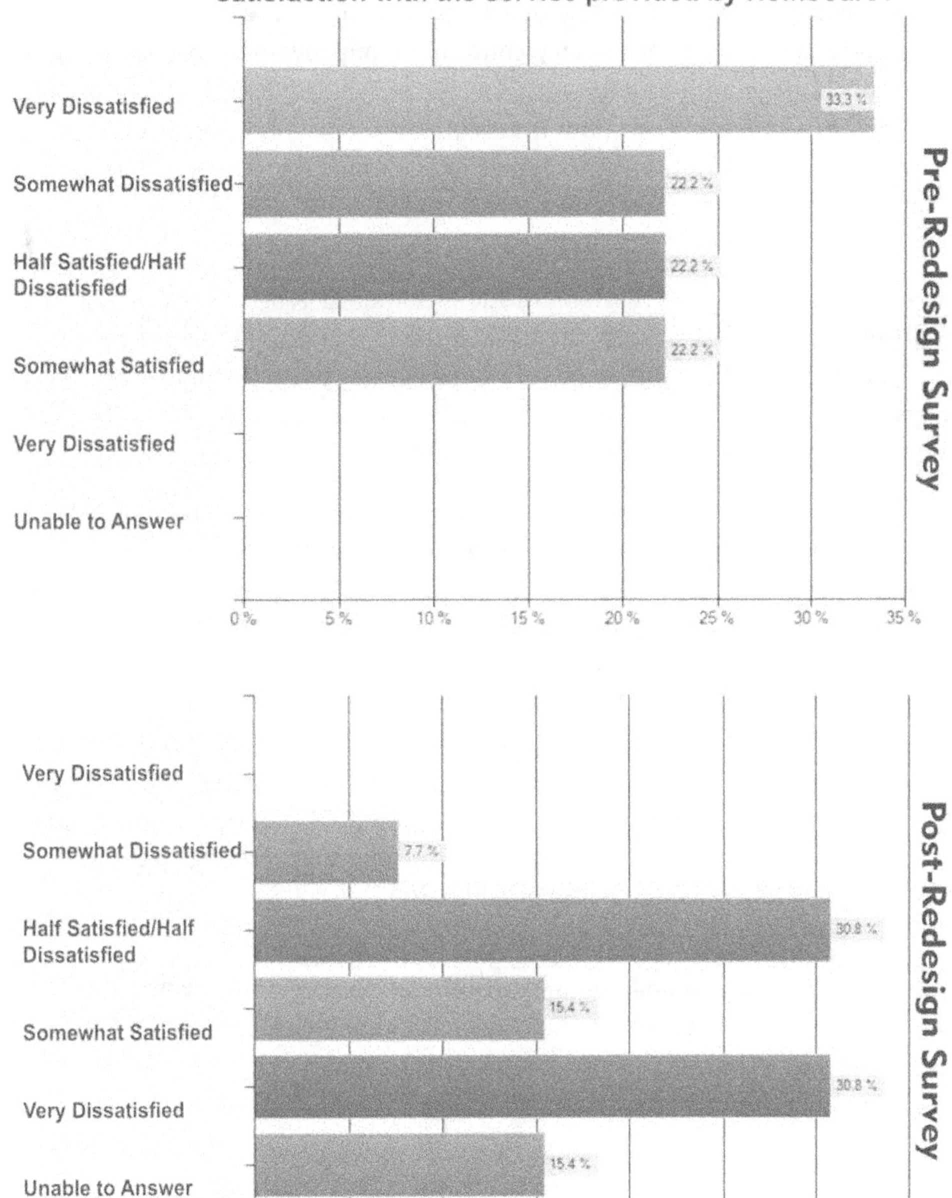
Toronto Nursing
From your personal experience, how would you rate your satisfaction with the service provided by HomeCare?
Pre-Redesign Survey
Very Dissatisfied
33.3 %
Somewhat Dissatisfied
22.2 %
Half Satisfied/Half Dissatisfied
22.2 %
Somewhat Satisfied
22.2 %
Very Dissatisfied
Unable to Answer
0 % 5 % 10 % 15 % 20 % 25 % 30 % 35 %
Post-Redesign Survey
Very Dissatisfied
Somewhat Dissatisfied
7.7 %
Half Satisfied/Half Dissatisfied
30.8 %
Somewhat Satisfied
15.4 %
Very Dissatisfied
30.8 %
Unable to Answer
15.4 %
0 % 5 % 10 % 15 % 20 % 25 % 30 % 35 %

Post-Script and Implications

Now that the redesigned process and organizational system have been implemented throughout all of the Central Region of HomeCare the improvement process is in a new phase, going from changes in systems and structure to the more evolutionary continuous improvement process. There have probably been a hundred small improvements made in how the design has been implemented across the Districts. But there is now an entirely new process of managing in the Central District of HomeCare and that is based on teamwork and continuous improvement.

HomeCare is now standardizing the redesigned work processes. They are also developing Standard Work and Leader Standard Work for each position. By developing standard work they understand that this does not mean to make these jobs rigid. It simply means "here is what we know works from our experience, so let's keep doing it" until someone decides to conduct an additional experiment and find improvements.

One often expects resistance to change when you are changing almost everything about how jobs are done, how decisions are made, and the culture of the organization. And, while some resisted change at HomeCare, that resistance was minimal. The reason for the lack of resistance was the use of a design process that was genuinely one of co-creation that trusted the expertise of those who do the work. Each site took the original redesign documents and then did their own design, modifying and customizing to their realities. There was also little resistance because it did become the accepted norm that there would be no blame or punishment of individuals, but rather we would all focus on how to improve the process. That relieved a great deal of fear that had been present in the organization.

This case provides a general model of how successful change can be achieved in a dispersed and complex health care organization where there is little immediate supervision. It illustrates both the successful application of lean thinking and the whole-system model of change.

Part Two

The Process of Whole-system Architecture

CHAPTER 5

ARE WE READY FOR CHANGE?

Every organization is in some state of change. Every country, family and individual is in a state of change. To be alive is to be in a state of change. The same can be said of any organization. The first question is *"Do we need transformational change or continuous improvement?"* The second question is *"Are we ready for the change that is coming?"*

CONTINUOUS IMPROVEMENT OR TRANSFORMATIONAL CHANGE

This author will assume that every organization needs to be engaged in continuous improvement, just as every human being needs to be engaged in life-long learning and exercise. The alternative is decay. Or, as Dr. Deming said, "You don't have to change. Survival isn't mandatory." For some companies continuous improvement is sufficient. When is it sufficient?

- When you are in a strong competitive position.
- When you possess all of the essential capabilities to compete in the market of today and tomorrow.
- When you know that your culture is strong and well suited to continuous improvement.
- When the external environment is changing slowly and is not presenting significant threats or opportunities.
- When your organization structure is not inhibiting, but facilitating innovation and continuous improvement.

If all the above describe your organization I will strongly recommend you to my *Team Guide to Continuous Improvement* which will help you engage everyone in the process of continuous improvement. If, on the other hand, any of those conditions are not true, you will be well advised to follow the transformational change process described in this book.

Are We Ready for Change?

The answer to this question is almost always "no." We are installing new computer software, we are rolling out a new product, we are making management change, etc., etc., there is always something going on that makes a significant change something worth putting off. It's a bit like putting off that diet or exercise. It always seems that it will be more convenient tomorrow – and, then somehow, it never is.

A genuinely transformational experience occurred when I was eighteen years old and enlisted in the Army. I was sent to Fort Dix, N.J. for basic training. My head was shaved, my clothes disappeared and I suddenly looked like everyone else. That was the beginning of transformation!

It was five o'clock in the morning and the five foot tall Puerto Rican drill sergeant came bursting into the barracks banging on garbage cans and bunks and yelling for everyone to get up and stand at attention. For some reason he spotted me. He came within a few inches of my nose and shouted "Recruit! It's raining outside. Are your ready to run five miles in the rain? (He didn't wait for an answer.) Well, you're going to run five miles in the rain this morning, and you know what you're going to do after that? (Again, it was a rhetorical question) You're going to crawl through the mud for a hundred yards with your rifle in your arms! And, do you know what you're going to do then? You're going to run another five miles in the rain! Isn't that right, Soldier?" I wasn't at all sure that it was right, but I did have the sense to know that "Yes, Sergeant!" was the right answer. Of course, he yelled back "I didn't hear you!" To which I repeated "Yes Sergeant!" a bit louder.

I was genuinely not ready for this experience. But a great realization occurred to me. This sergeant, and everyone else in that barracks or on the entire base, could not have cared less how I felt about running and crawling in the rain! I was going to do it whether I liked it, was ready for it, or not. There is something very liberating about that realization. And, I am sure that there are many times when the CEO of a company would just like to line everyone up and act out the role of that Puerto Rican drill sergeant. Unfortunately, he would not be held in high regard if he did. Unlike new Army recruits, employees can walk away, and they can pretend to be engaged, but go about their business as usual. Somehow, we have to get them engaged, understanding, and committed to change. Even though the reality may be no more pleasant than running five miles in the rain and it may be just as inevitable. One important thing... that drill sergeant ran right alongside our company through the rain, calling cadence all the way!

It is the responsibility of leaders to make the business case for why a significant change is needed. Transformational change must be linked to your strategy and the imperative to survive, to compete and to grow as an organization. There must be a common understanding that "we just aren't good enough the way we are today."

Challenge and Response

One way of understanding strategy is to see it as a challenge-and-response mechanism; the response producing a wave pattern of success or failure, each wave in its turn presenting a new challenge. Creatively responding to challenge is the essence of competitive strategy.

The challenge may be presented by the external environment. It may be a new technology, a shift in market preference, a decline in a market, or behavior of competitors. Companies often decline not because of brilliant moves by a competitor but because of their own loss of motivation and creativity. Bureaucratic companies lose the ability to respond, they lose the force of will, the ability of self-determination. Bureaucracies essentially commit suicide by their inability to creatively respond to challenge. The whole-system architecture process is about developing this creative response.

Companies also fail because they recognize a challenge but fail to create the internal alignment which permits an effective response. A company such as Sears may have originally been a creative company and responded to the challenge of a dispersed marketplace. However, Sears grew accustomed to its market position. Suddenly, Wal-Mart created new responses to the challenge of the market. These responses were clearly visible, but the culture of Sears was not able to exert its will and respond successfully. Intellectually, Sears knew it had to change its ways, but the systems and structure of the company made this almost impossible.

It may be that your executives have defined a strategy that will lead to competitive success in the future. Achieving that strategy is the challenge. But, do you have the capabilities in place to respond to that challenge?

Gap Analysis – The Case for Action			
Challenges	**How Critical**	**Current Capability**	**Required Future Capability**

A Consensus Building Workshop – Preparing for Change

Consider having a series of workshops to involve a large number of people, particularly the managers and employees who need to be engaged in the change process. The purpose of the workshop is to define the critical challenges facing the organization, prioritize those challenges, and then identify key responses to those challenges. The results of this exercise will be helpful input to the steering team when they write the charter. The following diagram can be blown up and put on the wall.

Use Post-It-Notes to write down each of the significant challenges.

Ask each table of participants to brainstorm what they feel are the following:

- Challenges from competitors.
- Challenges from changing customer preferences.
- Challenges from new technology.
- Challenges from changing demographics or social preferences.
- Challenges from the economy or political, or government regulations.

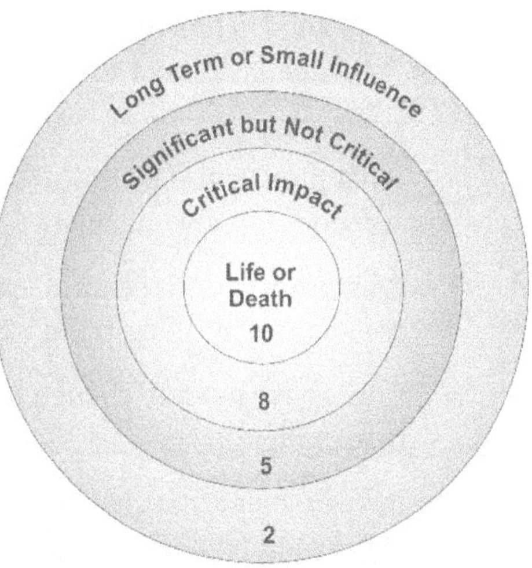

The participants may think of other sources of challenge, but the above questions will get them started. Give them a half hour to brainstorm all the possible challenges facing the organization. Then have the team prioritize them and place the post-it-notes on this diagram.

Once you have done this, have a pros and cons discussion. Those who feel most strongly about a challenge should make their arguments to the group by presenting the facts, insights, or expertise that may cause them to give a particular challenge a high rating. At this point it may be helpful to have some experts from outside the group present their impressions or knowledge. The team should then be given an opportunity to re-vote. Changing your vote should be considered a normal thing to do once you have had a discussion of the importance of each challenge.

The team should then take the three to five greatest challenges and state them as a "Case for Action." The case for action should state the threats and the opportunities represented by the challenges in the environment. The statement should include both the business case and the personal case. In other words, how will a failure to respond to these challenges affect the lives of employees of the organization? How will successful responses affect the lives of employees? What will be the impact on the shareholder, customers, and suppliers?

If you have different tables, or teams, doing this you can then ask for each group to report and share what they identified as the highest priority challenges. Which ones were considered "life or death" by all the groups? Each team should make their "case for action." Which challenges got the highest score? Rank order them according to the score assigned to each challenge by the combined tables.

This process will result in ranking the strategic challenges facing the organization. It is time to begin to formulate responses to these challenges.

The second round of this exercise is to identify responses to the most critical challenges. Have each table start with what they recognized as the greatest challenge. Then have them address the second and third highest priority challenge. Ask them to consider the following in their response to the challenge:

- What human and technical capabilities do we have that can be used to respond to that challenge?
- What human and technical capabilities do we need to develop or create in order to respond to that challenge?
- How do we need to change the way we do our work in order to meet that challenge?
- If we do meet that challenge, what will be the benefit to the organization and to employees?

These workshops could be a morning or afternoon in length. You may think of other questions to pose in addition to these. But, you are accomplishing two things by doing this. First, you are generating understanding as to why the organization needs to change, the case for action. You are also generating "buy-in" or support because you are engaging your employees and managers. You are listening to them. They are building their own house. This goes a long way in helping to prepare them for change. Second, you are creating a list of priorities for change, and possible changes, or responses that will be very helpful input to the senior team as they write the charter for change. It will also be helpful to the design teams as they begin to do their work.

Survey Your Customers and Associates

For several projects I have found it very helpful to survey both customers and associates prior to beginning the change process. Using web based surveys it is very easy to construct, administer and analyze the results. I can assist with several templates that I have prepared, but you will probably want to customize them to your specific situation. Seeing the results, particularly of customer surveys can do a lot to create readiness for change on the part of the senior team and can provide useful input to the design teams. This again, is part of the discovery process.

Train to Prepare for Change

It is possible that some of your managers and employees simply do not read books to prepare them for change. They don't know the difference between what they have now and what they could have. Understanding how Shigeo Shingo worked with the press operators to achieve single minute exchange of dies, or hundreds of other stories help to envision a different culture. This is what I call "getting out of the village" which we all live in. There are many books and many training experiences that can help to create this alternative vision. In the Appendix there are several cases that may help your steering team and design team "get out of the village."

The Psychology of a Change Process

While no two organizations go through a transformational change in the same way, there are predictable patterns. In the beginning of a change process there must be a felt need and the primary change agents, the executives, the internal or external consultant, must make the case for change and paint a picture as to why the future will be better than the current state. He or she must also "sell" the participants on the idea that the nature of the process will be not only challenging, but fun and a great opportunity for learning.

The change process will often begin the way many relationships begin - with a romance stage. In this stage we love the idea and we have great expectations for the future. But, no one has done any work yet. Ideas are loved before they involve work! Then the work begins... and the pain begins. Now it is pregnancy. As the work increases, the weight of the child increases, the stretching of your mind or body happens, and somehow your enthusiasm for the change begins to decline. You didn't realize it was going take this much effort! And, of course, there are no actual results to show at this point. So when the work gets to the maximum and there are no results yet, the enthusiasm drops dramatically. Then the baby or the new design is born, you begin implementing it, and there is a new burst of enthusiasm. Now you enter the nurturing stage. It is not as painful as pregnancy and labor, but it is still a lot of work. Gradually, results begin to appear. As the design is implemented it becomes less effort and more natural. With work going down and results coming up, enthusiasm returns and you experience fulfillment. This is the typical emotional life cycle of a change process.

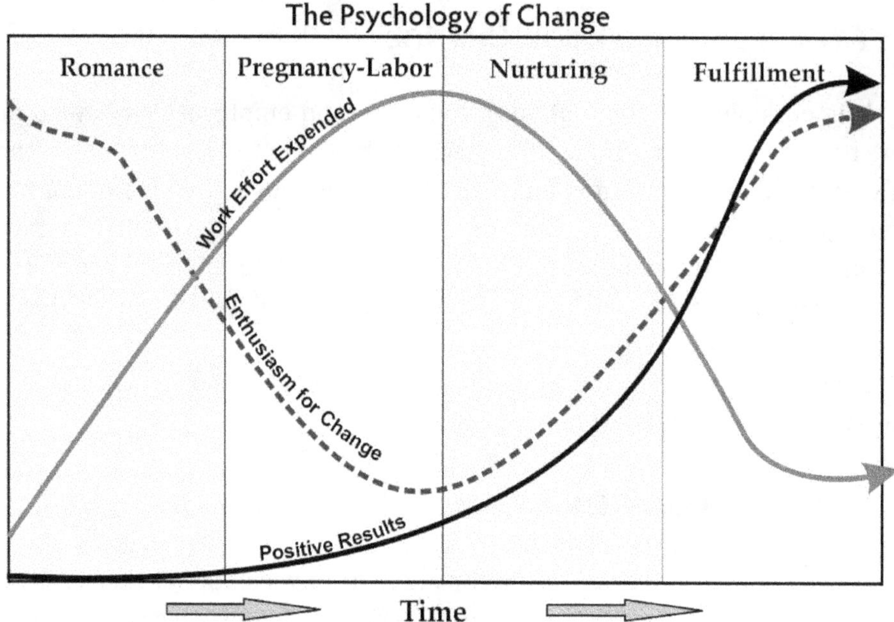

In the End – There is Leadership

Leaders do not wait until others in the organization are ready for change. Leaders cause them to be ready by making the business case clear and by inspiring others to believe in a better future. Leaders lead by creating and communicating a positive vision of the future for the people whom they seek to lead. And, eventually, leaders will have to hold people accountable for their action or inaction. Sometimes leaders need to make the imperative to change clear.

There is one quality of leaders that helps people adapt to change. It is not the obvious qualities of determination, charisma or intellect. It is illustrated in the following story.

I was conducting a workshop at the Intel Corporation headquarters in Santa Clara and, Andy Grove, Chairman and founder of the firm, one of the founders of the entire semi-conductor industry, was a participant along with about forty senior managers. At some point in the workshop, Andy Grove, not shy or soft-spoken, made a very declarative statement about something I had said. Immediately upon completing the statement, a young man, in the back of the room, raised his hand. I suspect that this young man was two or three levels below the Chairman in the organization structure. When he rose to speak, he too was not shy. "Andy, that's wrong. And we all know it's wrong, and you keep saying it, and it keeps being wrong!"

A pregnant silence filled the room while we waited for the Chairman's response. Andy Grove slowly turned around to face the young man and said, "OK, let's discuss it. What do the rest of you think?" Then followed a twenty-minute period during which the managers discussed the issue with their chairman, and I lost control of my workshop. But, I was more interested in observing this dynamic than in regaining control.

The bold young manager knew something about his chairman and the culture of his company. He was no fool. He knew the boundaries and he trusted those boundaries. When this discussion was over it was clear that he would be fine, he was in no danger of retribution.

Intel is a company built on intellectual and scientific rigor. What is valued most is the ability to think, to question, and to explore the truth of things. Andy Grove is a scientist, the opposite of an ideologue, who values people who can raise serious questions and engage in serious dialogue on important issues. This forms the social capital, one of the strengths of Intel, and the culture begins with the norms established by the founder and Chairman and demonstrated through his own behavior.

The ability to trust in the honest pursuit of the truth, to trust the value of intellectual inquiry enables innovation, creativity and change. Imagine the opposite culture. Imagine that a competitor of Intel was dominated by a leader who punished those who were outspoken, who would not listen to a challenging statement by an underling. Imagine the fear. And, then imagine how this company would be able to compete with Intel.

A leader who will listen and is not threatened by challenging ideas and differing opinions serves as a catalyst for change.

CHAPTER 6

WRITING YOUR DESIGN CHARTER

The design charter should begin with an understanding of the corporate level purpose, strategic business model and goals. It should present the vision of where we are going and why we are going there. That is strategy. The design of the future state should be for the purpose of creating the *organizational capabilities* that will enable the organization to achieve its strategy. Too many strategic plans begin in words and end in words. They are not translated into actions that create the capabilities required to achieve the strategy.

For example, if a company has a strategy to be an innovator in software development for health care applications, they will need a set of capabilities. Do they have the human capital, the competencies that are required? Do they have the processes that lead to successful software development? And do they have the organization structure and culture that will enable that development? These should be the goals of the design team; to design an organizational system with those capabilities that will achieve the strategic objectives.

Whole-system architecture is focused on building the capabilities to achieve strategy, not merely solving short term problems.

The design charter initiates the detailed redesign of the organization's work and human systems. The steering team will define the essential purpose, principles, goals, and the boundaries of design or redesign work. This is the purpose of the design charter.

The charter is the Constitution for the future organization. While the design charter initiates the design based on strategy, it is best if the steering team is somewhat humble about its product and is willing to listen to feedback and suggestions from the design team. In other words, "play catch-ball" in Hoshin Kanri language. This may result in useful changes in the charter. As the design work progresses, it may also be wise to revisit the charter if the design team discovers new and unanticipated obstacles or opportunities.

There are several reasons for writing a design charter:

- To create the vision for the design team to understand what they are trying to achieve.
- To be sure that the design is clearly linked to strategy and business goals.
- To clearly state boundaries: what may be designed and what must remain beyond the design team's scope.
- To share any expectations regarding the nature of the process to be used by the design team.
- To share any expectations that the steering team may hold regarding the final product in terms of the work process or culture of the organization.
- To clarify expectations for time and deliverables.

Most management teams have written some mission, vision, and values statements. Or, there may be a corporate-level statement. Many management teams have not given a great deal of thought to what capabilities, competencies, or technologies they believe will result in competitive advantage in the future. This thought process should be the basis of developing the organization architecture.

Once the charter has been written, the steering team meets with the design team and they read the charter together. It is important for the design team to look the steering team in the eye and see that they are serious about considering an entirely different type of organization, culture, or strategy. The design team is likely not to believe that, *"We can actually change this...."* unless they have this direct communication with the steering team. They may also ask clarifying questions such as, "Do you mean we can actually change the compensation?" A clarification may be, *"We do actually want your recommendations to change the compensation system but not actual compensation levels."* This clarification at the beginning of the design process is a simple matter, but the failure to obtain this clarification can result in wasted effort.

COMPONENTS OF A CHARTER

Generally, effective charters contain the following components:

- Purpose Statement
- Values, Vision, and Mission
- Business Strategy and Scorecard
- Organizing Principles
- Project Boundaries and Scope
- Reporting Expectations

PURPOSE STATEMENT

To the steering team the purpose of the change process may be obvious, while for others it may not be fully understood. Write a clear, simple one paragraph statement explaining why you are doing this. Don't make the mistake made by the mother who when asked by her five year old son, "Mommy, where did I come from?" proceeded to give a long lecture on the birds and bees. When finished the boy said, "Oh, because Johnny came from Indiana."

The purpose statement should answer these questions:

- "Why did we form a design team?"
- "What is the general result we want?"
- "What is the primary goal that should be the focus of the design team?"
- Is there a big business goal? For example, to cut cycle time in half; or, to improve productivity by 25%; or to enable us to enter and compete in a new market.

Do not get into all of the details of strategy, performance targets, etc., because that will come later. This is simply an introductory statement.

VALUES, VISION, AND MISSION

There is nothing wrong with motherhood and apple pie! We have often heard managers complain that broad principles or values are nothing but motherhood and apple pie - perhaps so. But, a clear statement of why you exist as an organization (our mission), the core values that form a foundation for your behavior, and a statement of where you are going to be in the future are essential first ingredients in a design charter. Toyota states there purpose as "to serve society." That is certainly a simple statement, but it has served them well.

Many organizations today have been through exercises based on Stephen Covey's books on principle-centered leadership[37] or his book *Seven Habits of Highly Successful People.* As a result they have defined personal and company statements of principles, values, and vision. In many cases these have been shared with employees, printed, framed, and hung on the wall. Unfortunately, in too many cases the reality of daily life has changed little. Life has changed little because the real things that dominate daily activity in an organization – the work process, the job definition, the decision-making process, and the structure of the organization – are not aligned to principles.

Whole-system architecture is *"principle-centered"* redesign. When most reengineering projects were done, they focused on cost reduction or cycle-time improvement. Rarely did they include a focus on changing the culture of the organization to be more centered on principles. Whole-system architecture does both: it focuses on business processes and creating a culture based on principles.

Knowledge of vision and values is the starting point for creating organization architecture. Imagine that you are going to build a house. You begin the process with an idea. You want a house that is casual and airy and you have three young children who you can picture playing in the backyard. You can imagine yourself at the barbecue on your deck with a dozen friends playing volleyball in your backyard. You have a vision of what this house could be, how it could affect lives. You imagine the children you are planning to have living and playing in this house. This vision is the beginning of architecture. The vision of a home for an elderly couple in retirement will be something very different.

---

[37] Covey, Stephen R. *Principle Centered Leadership*, New York, Fireside, 1990.

As you design the house questions will arise that can only be answered by your values and vision. Will the children's bedrooms have telephone and cable outlets? What if the school system is hooked up to the cable system to provide Internet connections over fiber optic cable, with all classroom material coming over the Internet or cable television? Now your decision may change. Your decision about the home information systems is based on both your understanding of technology and your assumptions about how you want your children to behave. These are value decisions. The decision to provide different types of information to employees will be based on value assumptions and cultural principles. It is important that the senior team consider these carefully.

One of the difficulties in writing a vision statement is that we have been well taught to think in practical, even conservative terms. To write an inspiring statement, we must leave that learning behind. The Declaration of Independence is an entirely impractical document. "We hold these truths to be self-evident that all men are created equal...." Really? That wasn't practical! It violated what was obviously true in the present state. Some men were created wealthy and some poor. Some were created with power and prestige, and some were created slaves. How could they make such an obviously impractical statement as to suggest that all men *are* created equal? The American Founding Fathers were architects of change. They were creating a new organizational architecture, and they based their architecture on what they wished the nation to be, what they imagined it could and should be. By doing so, they set in motion incredible forces that would alter the structure and systems of the entire planet. They were leaders!

Business Strategy and Scorecard

The primary motive for the whole-system architecture process should be to design those processes and culture that will enable your organization to achieve its strategic plan.

> *"Competitive strategy is about being different. It means deliberately choosing a different set of activities to deliver a unique mix of value. The essence of strategy is in the activities - choosing to perform activities differently or to perform different activities than rivals. Otherwise, a*

strategy is nothing more than a marketing slogan that will not withstand competition."[38]

The whole-system architecture process should be one of defining those activities that lead to competitive success and defining how they will be performed. It should be focused on creating strategic value, not only operational effectiveness.

Too often strategy is owned by the senior executives as a prized jewel. It is too often not deployed in a way in which everyone can feel ownership for the strategy. To the degree that it is exclusively owned by senior executives it will not be achieved. The more broadly it is owned, the more likely it will be achieved.

Professional employees, in particular, with skills that are easily transportable from company to company, are not content to simply trust in senior management's strategic wisdom. They know better. They know that the most senior managers are not the sole owners of great thoughts, dreams, imagination, and creativity. In fact, the best visions of what is possible in the future often come from those who are directly working on new technologies or working directly with customers. One of the reasons many strategies are never implemented is because they were created by the senior managers without involvement of those close to the work and therefore did not reflect the realities on the ground. Today the best strategic planning process is a dynamic dialogue that involves managers and employees at various levels as they create a common vision of the future organization.

Strategy is everyone's business. A few years ago I met with the union employees at a truck manufacturing plant. Among their greatest concerns was, "What is the future of this plant? How does it fit with the long-range plans of the company? What do we have to do to assure the long-term viability of this facility?" These questions translate into the understandable personal question, *"Am I going to have a job here five years from now?"* The hourly employees have a perfectly legitimate interest in the company's strategy and how their performance links to this strategy. They should be engaged in the process of assuring that they are doing everything possible to assure its competitive success.

---

[38] Michael Porter, Harvard Business Review, November-December 1996.

The following summarizes the strategy issues that should be included in the charter:

1. How will your market position change in relation to competitors in the next three years?
2. How will markets and customers change in the next three years, and what impact will this have on your work and organization?
3. How will your products and services change in the next three years, and what impact will this have on your work and organization?
4. How do you hope that the new design of work and organization will lead to an improvement in economic performance?
5. What are the specific financial targets? Do these include revenue, expense, and asset utilization targets?
6. What is the design attempting to achieve in terms of enhancing the assets, the capital, of the organization. (see the chapter on assets and liabilities)
7. What changes in our technology or information strategy will be required in order to fulfill your strategy?
8. What changes in core work processes will be required to fulfill your strategy?
9. What changes in the competencies of people will be required in order to do the important work?
10. And, what are the big changes in the culture of the organization that the steering team desires to see as a result of this process.

It may be that the senior team genuinely does not know the answers to all of these questions. It is perfectly legitimate to answer them as best you can, and then ask the design team to respond with their own ideas as they progress through the design process.

Organizing Principles

Organizing principles are more specific than the vision and value statements. The vision and values or mission statement may be a very broad and general statement such as "We will be the world's first choice in air travel," or, "We will be the leading provider of Internet software." These are missions or visions of who we want to be. While this is helpful, it will also be helpful to provide principles that give some guidance as to the nature of the desired organization and culture.

The following questions may provide clues as to guidance you may wish to provide:

1. How would you characterize the culture you hope to create in the future organization?
2. Do you want to tell them specifically to reduce the layers of management or any other measures of the structure?
3. Should they be instructed to consolidate horizontal organizational units?
4. Should they strive for performance-based compensation or other performance-based rewards?
5. How do you envision the use of information and information technology in the future organization?
6. Do you envision significant changes in access or utilization of information by employees?
7. Do you have any guidance regarding the relationship to customers or suppliers?
8. Should they focus on creating a team-based organization?
9. Has the steering team decided that walls between departments need to be broken down to emphasize a cross-functional collaboration and process flow?

Project Boundaries and Scope

There are always boundaries to any organization architecture process. This was clear in the very first design project this author was involved in. The company had just invested a great deal of money in new software and that software was essentially the factory equipment. It was the platform on which the work was done. And, it was controversial among the employees. Given the money they had invested, there was no way they were going to abandon this software. This was a boundary of the design work.

You cannot design everything that impacts the work process. You cannot design the educational system that conditions people coming into the organization. You cannot design your customer's stores that sell your products. You cannot design the monetary system or the legal system. There are similar internal boundaries. It is the function of the steering team to define the boundaries for the design team so they can focus their energies most productively.

The first type of boundary is the definition of the work processes. You may be designing the organization of a paper mill. Does the process begin with the input of pulp, or does it begin with the receipt of pulpwood to be converted to pulp? Does it include the packaging of the paper? State the definition of the work process from beginning to end.

Often there are questions about associated processes and about whether they are to be considered in the design. For example, software preparation may support an actual work process. Can the design team consider the process of software development or acquisition? Or should they consider information system requirements that can then be assigned to that department or another design team?

Be very clear about these enabling processes. You do not want to limit the ability of the design team to make changes by putting these out of bounds. On the other hand, you do not want to give the design team so much work that the task becomes an impossible burden.

Another boundary concerns the human system. Can the design teams consider performance appraisal, which may be a corporate process? Can they consider compensation? Whose compensation? Can they increase or reduce head count? All of these boundaries should be stated if they are indeed boundaries.

Reporting Expectations

The charter should include the steering team's reporting expectations. It is recommend that the design team meet with the steering team after they have completed the discovery phase to share their key findings; then again after they have completed the work process design; again after the social system design; and finally after they have developed an implementation plan.

There should also be a discussion about communication with the rest of the organization. Someone should have the task of sending out periodic updates to employees to let them know how the work is progressing. If you don't do this the rumor mill will be very actively at work and it is probable that the worst interpretations will be made, not the best.

Sample Charters

It is helpful to see examples of charters developed by other organization. There is a danger however. Too often steering team members want to copy sample charters and avoid the hard work of thinking. It is the exercise of thinking that creates understanding and commitment to the change process. We suggest that you review the following charters to get an idea of what others have done, then put them aside and think about your own situation and develop your own charter.

Super Corporation

Manufacturing Design Charter

Company Mission Statement

We commit to being the supplier of choice for our customers, the employer of choice for our associates and our communities, and the investment of choice for our stockholders. We will be the model of high ethical standards and excellent performance. Leadership from all associates will be encouraged within an environment of mutual trust according to the Super Corporation values statement. Our success will be realized by the timely delivery of superior quality products at competitive prices and by providing services that satisfy our customers' expectations, thereby ensuring the prosperity of our customers, associates, stockholders, and communities.

Design Purpose

The general purpose of the design team and the design process is to create the ideal process, organization, and culture that will enable the Super Corporation to fulfill its mission, to be the number one market leader in its markets, and to provide a workplace that satisfies the needs of its members and creates a learning community. The steering team expects the design team to study the world's best organizations and the competitive environment and use its imagination to create the best possible design, not for the next few months but for the next five years.

Environment and Capabilities Analysis

The steering team has given some thought to the current and future business environment and considers the following to have implications for the design process.

- The reduction in regulation will bring additional competitors into our marketplace and increase the competition.
- The market in the United States will remain flat for the foreseeable future and, therefore, we must expect growth to come from new markets, new products, and international business.

- The technology of our manufacturing facilities is adequate for the present; however, we foresee the need for faster cycle times in product development and order turnaround and a significant reduction in defects. The defect reduction in the next five years will need to be to one tenth of the current level. We believe new technology will be required to achieve these goals.
- Our products are largely bought on style. Our ability to respond to the increasingly fast changes in style will be critical.
- We can invest in those capital investments that result in a return that exceeds the cost of capital.

We believe that the new organizational architecture should increase the following capabilities:

1. The ability to design products to market cycle time.
2. The ability to sell overseas.
3. The ability to perceive and to react to market style preferences.
4. The ability of our employees to self-manage and to deal with more complex technology.
5. The ability of our people and our equipment to produce a far lower level of defects.

Design Principles

- Design to an ideal state by considering what could be achieved in a five-year time frame.
- Design the ideal manufacturing process by considering possible technology, equipment, and materials.
- The design should meet both short and long-term customer needs as well as the need for improved financial performance.
- The design should be based on increased employee self-management, skills, and teamwork.
- The design should provide a set of information system requirements that will enable every employee to have real-time knowledge of his performance including quality, productivity, and

costs. The goal should be to make every employee a business manager.

- The design should reduce the layers of management, processes, time, and activity through increased responsibility of employees.
- The design should maximize employee problem-solving, creativity, and innovation.
- The design should address the structure of the organization up to the division vice president.
- The design should address all systems that impact the performance of the organization including compensation, appraisal, training, discipline, promotion, recognition, feedback, and others.
- The design should consider symbols that impact the culture of the organization such as dress, parking, titles, etc.
- The design should include plans for improving employee skills including the types of skills, the training process, and the incentives for improving skills.
- The design should provide a process that will encourage interaction between employees and their customers and suppliers. All employees should know and receive feedback from their customers and provide feedback to their suppliers.
- The design should plan for the periodic update and improvement of the proposed design.

Design Boundaries

1. The technical boundaries include the process from the identification of customer needs and requirements through product design and engineering, manufacturing, and shipping.
2. Capital boundaries should be considered to be approximately the current year's capital budget for each of the next five years with increases for inflation. Budgeting beyond this is possible if sufficiently attractive return on investment can be demonstrated.

3. It is not the intention of the design to reduce the current number of people employed. It is, however, the objective to reduce total costs over time.
4. Product quality, specifications, and delivery cannot be compromised during this process.
5. The basic responsibility for division MIS, R&D, and finance will remain corporate activities, but some aspects of these functions can be designed into the plant for more immediate support.
6. All aspects of the design and the process must conform to federal, state, and local laws.

Reporting and Communication

The design team will report to the senior management team through John Smith who will serve as the senior executive responsible for this change initiative.

The steering team would like to receive a presentation and update after you have completed the discovery phase, after the design of the technical system, after the design of the social system, and finally, after the design of the implementation plan.

We will provide a monthly communication to the larger organization to inform them of your progress.

HomeCare Service Delivery

Design Team Charter

Purpose:

The purpose of the HomeCare Service Delivery Redesign Team is to ensure that our service delivery to clients and customers (funders) meet or exceed their expectations in a manner that will maximize the probability of customer, client and service provider loyalty and acquisition of additional contracts. The design should improve financial performance as well as customer and client performance.

Objectives:

Timelines

1. One (Nursing) will focus initially on designing the nursing service process, while another (Home Support) will focus on designing the home support delivery process.
2. By November 1st, 2011 present initial recommendations for a redesign of the work flow.
3. By November 15th present initial recommendations for changes to systems, structure, decision-making, responsibility or other factors that may enhance performance to customer expectations.
4. By January 1st begin implementation of those recommendations.

Deliverables

1. Reduce the number of process steps by at least 50% in order to reduce potential for errors, delay and rework.
2. It currently requires an average of five hours from acceptance of referral to the scheduling of a visit. The goal of the design team should be to reduce this to one hour.
3. A customer or client or service provider must be able to reach someone who can respond to their concerns 24/7.
4. The redesign should result in a missed visits rate below CCAC targets.

5. The redesign should result in a referral rate to exceed CCAC targets.
6. The redesign should result in continuity within CCAC targets.
7. The redesign should result in a reduction in ORTS (complaints) by 75%.
8. The redesign will ensure there is a focus on the quality of care delivered to the client. It will ensure that managers are able to facilitate necessary clinician education, supervisory visits and practice learning teams. This will be measured by up-to-date performance review practices for new and existing employees (as per policy) and by nurse satisfaction that learning needs are met.
9. Reduce billing rejections to a rate of less than .05 percent.
10. Quality feedback loops will be built into each process so they can monitor in real time effectiveness.
11. The design team will calculate the cost of planning and scheduling of visits to be less than five dollars per visit.
12. The design team will define productivity measures at the primary care provider team level and at the district level. These measures will align financial improvement measures at all levels.

Principles

1. All processes are to be viewed and judged through the eyes of the customer and client. Meeting their needs is our primary purpose and all processes should contribute to this purpose.
2. The voice of the service providers will be respected as experts in the service delivery process.
3. The voice of the client will be sought for client's experience.
4. The design team should consider and seek to optimize the quality of patient care, reducing any obstacles to quality of care.
5. The design team should consider the factors that contribute to care provider job satisfaction and seek to improve job satisfaction.
6. The design team should seek the participation, opinions and concerns of all those who contribute to the core service processes.

7. The design team should demonstrate respect for all of those acting within the service processes and consider all current improvement efforts to be good faith efforts. The design team, however, should not feel constrained by any existing improvement efforts.
8. The design team should set as a goal to establish a culture of continuous improvement and high participation or engagement within all processes and functions.
9. The design team should engage in appreciative inquiry to discover those practices that are successful and should be incorporated in the design.

Guidelines for the Design Team Work:

1. The design team will consider any and all changes to existing processes that will optimize customer and client satisfaction while optimizing staff satisfaction.
2. The design team should create a management process that unifies effort across the service delivery chain and gives managers both responsibility and authority to manage those processes while responding to the voice of the customer.
3. The design should consider the value of creating a team process at every level.
4. The design team will examine and recommend changes to not only the formal processes, but to the social systems and interactions within and around those processes which may enable or disrupt them. The design team should consider organization structure around the processes, the decision-making processes, responsibility and accountability.
5. The design team will consider the use of current standard operating procedures that facilitate customer satisfaction and improved client care. They may also propose changes to those procedures.
6. The design team should seek to remove any and all "walls" or barriers within the process to speed the process flow and decision-making.

Boundaries

1. The core processes to be addressed include intake; scheduling of staff; availability of staff; and assignment of client visits; care provider education and management; service delivery and verification. This will include all communications and problem resolution with clients, customers and staff.
2. The design team should define process requirements of those enabling processes that support the work of the core process. They should not, however, seek to design the work of those enabling processes. These include information technology, quality management, human resource management and development, financial management, and communication processes.
3. The design team may consider the use and application of information technology; however they must incorporate and employ existing software and hardware solutions. The team will work within the existing database set up and architecture. They may make recommendations concerning IT, however should not be dependent on significant changes in IT.
4. The design team may re-allocate resources; however, the design should be budget neutral, but in the long term should create improvement in productivity and financial performance.
5. The design team may consider the organization structure – the levels, titles, assignment of responsibility and decision-making processes.
6. The design team should consider and propose means of motivation that will reinforce desired behavior.

Reporting and Communications

1. The design team should do its work openly, with agreed upon communications with other members of the organization and external stakeholders. The design team members should be clear not to imply final decisions versus recommendations and ideas being considered.
2. The design team will first report its progress and results to the Vice President of Quality and Risk. She will then plan for meetings and reports to the senior management team.

3. The design team will participate in reporting its proposals to other members of the organization upon the approval of the management team. The design members will be ambassadors to present the design to the larger organization.
4. HomeCare commits to 2-way communication to enable the work of the team.

CHAPTER 7

DISCOVERING YOUR INTERNAL ASSETS AND LIABILITIES

This is the first of three chapters on the discovery process. They are longer than the subsequent chapters because you will find that as you are discovering the current state you are also creating the dream and identifying elements of your future design. The process of WSA is presented as linear - four sequential steps. However, the human mind does not work in a linear manner.

You will spend a good bit of time doing research. However, you are not a pure scientist, you have a stake in this organization and you have your own ideas and experience. Do not discount your own experience.

You are going to be thinking about the future as you do your work. It will be a good idea to capture your thoughts in a systematic manner. Of course, you can keep your own notes. But, a better way to do it is to have a "Future State Wall." This can be a wall in a room where your design team meets. On this wall you are going to place Post-it-Notes with ideas, requirements, or characteristics for your future system. At the top of the left side of the wall, make a heading that says, "Technical system" and on the right "Social system." Depending on your schedule, your design team may be meeting for weeks or even months.

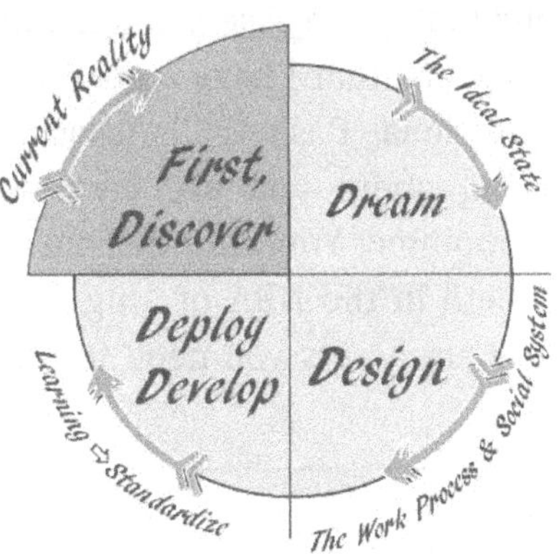

Don't lose your brilliant ideas.

Your facilitator should ask each day, "Have we created any requirements or characteristics for our future system?" You don't have to discuss them, prioritize them, or make any decisions. You will do that when you are in the design stage. This is purely an on-going brainstorming process. Just write them down on a sticky, and put them on the wall. As other members of the team read your notes, that will generate ideas of their own.

By the time you finish with the different discovery activities you will have dozens of good ideas that you will later organize and incorporate in the future design.

The New Capitalism of Your Organization

The ability to achieve a strategy is dependent on capital or assets. The assets of the organization include much more than financial assets and liabilities. The forms of capital that enable any culture to perform, whether the culture of a country or a company, include spiritual capital, human, social, innovation and financial capital. This is a new way of thinking about how the organization creates value. It is a different understanding of value then most will be used to.[39] However, it is increasingly well recognized that money does not produce money. Money is the end result of human motivation, values, social relationships and the ability to innovate. Making money is an end result of all of these other capabilities.

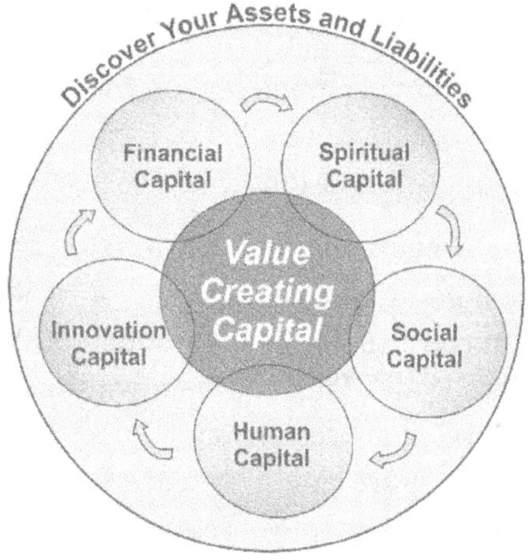

Just as the capability of an organization to achieve its goals is dependent on its assets, we as individuals have assets and liabilities. If you tell me that I have a goal to play in the National Basketball Association or to sing opera you are certain to be disappointed. You can offer me a million dollars and I will still not be able to compete in the NBA or sing opera. I simply do not have those capabilities. There are assets you need to play in the NBA that this writer certainly does

[39] The author has an electronic survey to assist in making this assessment.

not have. Similarly, every company or organization has assets that enable them to perform.

Imagine that a company decides on a strategy to enter and win the Formula One World Championship. They set targets for the number of races they will win, the advertising income they will receive, and the measures of customer recognition or brand value that they will create. This is their external or business strategy. What about internal or capability strategy? What human talents, competencies and motivation will be required? What types of innovation will be needed to compete against the other Formula One teams? What driver and engineering capabilities are required? What is their plan for developing driver and engineering skills? Without effectively answering these questions about internal capabilities and culture, the external strategy is no strategy at all, it is merely strategic wishing!

The purpose of this chapter is to help you know and assess your current assets and to identify assets that you will need to build in order to achieve your strategic goals.

What is Capital & How is it Invested?

The plant and equipment, computers, land, and cash on the balance sheet are all material assets of the organization. But, in today's world they are not the primary assets that will create future value. Human capabilities and culture are the much more significant value-adding assets held by an organization. If you had zero money, but if you had a team of dedicated scientists who knew how to cure cancer, you would be in possession of an incredibly valuable asset. Yet, it would not appear on the balance sheet or be

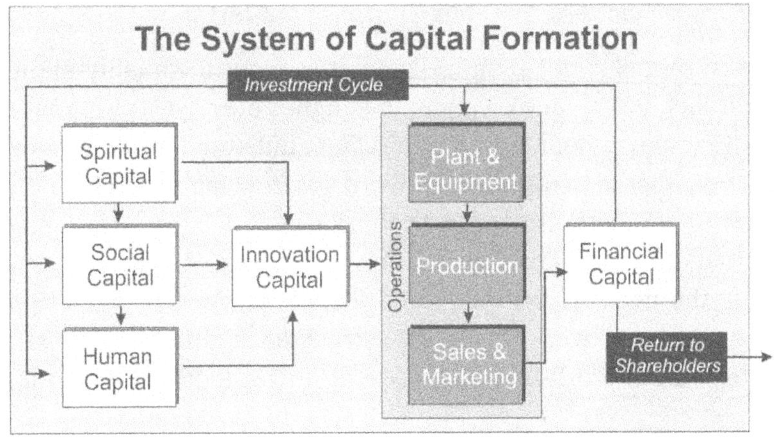

visible in cash flow. Similarly, what has distinguished Honda and Toyota and companies like Google, Apple and Facebook, is their human abilities to generate innovation that result in brand loyalty and new revenue.

What is wealth? What are the valuable assets of a person or organization? We think of money, but money is not in the beginning. The "Word," the creative spirit, purpose and values, are in the beginning. The cycle of wealth begins with a creative act of leadership that inspires unity of energy and effort. The ideas, the creative spirit, purpose and values - spiritual capital - come first. This then generates the wealth of social and human capital that stimulates innovation capital and finally results in financial capital.

Spiritual Capital

To the degree that an organization can enable, support, or encourage a depth of personal morality and dedication to a noble purpose, it possesses spiritual capital. This form of wealth accrues both to the organization and to the individual. It will interact and support every other form of capital and ultimately will have its effect on the financial bottom line. In many ways it is the first cause.

The pursuit of worthy purpose is the primary means of achieving energy in an organization. Human beings are energized by, and will sacrifice for, that which they believe to be noble and therefore ennobling of them. Leaders create energy that may later be directed by managers, but absent the energy that comes from a worthy purpose, there is little motion. Any manager who believes that only technical processes, skills, or financial capital are required for competitive success is much like the racing team that spends a million dollars for the latest race car but then hires a driver who doesn't care about winning. Purpose matters. Ennobling purpose matters most.

Spiritual capital is not about religion. It is about the quality of the human spirit – morality, virtue, and a calling to a higher purpose. It is about spiritual capacities that may be influenced by religion, but stand on their own merit. I am fully aware that to many ears the word *spiritual* may sound out of place in the context of business. However, the perceived division between work life and spiritual life is a false separation and more and more people are recognizing the need for an integrated life. A high percentage of our social interactions occur at work. Many of our anxieties, ambitions, passions and fears center on our work life. Our sense of purpose or self-worth is directly related to our work. The nature of the organization in which we work has a profound effect on our spiritual life.

Many entrepreneurs have been motivated to leave the traditional corporation and start anew, not simply to pursue their dreams of wealth, but to pursue the vision of an organization that contributes to the human spirit as well as the bank account, an organization that satisfies their own spiritual quest. In practice, many organizations have done great harm to the spiritual life of their members. The reader no doubt has sufficient examples without the author providing depressing illustrations. If not, then simply watch Arthur Miller's play *The Death of a Salesman* and know that the graveyard is well populated by kindred spirits of Willy Loman.

I am certainly not the first writer to write about the importance of the human spirit in business. Stephen Covey in his *Principle Centered Leadership* and more recently in his *The 8th Habit* has addressed the importance of spiritual capacities in leadership. Covey writes that his "8th Habit" is *"the voice of the human spirit – full of hope and intelligence, resilient by nature, boundless in its potential to serve the common good. This voice also encompasses the soul of organizations that will survive, thrive and profoundly impact the future of the*

world."[40] And, Ken Blanchard, best known for his One Minute books that address leadership and motivation, has designated himself to be, not the CEO or Chairman of his company, but the Chief Spiritual Officer. This is a profound insight into the actual function that should be performed by leaders.

Spiritual capital has two components: first, the degree to which members of the organization are committed to a *worthy purpose* beyond their self-interest; and second, a commitment to *shared values* that guide ethical behavior.

The Pursuit of Worthy Purpose

The pursuit of *worthy purpose* is the primary means of achieving *energy* in an organization. Human beings are energized by, and will sacrifice for, that which they believe to be noble and therefore ennobling of them. Leaders create energy that may later be directed by managers, but absent the energy that comes from a worthy purpose, there is little motion. Any manager who believes that only technical processes, skills, or financial capital are required for competitive success is much like the racing team that spends a million dollars for the latest race car but then hires a driver who doesn't care about winning. Purpose matters. Ennobling purpose matters most.

Purpose is the most pure energy source emerging from the deepest well of our soul. It is the answer to every important question about our being. Why are we here? Where are we going? What difference will it make if we get there? It is the motivation of motivations; it is the reason to seek reason; it is not merely what people will work for, it is what people will die for. The pursuit of purpose was in the beginning and in the Word. Without it you are spiritual dust, because you are going nowhere and don't know why.

The capacity to lead is directly related to the pursuit of worthy purpose. Purpose may be the most powerful link to join people and processes in common effort. Authentic leaders know and display purpose in their lives. Why? The degree to which we pursue an ennobling purpose is the degree to which we attract others. Leaders must attract others if they expect to have followers. Purpose attracts and therefore serves as a unifying force. There is unity of effort and energy to the degree of shared purpose. Our level of satisfaction and our level of energy are directly related not only to our

---

[40] Covey, Stephen R. *The 8th Habit.* Free Press, New York, 2004. P. 5.

understanding of our own purpose, but also to whether the organization to which we contribute, share that same purpose.

Business purpose is found in knowing and serving customers. Some years ago, I was working with a foundry in Monongahela, Pennsylvania, deep in the heart of the adversarial culture of steelworkers and coal mines. A foundry is a tough environment where the buildings aren't heated, where they pour molten iron to form castings, and where union and management are often at war. Listening as best I could to the experience of workers, I discovered that even though some had worked there for thirty years, they had never met a customer face-to-face. They knew that their castings were put on a truck and shipped to another company, but that company had no human face.

Sometimes the simplest things have the strongest effect. We found that one of the customers was no more than fifty miles away. We gathered some of the experienced union members and drove to the customer's plant on a day when their product was going to be delivered. There, they watched the workers of that plant unload and inspect their castings. These other workers, it turned out, were members of the same steelworkers union. They were brothers, brothers they had never met. And these brothers explained to them the problems they had with their castings, in language more direct and more forceful than their managers would have dared. Suddenly the purpose of their work, rather than meeting the requirements of managers they did not trust, became doing work that met the needs of their brothers. Their entire purpose had changed.

These workers had been denied a sense of purpose, not by any fault of their own, but by the system in which they worked.

The question the steering team and the design team must ask is "How does this organization give its members a worthy purpose?" How can that purpose be enhanced and how can we connect daily work activity with a greater purpose?

The Asset of Shared Values

Shared values are the basis for trustworthy relationships and sociability. Belief systems have enormous impact on the culture of organizations, and it is the function of leaders to exert efforts to intentionally shape these beliefs. A common set of values is the lubricant of fluid associations. It is the basis of unified action and trustworthy behavior.

Countries that are unified have a clearly articulated set of values stated in a constitution or "Bill of Rights" that forms the basis for relationships. We know that (in the United States) we believe in freedom of speech, press and religion. We know that one is innocent until proven guilty. And we know that everyone is entitled to equal treatment and opportunity regardless of race, religion or gender. And, we also know that we have often not lived up to these values, but we know that pursuing them leads to a better outcome than abandoning them.

These values are not innate. We were not born with them. These values must be taught. The degree to which these common values are successfully taught becomes a basis for social cohesion, unity or trust. When the common values are lost a civilization begins the process of disintegration and internal warfare. The same happens in companies. The decline of the American auto companies began in the middle of the last century when they appeared all powerful, but like the Roman Empire, their internal divisions between operating units, functions, and between leaders and led, was a cancer eating away at their strength.

Because of our humble human condition, organizations which desire a high level of sociability or trust, internally and with external customers and partners, must clearly articulate their values, demonstrate adherence to those values, and hold all members accountable for their compliance.

We need shared values precisely to rise above the cultural norms of the moment. We need an anchor in a storm, a deep keel to set our course upwind, a truth that transcends the moment. We have all confronted the teenager who explains his behavior with "Everyone else was doing it!" And Mom or Dad will certainly reply "But, I don't care what your friends are doing; you should know the difference between right and wrong." We try to train our children to have that deep keel to keep them on course in the storm. Yet, the entire adult "smart money" culture of Wall Street in the years leading up to 2008 were packaging exceedingly complex and risky investment vehicles "because everyone else was doing it." The pay packages of not only executives, but moderately successful traders and brokers, were in the many millions and made no sense according to any value system other than the adolescent "Everyone else was doing it!"

Spiritual Capital in an organization is instilled from the top down. It is the function and responsibility of leaders to create and reinforce a set of values that are those to which the organization is dedicated. Commitment to a common purpose and a common set of values must be an explicit component of every employment contract. It is not reached through consensus by first level teams. Nor can senior executives stand aloof as if this is some commitment of underlings. Rather, it is the job of the senior executives to define, practice, and communicate values and purpose from the top. The emphasis should be on practice, because it is deeds far more than words, which will instill Spiritual Capital in the organization.

Shared values are the basis for trustworthy relationships and sociability. Shared values hold a family together. They hold a country together. The decline of every civilization has been marked by internal disintegration into interest groups with conflicting values and a loss of values at the core. Countries, communities and companies work best when committed to core values.

We all have beliefs about human nature that guide our behavior. When someone holds the belief that human beings are created evil and are naturally devious, then it is logical to assume that they must be watched and controlled. However, if we believe that people are essentially created noble and worthy, we treat them with an assumption of trust. Business partners, fellow managers and employees all have a tendency to conform to our beliefs about them. These belief systems have enormous impact on the culture of organizations, and it is the function of leaders to exert efforts to shape these beliefs.

I was once told by a Japanese quality leader that the difference between Japanese and American companies was in religion. He claimed that in Japanese religion (Shinto and Buddhism) man is born good and trustworthy and is to be treated that way. In Japanese culture it is assumed that bad behavior must be taught, a result of the environment or the system. On the other hand, in Western, or "Christian" cultures we believe in original sin, that man is born with sin and must be "saved" from that original sin. According to him, this resulted in completely different types of systems within organization. This may or may not contain some element of truth, but it is an interesting perspective. There is good evidence that the assumptions we hold about people, how we "value" them, will affect their behavior toward us. It is, therefore, good business to hold a set of values toward employees that increases the likelihood that they will act in the common interest of the firm and its customers.

(A Note About the following assessments: After each of the sections on the different forms of capital there is a quick, ten item assessment. The primary purpose of this is to stimulate conversation within the design team and help the design team reach a consensus view on what assets need to be enhanced and how that could be done. They are simply to help you think. It may also be beneficial to conduct a survey to a larger body of employees and managers to gain their insight in these same questions. The author can provide an electronic, web based, assessment for this purpose.)

An Assessment of Spiritual Capital in the Organization

1. Our orientation for new employees seeks to instill a sense of calling, or dedication, to a noble purpose to which the organization is committed.

1____________2____________3____________4____________5

Not True Somewhat True Very True

2. An examination of presentations made by the leaders of the organization will reveal regular references to the worthy purpose of the organization.

1____________2____________3____________4____________5

Not True Somewhat True Very True

3. Individuals decide to work for our organization while accepting compensation that may be less than other companies offer because they believe in what we do.

1____________2____________3____________4____________5

Not True Somewhat True Very True

4. We make business decisions, decisions regarding products, services or markets, in part based on their contribution to our worthy purpose.

1____________2____________3____________4____________5

Not True Somewhat True Very True

5. When some acquaintance of yours asks "why do you work for this company?" you answer this question, not referring to your self-interest (pay, promotion), but with the good that is done by your company.

1____________2____________3____________4____________5

Not True Somewhat True Very True

6. All employees have a written document that defines the core values and principles of the organization.

1____________2____________3____________4____________5

Not True Somewhat True Very True

7. When making decisions about human resource practices (hiring, incentives, training) these values are frequently a factor in our decision-making.

1____________2____________3____________4____________5

Not True Somewhat True Very True

8. We can all remember a case in which leaders of the organization made a decision to adhere to our shared values despite sacrificing personal or business gain.

1____________2____________3____________4____________5

Not True Somewhat True Very True

9. Most employees believe that this is a "high trust" organization.

1____________2____________3____________4____________5

Not True Somewhat True Very True

10. The anxiety most likely to be experienced by employees concerns customer satisfaction, and not the internal support of co-workers or managers.

1____________2____________3____________4____________5

Not True Somewhat True Very True

Social Capital

Social Capital is the value of trust. Almost all business transactions are based on trust. Trust will determine the likelihood of customers purchasing your products or services; or, the willingness of employees to sacrifice for your company. Trust is the social lubricant that enables employees to engage in solving problems. It is a key to the effectiveness of all teams, families, communities, or companies. It determines brand equity and market capital.

Social capital can be divided into two forms: first, the trust and sociability within the organization; and second, the trust between the organization and the external market place. The first enables problem-solving and creativity, the second defines your relationship with the markets you serve. In both cases, high trust or social capital is a benefit and low trust is crippling.

The World Bank, recognizing the importance of social capital in economic development, has said, *"Social capital refers to the institutions, relationships, and norms that shape the quality and quantity of a society's social interactions... it is the glue that holds them together."*[41] There is a great deal of evidence that social capital is a critical force for economic development. The quality and productivity of a society is directly related to social relationships. For example, the number of parents who participate in school activities is directly related to the quality of education and further economic success. There is even a demonstrated relationship between social capital and health. *"As a rough rule of thumb, if you belong to no groups but decide to join one, you cut your risk of dying over the next year in half. If you smoke and belong to no groups, it's a toss-up statistically whether you should stop smoking or start joining.'"*[42] In our personal lives, social capital, the quality of our relationships, interacts with our physical well-being. In our businesses, social capital precedes and determines financial capital.

If, as the World Bank and others have concluded, the quality of social capital in a society has a positive effect on all measures of social and economic development, it is logical that these same qualities of sociability have a similarly positive effect both within the mini-society of an organization and in relationships with the market place.

---

[41] The World Bank 1999: *What is Social Capital?*

[42] Putnam, R. D. (1995) 'Bowling Alone: America's Declining Social Capital', *Journal of Democracy* 6:1, Jan, 65-78.

Individuals are most aware of the value of their own social networks when they start looking for a job. We hire people we trust. We help those whom we know and trust. To the degree to which you have a trusting social network, a group of people who consider you trustworthy, you have the security of social capital.

Internal Social Capital - Trust

Lean manufacturing is a social system that is built on teams and trust at every level of the organization. It is the strength of these teams that is the mechanism for problem-solving and innovation: the more effective the teams the faster the rate of learning and improvement. This speed of improvement is itself a form of wealth in the organization.

Trust operates both horizontally and vertically within the organization. Horizontal trust is between peers and across functional groups in the organization. Vertical trust is trust in leadership and leaders trust in their employees. In both cases, social capital is the glue that bonds people together.

Internal sociability may have the most significant impact on the ability to solve problems. All organizations are a continual stew of problem-solving. Whether it is solving the problems presented by a customer, a new technology, or a competitor, business is a game of constant adaptation to a changing environment. The apparently small act of walking down the hall to an associate's office and sharing a problem, casually brainstorming without regard to who gets credit, or who bears what responsibility, is the most frequent, and probably the most effective way to solve problems. These encounters may escalate into a formal meeting or problem-solving process. Whether the interaction remains highly informal or becomes more formal, the critical ingredient is the simple willingness to be engaged, to care about the problem, to listen deeply, think together, and brainstorm solutions.

Social capital is an intangible form of capital and cannot be measured on the balance sheet. Yet, in many ways, it may be the most powerful asset. Francis Fukuyama has defined social capital as *"a set of informal values or norms shared among members of a group that permits cooperation among them. If members of the group come to expect that others will behave reliably and honestly, then they will come to trust one another. Trust is like a lubricant that makes the running of any group or organization more efficient."*[43] He points out that every society has some social capital, the important distinction that results in economic differences is what he calls the "radius of trust" that extends outward from the individual to the family, the community, the state and other associations. Similarly, with the corporation, there is a radius of trust that extends out from its employees to its suppliers and business partners, its customers, and to the marketplace. The much sought after financial returns will only follow the creation of social capital.

Francis Fukuyama got it right when he said that *"one of the most important lessons we can learn from an examination of economic life is that a nation's well-being, as well as its ability to compete, is conditioned by a single, pervasive cultural characteristic: the level of trust inherent in the society."*[44] Fukuyama presents an argument for individual virtues which are the bedrock of social relationships, or the tendency toward fluent association, what he calls spontaneous sociability. *"Spontaneous sociability is critical to economic life because virtually all economic activity is carried out by groups rather than individuals. Before wealth can be created, human beings have to learn to work together, and if there is to be subsequent progress, new forms of organization have to be developed."*[45] Fukuyama directly relates social capital to the prevalence of trust in a society. High trust societies are more successful at wealth creation. Those which are low trust societies demonstrate less ability to generate material wealth.

There is increasing research demonstrating that the strength of social networks within an organization correlates positively with higher rates of productivity. *"A social environment rich of participation opportunities, allowing people to meet frequently, is a fertile ground for nurturing shared values and social norms of trust and reciprocity. Where such values and norms develop, the likelihood of cooperative behaviors is higher, and workers may be more motivated and not inclined to shirking behaviors."*[46]

---

[43] Fukuyama, Francis. *The Great Disruption – Human Nature and the Reconstitution of Social Order*, The Free Press, New York, 1999. p.16.

[44] Fukuyama, *Francis: Trust: The Social Virtues & The Creation of Prosperity*, New York, The Free Press, 1995, p. 7.

[45] Ibid. p.47.

[46] Sabatini, Fabio (2006) *Does Social Capital Improve Labour Productivity in Small and Medium Enterprises?* Working Paper, Dipartmento Di Economia Pubblica, Rome.

In *Better Together* Robert D. Putnam and Lewis M. Feldstein present positive case studies in which social capital was successfully increased. They make a useful distinction that can be applied to any organization. *"Among the many different forms of social capital one distinction will be especially important... Some networks link people who are similar in crucial respects and tend to be inward looking – bonding social capital. Others encompass different types of people and tend to be outward-looking – bridging social capital. Bonding social capital is a kind of sociological Super Glue, whereas bridging social capital provides a sociological WD-40."*[47] They point out that a pluralistic society, composed of many diverse groups, requires a lot of bridging social capital, but the problem is that bridging social capital is harder to create than bonding social capital. It is relatively easy for "birds of a feather" to flock together. It is not so easy to create bonds between diverse birds.

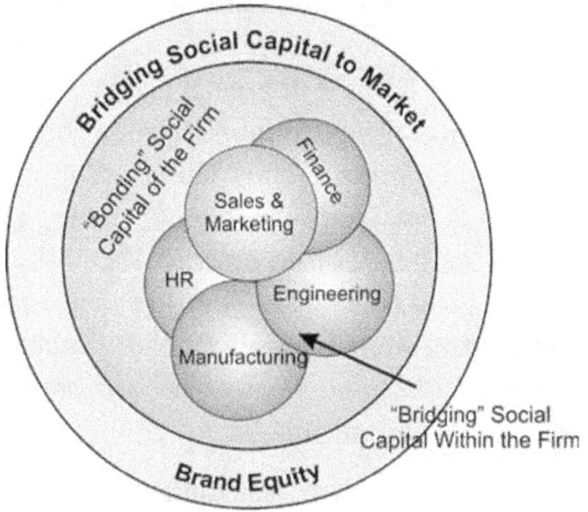

This same effect occurs within the corporation. Within a corporation you may have strong bonding social capital within the engineering or the sales organization. Within each department, employees have the same training, speak the same language and deal with similar problems. However, they may have few bridges or shared social capital with each other or with the manufacturing organization. While there is an obvious interdependency between engineering, manufacturing and sales, the three groups of employees are often located in different buildings, eat in different cafeterias, dress differently, and consequently, each group increasingly speaks a language that cannot be understood by the others and is likely to assign blame to the other groups.

You might ask "So what?" What does it matter if these three "flocks of birds" fly with their own kind and not with other flocks? Too often the

---

[47] Putnum, Robert D. and Feldstein, Lewis M. *Better Together*. New York, Simon & Schuster. 2003. P. 2.

engineering organization comes up with a solution that is almost impossible to manufacture. Sales people encounter problems in their discussions with customers that can only be solved by engineering solutions. Manufacturing can solve or create problems that show up at the customer and must be explained by the sales organizations. The ability of the larger organization to respond to customer needs and create improved solutions for customers is directly related to the degree of sociability between these three organizations. This bridging social capital is a primary determinant of the creation of brand equity and economic value. This is exactly why the engineering organization at Honda is located in the manufacturing plant. It is why all engineers start their career by working on the assembly line. It is why assembly workers, engineers, and executives wear the same clothes. Bridging social capital takes priority over bonding within sub-groups. This is a value that requires deliberate attention by leaders in every organization. It is a result of organization architecture.

The case can be made that the ability to create bridging collaboration across dispersed organization units is a distinct capability that provides competitive advantage.[48] Hansen and Nohria list four barriers to inter-unit collaboration: 1) Unwillingness to seek input and learn from others; 2) Inability to seek and find expertise; 3) Unwillingness to help; and 4) Inability to work together and transfer knowledge. They then list three "management levers to promote collaboration." These are 1) Leadership values and goals; 2) Human resource procedures; and 3) Lateral Cross-unit mechanisms.

As a design team, it is your job to build the mechanism of both bridging and bonding social capital.

Brand Equity

External brand equity is the recognition and respect given to your firm by the market place. Just as the quality of an individual's life is largely determined by the quality of their social relationships, the same may be said of a company. The value of a company is directly related to its brand equity. The success of lean management is not only in the elimination of waste. For many years Honda and Toyota brands have had among the highest customer loyalty ratings and that translates directly to the sales of their products. The

---

[48] Hansen, Morten T. and Nohria, Nitin. "How to Build Collaborative Advantage." MIT Sloan Management Review, Fall, 2004.

latest R.L. Polk study of brand and vehicle loyalty in the auto industry, found that 48% of people who bought a car in 2012 bought from the same brand they were already driving. Polk says the four brands with the most loyal customers were Ford, with 61.2% repeat buyers, Mercedes-Benz (57.7%), Toyota (55.5%), and Honda (54.8%).

Brand equity is almost as good as money in the bank. Some have measured market capital by subtracting the financial value of all material and cash assets from the firm's market capitalization. In other words, if the stock market values the total equity of the firm at $1 billion, and the firm has cash, accounts receivables, building, equipment, and other balance sheet items worth $500 million, it is logical to assume that the value of the brand, the trust of the marketplace represents the other $500 million. Of course, it can also be argued that this value may represent future cash flows but those cash flows are predicated upon trust in the marketplace.

If Honda, Toyota or any company with high brand loyalty, produces a new car, people without any direct knowledge of that car will have a high degree of respect for it simply because it is produced by a company to which they feel loyal. This is market capital. This brand loyalty reduces the marketing cost of each sale. The dollars that would otherwise be spent on marketing to acquire a new customer can be invested in new product development. Similarly, if Pixar comes out with a new movie, even without any reviews or promotion, families will have a positive bias that this will be a good movie to see with their children. This again, has direct monetary value.

Arthur Andersen, the major accounting firm that sank in the Enron scandal, went out of business, not because they lost financial assets or human capital but because they completely lost the trust of those who read financial statements. This quickly translated into bankruptcy as customers fled to other accounting firms.

AN ASSESSMENT OF YOUR ORGANIZATION'S SOCIAL CAPITAL

1. I feel that my manager cares about my personal well-being.

1__________2__________3__________4__________5

Not True　　Somewhat True　　Very True

2. Besides my immediate team, I frequently meet with other groups or teams within the company to share information or solve problems.

1____________2____________3____________4____________5

Not True Somewhat True Very True

3. I volunteer to participate on groups that solve problems at work.

1____________2____________3____________4____________5

Not True Somewhat True Very True

4. If I have a high level of trust in my co-workers.

1____________2____________3____________4____________5

Not True Somewhat True Very True

5. I am confident that my voice will be heard when solving problems.

1____________2____________3____________4____________5

Not True Somewhat True Very True

6. Our customer's loyalty to our products or brand is the highest in our market.

1____________2____________3____________4____________5

Not True Somewhat True Very True

7. Our brand is associated with quality and excellent customer service.

1____________2____________3____________4____________5

Not True Somewhat True Very True

8. If we introduce a new product, we can expect a positive reception in the market even prior to evaluation.

1____________2____________3____________4____________5

Not True Somewhat True Very True

9. Research indicates that repeat buying by our customers is in the top quartile of competitors.

1____________2____________3____________4____________5

Not True Somewhat True Very True

10. When considered against our competitors we are the employer of choice for professionals in our market.

1____________2____________3____________4____________5

Not True Somewhat True Very True

HUMAN CAPITAL:

Human capital is the sum of all of the competencies and motivation of the people within the organization. Human capital has always been a critical component of the performance of any business, but today's entrepreneur is likely to bring with him, not money, but *competency* and *motivation*, the two key ingredients of human capital. Attracting and retaining human capital will be one of the most critical challenges as a business grows.

It was assumed in the industrial age that the brains were at the top and the mindless labor at the bottom. In the feudal kingdoms of Europe the King was believed to have a divine connection, endowed by God with the "Divine right of Kings," and therefore, unquestioned authority. How could you argue or dispute with one appointed by God? But, the American Revolution began the process of turning the idea of authority on its head. "We the people... in order to establish a more perfect union... do ordain and establish this Constitution." With those words the revolution began, and it isn't over. With those words the bottom became the top, and the top depended on the bottom for its authority. From that moment forward, every kingdom of Europe, every despotic dictatorship, and every authoritarian corporate executive began to lose power and control. The democratization of education, the printing press, public schools, and now the Internet have made knowledge the property of the masses. And, knowledge is power!

In the Industrial Age the labor in the factory was referred to as "hands" employed on the "floor" of the factory: brains at the top, hands doing "labor" on the floor. But, that is now all changed.

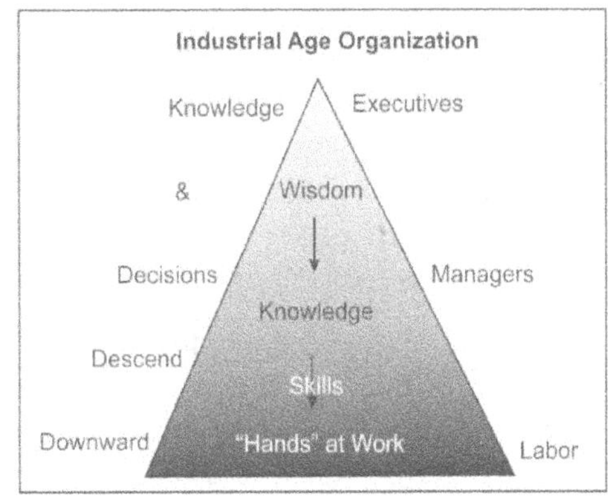

In lean and other modern organizations expertise is at every level. The assembly worker at Honda is trained and expected to be "the world's greatest expert" who is "on-the-spot." The worker's job may be to install the headlight or tail light assembly that is at the corner of every Civic or Accord. He or she is trained to inspect every headlight assembly and reject defective ones. If she finds a bad headlight assembly, there is a phone at the work station that she picks up, even with just one bad part. In the quality assurance department there is a first level employee at a desk with two telephones. The black phone rings. This individual gets out of his chair, goes out and takes the bad part. Only minutes have passed. This same individual then picks up the other phone, which rings at the supplier who is twenty miles away. At the supplier, a first level employee answers the phone. These two people know each other. The employee at the supplier has one hour to get back to the quality assurance employee at Honda and explain what they have just done to assure that they are not right now making parts with the same defect.

Several things are important in this story. First, the flow of parts is continuous and with minimal interruptions. There are small piles, not big piles, no warehouse, and in many cases the pile is a two hour pile. In other words, the part made at the supplier this morning is assembled this afternoon. This is "just-in-time." In order for this *technical system* to work successfully, the *social system* must provide for immediate feedback and immediate problem-solving. Every social system functions according to the capacity of the people, human capital. Second, notice that no manager got in the way to slow the process down. The process was entirely horizontal, not vertical. Nothing went up. No decisions came down. If you had inserted one manager who was required to approve or think about anything, you would have slowed the process down and immediately you would have to have a warehouse to store inventory of goods. The elimination of waste, reduction of inventory, wasted time, useless activity, meetings, etc., is directly related to the competence of the employees at the first level and the trust placed in them. These are not "hands," these are brains. It is the job of managers to assure that those who are on-the-spot are, in fact, the world's greatest experts in their work. To the degree that this is true, you have the competitive advantage of human capital.

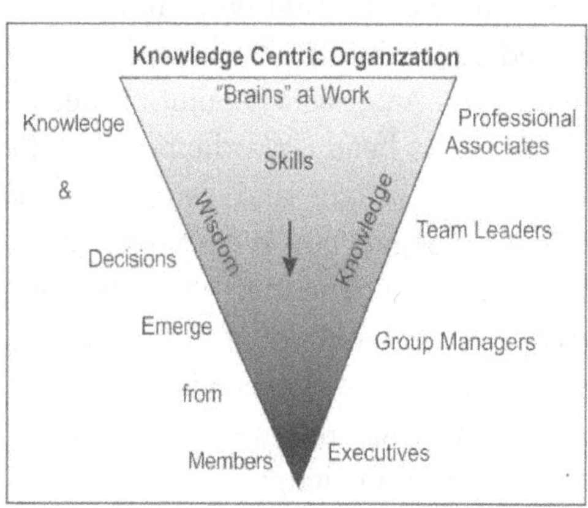

This example is also important precisely because Honda is not what people normally think of as a "knowledge organization" such as an advertising firm, a medical practice, or research lab. No. This is good old fashioned manufacturing, and the idea of the separation of labor from knowledge is dead! It is obvious that in a hospital the most important competence is that of the surgeon in the operating room, or other medical professional. These are the first level "workers" in a hospital. But, in our world today, it is also true that the most important competencies are on the floor, on-the-spot, at the frontline of manufacturing and every other kind of organization. Recognizing this and acting on this recognition is the first step in developing human capital.

Motivation + Competence = Performance

Motivation has been the subject of hundreds, if not thousands of books. However, the keys to motivation are relatively simple: work that is interesting and ennobling; sincere recognition by peers and superiors, opportunities for career advancement, positive feedback that can guide performance, strong and supportive social interaction by a team and, of course, fair and attractive financial rewards. There is little reason to waste time in the endless debates about which is more important: money, recognition, or enriching work. They are all motivating and different personalities are more or less influenced by different types of incentives. The job of designing an organizational system is to optimize all of the various forms of motivation. Over-reliance on any one form is a prescription for poor performance.

Human competence is the only modern parallel to production technology of the past century. Modern production most often occurs in the mind, or the collective mind of a small work group. If you have highly trained marketing professionals, skilled sales men and women, great engineers and brilliant financial managers, you have an important form of capital. These competencies are a foundation of performance. Investment in these assets is likely to pay off in the creation of other classes of assets.

Those organizations that have exhibited the greatest dedication to the development of human competence have consistently outperformed those who have only given lip service to training and development. General Electric, Microsoft, Toyota and other companies that have grown into great economic powers have done so as a result of both attracting and developing the most competent people.

Competence can loosely be divided into the functional skills, managerial skills and social skills. While there are many important functional skills, the most important are those that enable the core work process in the organization. If the organization is a software development company, the competence of software design and engineering are the core competencies. Managerial skills - decision-making, planning, project management, etc., are all critical to every organization, as are the social skills of communication.

A Philosophy that Builds Human Capital

We have all heard the speech that people are our most important product. It seems that every company has a statement of principles that articulates the importance it places on people. However, in too many cases the reality of daily life does not conform to the stated value. Whether in our personal life or in our professional life, it is easy to take people for granted.

A former consultant of mine worked for Hewlett-Packard during the reign of Carly Fiorina. He met with her to discuss the state of the culture in the organization, which was not good, and to make recommendations for its improvement. What was her response to him? "Look, for every unhappy person here, there are six people out there who want to work here. If they don't like it they can leave and we will hire someone else." She seemed to think that the people of HP were little more than disposable units. This attitude toward people was reflected in her relationships not only with employees, but also with the most senior managers and board members. Her philosophy toward people determined her failure. Her personal attitudes and behavior were in stark contrast to what had traditionally been an excellent people centered culture. It turned out that it was the CEO who was disposable.

Toyota is the opposite case. From the founding of Toyota, its leaders have put into practice a philosophy upon which their quality and innovation has been built. When a company grows to the size that Toyota has, with its world wide scope, there is no single leadership practice, no information system, no system of reward and punishment, powerful enough to hold it together and keep it moving forward. It is only an overarching philosophy, a system of beliefs, which can be sufficiently powerful to create unity of energy and effort. Toyota's founders understood this at an early stage.

The following founding philosophies do much to explain the success of Toyota and its ability to create and manage human capital. There are four key elements: tomorrow will be better than today; everybody should win;

customers first, dealers second, and manufacturer last; and Genchi gengutsu (go and see things for yourself, firsthand).[49] As you read these, consider what the overarching philosophy of your own company is because this is critical to the design of the social system.

Tomorrow Will Be Better

The extremely simple idea that "tomorrow will be better than today" may sound like some Pollyanna immaturity. However, it has significant meaning and psychological benefit. It defines the culture as fundamentally optimistic. Martin P. Seligman pointed out in his book *Learned Optimism*[50], that optimistic people are more successful, healthier, happier, and achieve more. Optimism is enabling and contagious. If you believe that tomorrow will be better than today, then you act on that belief, and that act is constructive. Optimism about the future of your company or your person is a self-fulfilling prophecy. If you are optimistic, you are thinking about the future. What will it be like? What are the opportunities? What do I need to do to take advantages of those opportunities? This is the thinking of an entrepreneur. All entrepreneurs are optimistic. You always start a company on the optimism of your idea and your ability to realize that idea. If an entire culture can be infused with the idea that tomorrow will be better than today, then it is very likely that the culture will produce innovation, continuous improvement, and financial success.

There is something that I have always called "creative dissatisfaction". It is an understanding of whom I am and where I am, as compared to whom I could be, and where I could be. It is an understanding of the gap between the current state and the potential future state. Knowing, or believing, that there is some future state, some better condition or place that I could be, creates the energy of creative dissatisfaction. This is present in the Toyota culture. Tony Fujita, Toyota Motors Sales, U.S.A., Vice President described it this way:

"I can't imagine Toyota being satisfied with any facts, any situation, any era, or any success. It's impossible. It shows in Mr. Watanabe's policies. I think it is Toyota's culture not to be satisfied, not to allow itself to be satisfied. The

---

[49] Osone, Emi, Shimizu Norihiko and Takeuchi, Hirotaka. *Extreme Toyota: Radical Contradictions that Drive Success at the World's Best Manufacturer*. New York, John C. Wiley, and Sons. 2008.

[50] Seligman, Martin P. *Learned Optimism*. New York. Alfred A. Knopf, 1991.

company always demands progress. Kaizen is not only a word; it is everything to Toyota. It's implanted."[51]

But this creative dissatisfaction is not unique to Toyota. It is present in every entrepreneur, every great athlete, every great scientist, artist or writer. It is the foundation of excellence. It is also the foundation for developing human capital.

Everybody Should Win

The philosophy that everyone should win at Toyota is all encompassing. It includes suppliers, employees, customers and society. The mission of Toyota is "To contribute to society through the manufacture of automobiles." The idea of contributing to society, as well as to the well-being of the company, has always been at the heart of the Toyota culture. This, of course, is spiritual capital and is an antecedent to human capital.

The idea of everyone winning is hard for many managers in the West to accept. In the minds of many when there is a winner there is a loser. This is a zero-sum assumption. However, when it comes to economic matters winning is a non-zero-sum game.

Robert Wright, in his excellent book *Nonzero – The Logic of Human Destiny*[52], argues that human history and human evolution have a direction. That direction, simply put, is from simple to complex organization, requiring ever-wider circles of trust and cooperation. The challenge of unity grows as we move from the simple organization of the family to the complexities of modern organization. He also argues that genetic selection is hard-wiring a tendency toward what he calls "non-zero-sum" behavior. Just as we may focus on the competition in sports and fail to see the cooperation, we may fail to see the ever-expanding forms of cooperation required for us to survive, and even compete, as a human species.

The fact is that credit, or respect, is highly elastic, as are financial resources. Everyone can win. In other words, if the team performs extremely well, they win the NBA championship; consequently, the amount of credit expands greatly. Therefore, the real game is a win-win game in which the

---

[51] Osono, Emi, et al, Extreme Toyota. Page 128.

[52] Wright, Robert. *Nonzero – the Logic of Human Destiny*, New York, Vintage Books, 2000.

amount of credit is what Wright calls "non-zero-sum," or highly elastic. The goal of the player in sports is not only to win against his competition, but to increase the amount of total credit available to all team members. Our ability to see a sport as non-zero-sum leads us to develop cooperative relationships. Non-zero-sum games lead to unity; while zero-sum games, lead to disunity. The biggest sport of all is the sport of business, which is also a non-zero-sum game. Wealth is elastic.

As Toyota grew in complexity, the challenge of unity became more difficult and required constantly evolving sophisticated means of trust-building. The philosophy that *Everyone Wins* was critical to the development of this trust. Wright says this is an historical necessity, *"As history progresses, human beings find themselves playing non-zero-sum games with more and more other human beings. Interdependence expands, and social complexity grows in scope and depth.*[53]

Customers First, Dealers Second, Manufacturers Last

Keep in mind that this is the philosophy of the manufacturer. It is paradoxical. Do you come in last if you put your own interests last? By putting their customers and dealers first, does Toyota lose? This has been their philosophy since their founding. And they haven't lost!

Good management is good listening, more than good talking. If you put your customers and dealers first, you listen to them. They are the boss. They buy your cars and send you money. It is good to listen to the boss. Toyota has always listened well to its customers as well as studying the future. Listening is a human capacity. It is not something that everyone does well. It must be trained and developed.

For many years it was an assumption at General Motors that they could drive marketing expectations, create market demand, and inform the customer what they should want. They should want big tail fins. They should want sleek and sexy cars. They should want more horsepower. If we can make it, we can create the demand. This push, rather than pull, philosophy destroyed the ability to listen well to customers. Even as customers were

---

[53] Ibid. p. 19.

continually buying more and more foreign and smaller cars, GM believed they could drive market demand. It has cost them dearly.

Go and See For Yourself (Genchi Genbutsu)

At Honda this same philosophy is stated as "the world's greatest experts are on the spot." I have sat in senior level decision meetings at Honda and some manager will offer his opinion about what to do to solve a problem and another manager will ask "Have you been on the spot." If you have not been on the spot or spoken to the world's greatest experts, then you do not really know.

Dr. Deming preached that we should manage by the facts. Toyota is a fact based culture, constantly striving to learn from the facts. Continuous improvement based on studying the data is a scientific attitude toward management. Rather than convincing yourself and trying to convince others, go and see, and learn the facts. Then form your opinions.

This philosophy is not only the philosophy of scientists who are in the business of learning from experience, empiricism, but it is also the philosophy of the most practical managers. There is a popular story at Toyota: The CEO, Kiichiro Toyoda was on a tour of the manufacturing plant. He came upon an operator of a grinding machine that would not work. He was scratching his head and looking at the machine. Kiichiro Toyoda looked at the man, rolled up his sleeves and stuck his hand down into the oil pan, pulling out a handful of sludge. He said, "How can you expect to do your job without getting your hands dirty."[54]

The meaning of this story is not that workers should get their hands dirty. It is that everyone, from the CEO on down, should get their hands dirty. They should "go and see" even if that means rolling up your sleeves and sticking your hands into a pile of sludge.

The above four philosophies are just one example of a corporate philosophy that has promoted human capital. Of course, other companies have philosophies that have also proven successful. The important thing is that you know your philosophy, you train every employee in your philosophy, and you carry it out over the long term.

---

[54] The Toyota Way 2001 (internal Toyota Motor Corporation publication, Tokyo) April, 2001.

Organization Assessment of Human Capital

1. We have identified the core competencies that enable the core processes within our organization.

1__________2__________3__________4__________5

Not True Somewhat True Very True

2. We benchmark our process of training and development against our industry competitors.

1__________2__________3__________4__________5

Not True Somewhat True Very True

3. We provide our managers world-class training in management skills.

1__________2__________3__________4__________5

Not True Somewhat True Very True

4. We provide world-class training, or encourage our professionals to seek external training in the areas of our core competence.

1__________2__________3__________4__________5

Not True Somewhat True Very True

5. Members of the organization consider one of the attractive features of working in this organization the learning and development process.

1__________2__________3__________4__________5

Not True Somewhat True Very True

6. Members of the organization are specifically recognized or rewarded for progress in the development of their professional competencies.

1__________2__________3__________4__________5

Not True Somewhat True Very True

7. Individuals share, in some form, in the business success of the organization and receive regular (weekly, monthly or quarterly) reports that inform them of business success.

1__________2__________3__________4__________5

Not True Somewhat True Very True

8. Members of the organization are members of work groups or teams that control their own process and regularly consult together on how to improve that process.

1____________2____________3____________4____________5

Not True Somewhat True Very True

9. Work groups have public celebrations of business success.

1____________2____________3____________4____________5

Not True Somewhat True Very True

10. Our rate of turnover of valued employees is lower than comparable organizations.

1____________2____________3____________4____________5

Not True Somewhat True Very True

INNOVATION CAPITAL:

Nothing has greater benefit to a corporation than innovation. Innovation creates markets, establishes market position, and creates customer loyalty. Without innovation you will die for the simple reason that your competitors are innovating. The ability to innovate is both an imperative and an asset.

The architecture of organizations may stimulate or stifle innovation. Innovation grows in the soil of spiritual, social, and human capital. To the degree to which there is commitment to a worthy purpose members of the organization will engage in the discretionary effort of thinking, exercising their brain on a problem or opportunity. Many creative ideas occur on the weekend or in the evenings, when a member of your team is choosing, even unconsciously, to think about a problem at work or a customer's needs. This is discretionary effort, effort that cannot be forced, measured, or required. It only occurs when employees genuinely care about the success of the organization.

Innovation thrives in an environment of high trust, social capital. Most innovations are not the result of one person thinking alone. Rather they are the result of thinking together, sharing ideas, brainstorming and allowing your idea to be criticized by your associates. High trust cultures are high innovation cultures. If you examine low trust cultures, such as in the Middle

East or the old Soviet Union, you will find very low rates of innovation. Companies in which there is a culture of fear, rather than a culture that celebrates successes, will have low rates of innovation.

The degree of competence and continual education of employees, lays the foundation for high innovation. When an individual is continually seeking the latest knowledge, the latest experiments, the latest inventions or theories, his or her mind is playing in the intellectual waters in which innovations float to the top.

The success of Honda and Toyota over U.S. automobile companies was the result of their fanatic dedication to process and product innovation. The successes of Wal-Mart, Home Depot, L. L. Bean or McDonald's were all about process innovation in their industries. Processes either create or minimize cost. They assure either consistency and reliability or the unfortunate alternative. Like other forms of capital innovation, creates a significant asset.

Types of Innovations – Big and Small

Innovations may be one of four types or a combination of types: They may be innovations in a product or service delivered to customers, or they may be innovations in process, how they are delivered or produced. Either product or process innovations may be small incremental improvements; or they may be large game changing breakthroughs. The way each of these is encouraged is different.

Process Breakthroughs

	Process	Product
Breakthrough	FEDEX Amazon.com Dell	Facebook Ipod Prius
Incremental	Continuous Improvement Lean Manufacturing	Iphone Civic/Accord Corolla/Camry

Federal Express is an example of a breakthrough in process innovation on which a company was built. There is no new product or service at FEDEX. Before FEDEX's guaranteed overnight delivery, you could still get packages delivered. But, Fred Smith, founder of FEDEX, studied the process of package pickup and delivery while in his MBA program. He studied all the potential technologies and processes and came up with a significant breakthrough. He changed the process, not the product.

There seems to be a pattern of major breakthroughs in process occurring among students. Fred Smith is joined by Michael Dell, Mark Zuckerberg and others in this distinction. Dell Computer had no innovation in product at all. The early Dell Computers were essentially IBM PCs, assembled from off the shelf components. However, the process of assembling and marketing was the innovation. Michael Dell understood the potential of Internet commerce as IBM and Apple did not. He decided to cut out all the middle layers of marketing and distribution, place his own ads in magazines and on the Internet, and ship the computers directly. It was a huge success although it would take only a nanosecond for dozens of competitors to catch on.

Amazon.com is also a business created as a breakthrough innovation in the process of marketing and distribution. Amazon was just a bookstore, nothing more. But, its founder also understood the potential of Internet commerce technology and how much less expensive it would be to simply ship the books out of a central warehouse while taking orders online. Many process innovations involve the elimination of steps in a process, thereby reducing costs and creating an economic advantage. This is market disruptive innovation and every business should be paranoid that some innovator is creating a business model that circumvents their own.

Product Breakthroughs

Many breakthroughs upon which new business are founded are new technologies, inventions, or products; rather than the process of how they are made or delivered. Facebook, once again, like Yahoo and Google, was born in a college dorm room by young people who struggled to find money for pizza. Facebook is an innovative service, one that is free, the idea of social networking online. Of course, there were predecessors, Microsoft's Instant Messenger, chat boards and email lists, and personal blogs. But, the idea of having your own space, where you share your thoughts, photos, and links with all your friends and where they can introduce you to new friends, is truly a new product simply using existing technologies.

The IPOD, not surprisingly from Steve Jobs and Apple, was also a breakthrough product innovation, taking some existing technologies and existing market for music in your pocket, but was so radically different in its ease of use and capability that it built a market where it had not been before.

Why is it that many breakthrough products are the creation of young people? What is it about their culture and the workings of their mind that allows them to imagine that Apple II when all the brilliance and wealth of IBM was blind.

I very well remember a trip I took to IBM's New York headquarters many years ago when I was working for Fran Tarkenton. Of course, we were hoping to sell them some consulting services, and they were interested in talking to the popular football player, much more so than to me about any need for consulting. Just a few months before this trip, I had purchased my first personal computer, a Radio Shack TRS80 Model III. It was terrific. I was mastering VisiCalc (which was the spreadsheet before Excel) and creating a spreadsheet that projected the billing days and dollars of my consultants forward for the year. I could figure out what would happen if we sold this client or that. And, I could do it all myself. Wow! That was my first experience with hands on computing.

When we met with the Senior Vice Presidents at IBM, in a casual conversation, I mentioned that I had just bought this Radio Shack personal computer and that I was pretty excited about what I could do with it. The moment I said that I was sorry. They looked at me as if to say "You child! How little you know about computers." What they actually said was that it was a toy. It would be fun for games and maybe for a few uses in the home, but it would be useless for business. Their business was selling huge million dollar mainframes to large businesses. They couldn't conceive of this silly little Radio Shack toy being of any use. About two years later, they were trying to figure out how to get into the personal computer business and meeting with the floppy haired Bill Gates. When they met with Bill Gates to talk about their adopting his MS Dos operating system, they still talked down to him as if he knew next to nothing about computers. As of this writing, IBM's market value is about 233 billion dollars; while, Microsoft's is around the same; and that ridiculous little company formed by two hippies and using an apple as a logo is now worth more than both.

This and a thousand other examples illustrate the danger of success, size and wealth. It makes the mind lazy; it reduces the ability to see the possibilities of new technologies. This is why Facebook was invented in a college dorm, and not by Microsoft. All this proves is that material wealth and resources has little to do with innovation. In fact, there is good evidence that the larger and wealthier an organization, the lower the probability of breakthrough innovations. Once you realize this, you realize how important the culture of the organization is.

Incremental innovation

Innovation is something like the race between the turtle and the hare. The speed of the hare is likely to gain more admiration, but it is often the turtle that creates more wealth over time. The value of innovation is not only in the breakthroughs of Facebook or FEDEX. Whether more wealth is created by these breakthroughs or by continuous improvement is very debatable. The dominant companies in retailing, manufacturing, hotels and many other industries are not the result of some dorm room breakthrough, but rather the result of continuous improvements.

Learning to Lead (and Innovate) at Toyota

In May 2004, the Harvard Business Review published an article by Steven J. Spears[55] that documented the education of one American manager hired by Toyota for a relatively senior position in their manufacturing organization. It describes in some detail how he is indoctrinated, not so much in the technical system of the organization, but in the mindset that drives continuous improvement. Bob Dallis (a fictitious name) is first assigned to the U.S. engine plant, where he is to help nineteen engine-assembly workers improve labor productivity, operational availability of machines and equipment, and ergonomic safety. He is also assigned a mentor who will follow his progress and provide feedback. In the first six weeks, Dallis identifies and implements 25 changes to individual tasks. For instance, a number of parts racks were reconfigured to reduce operator stress. Dallis and his work group also made 75 recommendations for redistributing their work, changes that required some reconfiguring of the work area equipment, wires, etc.

After 12 weeks of on-the-line work and improvement in the U.S. plant, his mentor then decided to take the student to Japan, where he will work in the Kamigo engine plant. To understand what follows, it is important to know that this is the plant where Ohno and Shingo developed the majority of their innovations. This plant is one of the best in Toyota and has been the subject of continuous improvement for forty years. There is nothing "wrong" with this

---

[55] Spears, Steven J. *Learning to Lead at Toyota*. Harvard Business Review, May, 2004.

plant by any standard. Despite this, Dallis was to work alongside first line employees in a production cell and was instructed to make 50 improvements, actual changes in how the work is done, in the short time he would be there. This worked out to one change every 22 minutes. By the morning of the second day he was there, he and his coworkers had built a list of 25 ideas for improvement.

Dallis found that his own ability to identify and make improvements grew with practice. This new American manager, who had held a senior position with a U.S. auto company and would hold a senior position in the Toyota manufacturing operations was just learning to make improvements, but not revolutionary ones. Rather his mind was changing the way it worked. He was learning that by being on the line, engaging in the actual work, he could find a large number of improvements even in a manufacturing plant with legendary quality. It is this mindset that Toyota was trying to instill. And the mindset he was developing is not one of superiority as a manager; rather he was developing the mindset of practical experimentation and respect for people.

Spears notes that *"Toyota's real achievement is not merely the creation and use of the tools themselves; it is in making all its work a series of nested, ongoing experiments, be the work as routine as installing seats in cars or as complex, idiosyncratic, and large scale as designing and launching a new model or factory."* Spears also concludes that the subject of this training learned, not to make changes himself, but rather to work through the workers on the line, to encourage them to experiment, and to monitor results of each experiment.

Incremental innovation is not only in the process of manufacturing or service. It may be in the product as well. But, there is a relationship between the two. It is not an accident that the Honda Accord and Civic, and the Toyota Corolla and Camry, have all been in production for about thirty years. No change in their names. No change in the market segment at which they are targeted. And, there has been no change in the reputation for excellent value and reliability in their market segment. There has been no dramatic breakthrough in these products, simply continuous improvement in their design, engineering and manufacture. There is no American manufactured equivalent to these products in terms of their market value, brand equity. U.S. auto companies do make comparable cars, but how many people can name them? U.S. companies have constantly been coming out with new cars, with new names, with little marketing, and little time to develop brand loyalty.

Lead with Questions, Not Answers

Leaders are supposed to have answers, not questions. Right? Wrong.

To stimulate innovation it is not essential that a leader have the answers, but more importantly that he or she knows how to ask the questions.

Shigeo Shingo and Taiichi Ohno are the fathers of modern production methods. In his excellent book Kaikaku,[56] Norman Bodek tells a Shingo story that may help understand the attitude of eliminating waste. Norman used to put on "Productivity" conferences at which I spoke for many years. These should have been called Lean conferences, but that term had not been invented yet. His conferences usually included talks by one of the masters of the Toyota Production System as well as lesser folks like me. Norman made trips to Japan and made it his mission to translate and bring to the United States the lessons from these innovators.

This story is from one of the trips to the U.S. he arranged for Dr. Shingo.

"On Dr. Shingo's first visit to America I took him to a Dresser, Inc. manufacturing plant, where they were producing gasoline fuel dispensing systems. After meeting the management team we walked around the plant floor with a small group of engineers and managers.

"Dr. Shingo stopped in front of a punch press. He asked us all to look at the operation and to tell us the percentage of *value-adding time*. He then took out his stopwatch to time the operation.

"We watched two workers in front of the punch press bend down and pick up a large sheet of thin stainless steel from the left side of the press. They placed the steel into the bed of the press. Then they removed their hands to press buttons outside the press, which indicated that their hands were out and clear of the press. The large press came down and formed the metal into a side of a gasoline pump. Then the two workers reached into the press, removed the formed sheet and placed the formed sheet at the right side of the press.

"'What was the value-adding percentage?'

"One engineer said '100%, the workers never stopped working.'

---

[56] Bodek, Norman. Kaikaku: The Power and Magic of Lean. PCS Press, Vancouver Washington, 2004.

"Another engineer said '75%' and, another said '50%.'

"Dr. Shingo laughed and looked at his stop watch. 'Only 12% of the time was the process adding value. Adding value is only when the dies are pressing against the metal to create a formed sheet. The rest of the time is waste.'

"Dr. Shingo then asked 'what can be done to increase the percent of value-adding time?'

"An engineer immediately said, 'You could place a table over here and put the raw inventory sheets on top of the table. This would help the workers. They wouldn't need to bend down. They could just slide the sheets directly into the press.'

"Another engineer said, 'We could install a leveler to automatically raise the sheet metal and keep it at a constant height, similar to what you might see in a cafeteria when you reach for a dinner plate.'

"A third engineer said, 'We could put a spring into the back of the punch press to force the formed metal to leap forward after the stamping.'

"Dr. Shingo laughed and said, 'Yes, you all know what to do, so do it!'"

An important point to notice in this story is that Dr. Shingo did not tell or instruct them to do anything. He merely asked the right questions and defined things as they really are. He knew waste when he saw it. This is the primary characteristic of successful managers in lean operations. They ask the right questions. They constantly seek to improve by eliminating waste. Also notice that Shingo never suggested that there was anything wrong with the workers or that they weren't working hard enough. He did not blame the person; he assumed the improvement was in the process.

As you design your technical and social systems you will want to take into account the essential lessons and practices of continuous improvement.

- Teach managers to ask questions, rather than give answers. Questions stimulate thinking and innovations; answers do the opposite.
- Encourage constant experimentation. Define a shop floor, or frontline process for submitting ideas and experimenting with the implementation of those ideas.
- Make work visual (process maps), make cause-and-effect diagrams visual reminders to think, and make performance (graphs) visual

so everyone is reminded how we are doing and is thinking about how we can do better.

- Make the submission of ideas as easy as possible.
- Review ideas quickly (24 hour turnaround from idea to feedback to the person who submitted it).
- Implement a very high percentage of those ideas.
- Reward both idea generation and idea implementation. Reward both tangibly with money, gifts, and socially with publicizing ideas and praising those who submit them.
- Eliminate criticism and fear of failure when submitting and trying out new ideas.
- Teach frontline managers to do their job in a systematic way. This should include designing a structure for their "Gemba walk". Gemba means where the real work gets done, on-the-spot. Managers in operating organizations should take a Gemba walk each day and they should know what to do. What they should do is NOT criticize. Rather they should ask questions, recognize good performance, encourage their employees, and study the process being used to see if it conforms to standard processes, and if not why not.
- Every employee and manager should be on a team that owns a value-adding work process. That team should consult together regularly on that process. They should have a visual graph, on the wall, of the key variables that define performance of that process. They should know the customers for that process and ask them for their requirements and level of satisfaction. They should continuously improve that process, and they should be recognized as the world's greatest experts in that process. They should keep account of the number of ideas they generate and implement for improving that process.

The questions that you must now ask are "How does our organization promote innovation? Is our organization and culture designed to promote both incremental and breakthrough innovation? How would its systems, structure and skill need to be changed in order to speed the process of innovation?"

ORGANIZATION INNOVATION AUDIT

1. We have a well-defined research process trying to develop a breakthrough product for our market.

1____________2____________3____________4____________5

Not True Somewhat True Very True

2. In the past two years, my company has brought at least one new product to market that has made a significant contribution to our financial performance.

1____________2____________3____________4____________5

Not True Somewhat True Very True

3. My company is able to charge a premium for its products or service because of their unique characteristics.

1____________2____________3____________4____________5

Not True Somewhat True Very True

4. People who are highly creative enjoy working for this company.

1____________2____________3____________4____________5

Not True Somewhat True Very True

5. My company promotes internal entrepreneurs, individuals who create a new business opportunity.

1____________2____________3____________4____________5

Not True Somewhat True Very True

6. Members of the organization are specifically recognized or rewarded for innovation.

1____________2____________3____________4____________5

Not True Somewhat True Very True

7. Individuals in this company work together in teams whose purpose is to find innovate ways to improve our work process.

1____________2____________3____________4____________5

Not True Somewhat True Very True

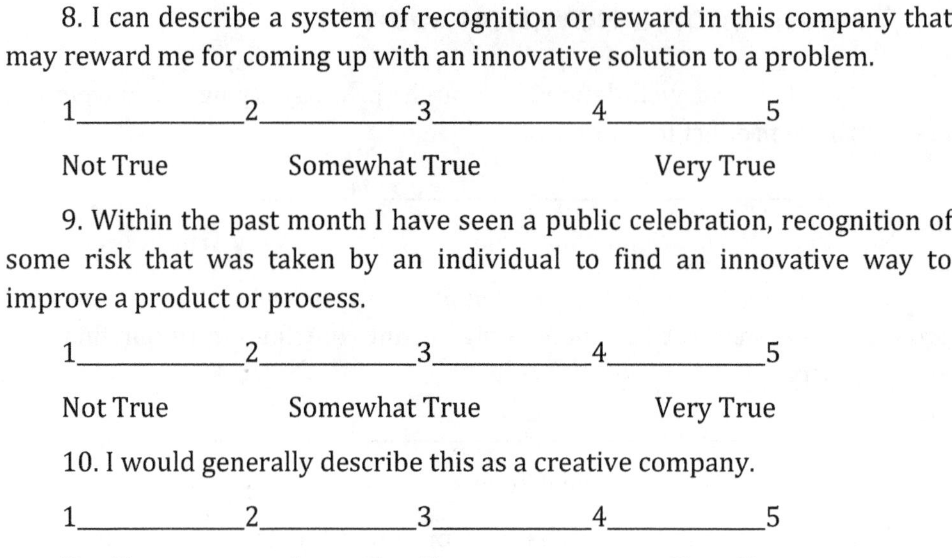

8. I can describe a system of recognition or reward in this company that may reward me for coming up with an innovative solution to a problem.

1____________2____________3____________4____________5

Not True Somewhat True Very True

9. Within the past month I have seen a public celebration, recognition of some risk that was taken by an individual to find an innovative way to improve a product or process.

1____________2____________3____________4____________5

Not True Somewhat True Very True

10. I would generally describe this as a creative company.

1____________2____________3____________4____________5

Not True Somewhat True Very True

Financial Capital:

Financial capital is the traditional understanding of assets. It may be measured as balance sheet assets or as the value of present and projected cash flows.

It is not our purpose in this book to redefine financial assets or accounting. Most companies already do that well. Our purpose is to identify and improve those things that create financial assets. Lehman, Bear Sterns and AIG did not collapse because of the lack of money. On the contrary, they had access to most of the wealth of the world. What they lost was not money. They lost the antecedents to money. They lost a system of values and purpose that had created trust with their clients. It then required only minor triggering events to cause a rapid loss of trust in the market place. This loss of trust then caused the immediate outflow of capital. It was the failure of spiritual, social and human capital that caused the collapse of these institutions.

My advice to design teams is to have a conference with the financial executive responsible for the organization which you are designing. Ask him or her to bring two documents as a basis for discussion. These two documents are the current income statement (also known as the profit and loss statement) and the current balance sheet. Then have a discussion around the following questions:

1. Regarding the Income Statement:

For those not familiar with financial statements, the income statement is the monthly statement that reports income, revenues received by the organization, and expenses; in other words, the money coming in and money going out during that month. Some income statements include a year-to-date or quarterly report, as well. One hopes that there is a bit more money coming in than going out, in which case there is a positive number on the bottom line. If not, there is a negative number, a loss.

What you want to understand is how the design of the organization and its processes can improve the financial picture. It may be that the steering team has given some targets for either revenue improvement or expense reduction. But, whether they have or not, you want to understand how you can help improve financial performance. So, here are some questions to ask about the income statement:

- Regarding the revenue or income side of the statement:
    - There are usually a number of different sources of revenue, based on different products or services or different regions. Which of these are currently trending up, increasing; and which are trending down or decreasing?
    - Do we know why they are trending up or down?
    - What do these trends tell us about the future of the business?
    - Given the strategy for the coming year, which of these income sources most need to improve?
    - If we designed a system that resulted in absolutely delighted customers, which revenue items would most likely improve?
    - Do we know how our firm compares to other similar firms in terms of revenue per employee?
    - Do we have a productivity number in terms of number of units of product or service delivered per employee? And, do we know how that compares to other similar companies.
    - Is there a productivity number for space utilization? In other words, if we utilize a million square feet of factory, warehouse or office space, if you divide that by the dollars of revenue, that

would give you a dollar per space utilization figure. This would be a measure of the productivity of space.

    - Is there a computation for work-in-process inventory or materials per revenue dollar?

- Regarding the expense side of the income statement:
    - Some expenses are fixed and some are variable. In other words, you may pay rent or payment on loans that is the same every month. That is a fixed expense. On the other hand there are variable expenses that go up and down with the level of business activity. For example, business travel. What are the fixed expenses that are not likely to be affected by the design project, and which expenses could be affected by the design project?
    - If we designed the organization that was recognized as the best place to work, in which employees were most satisfied, what expense items would be affected by that?
    - Can we see material waste as an expense item?
    - Can we see wasted time as an expense item? In other words, if we designed a work process that got the job done in half the time, how would that appear as a reduced expense?
    - Are there ways that making better use of technology could reduce expenses?
    - Are there other efficiencies that could be achieved that would reduce expenses?
    - Is there a cost of poor quality or rework that can be measured as an expense item?
    - Is there a cost of accidents or safety violations?
    - Is there a cost of environmental incidents that could be reduced?

2. Regarding the Balance Sheet:

To put it in very simple terms, the balance sheet reports the value of the "stuff" you own. While in our homes we are used to thinking that the more "stuff" I have the better, in a business there is a different idea. This has to do with the concept of "return-on-capital employed" in operations. In other words it is good business to do more with less. This is important because most companies borrow some amount of money or they are holding the assets of stockholders. In either case, the owners of the company, the owners of the assets want to know that their capital is productive. Therefore, if you can deliver the same amount of goods and services, but while employing less capital, you are increasing the return on assets, which is an important measure of financial success.

Larry Selden of Columbia University did research on what causes stock prices to move upward or downward, in other words, creating value for shareholders. Of course there is short term "noise" that affects every stock, but he factored that out to discover the important factors that could be counted on to move shareholder equity over the long term. The two most powerful variables are revenue growth and return on operating assets. In other words, investors are willing to pay more for a company, value it more highly, if revenues are increasing rather than staying the same or declining. They are also willing to pay more if the return on the assets employed in operations is high.

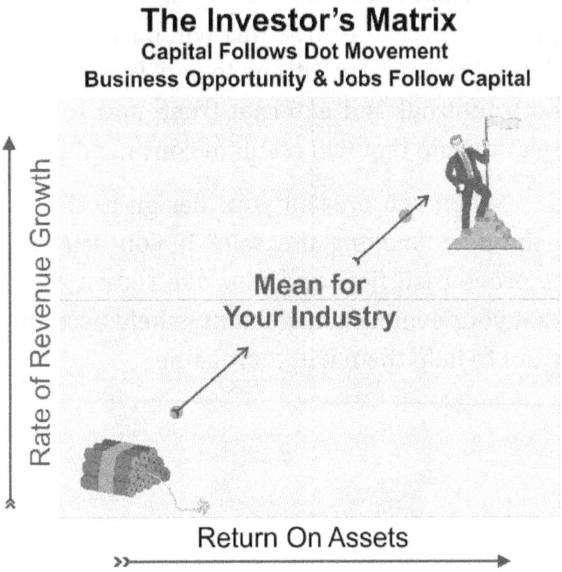

The Investor's Matrix
Capital Follows Dot Movement
Business Opportunity & Jobs Follow Capital
Rate of Revenue Growth
Mean for Your Industry
Return On Assets

One of my clients, a petroleum company, took this matrix and applied it to every business unit, down to the level of a small team at a well-head drilling for oil. Every team plotted the growth or decline in revenue and the growth in return on operating assets. They soon realized that if instead of buying a piece of equipment, they could share that equipment across several sites; they would improve their return-on-assets by producing the same with less. The CEO of the company was held accountable and rewarded by the Board of Directors for "moving the dot" northeast on this matrix. Every team in the company was playing the same business game, of moving the dot northeast. You can imagine that if you are the CEO it is a thing of beauty to have every employee in the company playing the same game that you are playing. That's how you win!

With that understanding as background, ask your financial manager the following questions:

- What are the different types of financial or material assets (space, etc.) employed in our business?
- Do we have a measure of productivity, or return on these forms of capital?
- Can we compute a return on operating assets, those assets actually employed within the operations?
- Can we create a matrix similar to the one illustrated here?
- What does he advise may be the assets that we could reduce or utilize more effectively?
- Does he see other ways, that if we designed the "ideal" organization and work process, we could improve the balance sheet?

The above analysis of financial capital and performance will help the design team understand the goal, which is almost always to improve financial performance. Of course this will best be achieved in a sustainable manner by designing your operations to satisfy the needs of your customers, to generate both internal and external trust, and to have the human capital and social relationship that will result in continued product and process innovation.

When you present your design to the steering committee it will be most helpful in "making the sale" if you can explain why your new design will improve cash flow and improve return on operating assets. It is most likely that your senior management is held accountable for these measures and you want to help them win their game.

CHAPTER 8

DISCOVERING YOUR EXTERNAL ENVIRONMENT

Everyone has heard John Donne's poem that begins... *"No man is an island, Entire of itself, Each is a piece of the continent, A part of the main."* And, so it is with people and companies alike. To understand where you are going you must understand what is happening beyond your island, or outside your own organization. To survive you must change for the simple reason that the landscape is moving and changing around you. The only serious question is not whether to change, but rather what that change should be and how best to accomplish it. In today's hyper-connected world the speed of change, your ability to adapt quickly, will determine the probability of your survival.

All living organisms survive by adapting to their environment. All systems that are sustainable are "open-systems," which simply means that they are open to influence, to feedback from their environment. The strategic house of every corporation sits on a landscape and that landscape is constantly shifting.

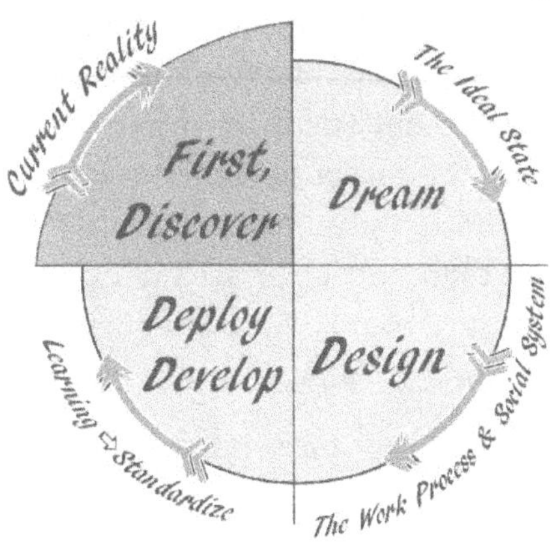

For every organization there are different external priorities. In other words, for some businesses the political environment may have little or no effect. For some the natural resource environment or climate, may have no effect. However, if you are in the energy business, both of these have a huge impact on your business. If you are in the healthcare industry you are impacted by political changes, such as the recent Affordable Care Act, by technology changes, and by social trends, particularly the aging population. Healthcare organizations have a serious challenge adapting to all of the changes in their external environment. You may want to discuss with the steering team and within the design team, which of these external factors are likely to be most important in the coming years and then focus your energy on assessing the impact of those.

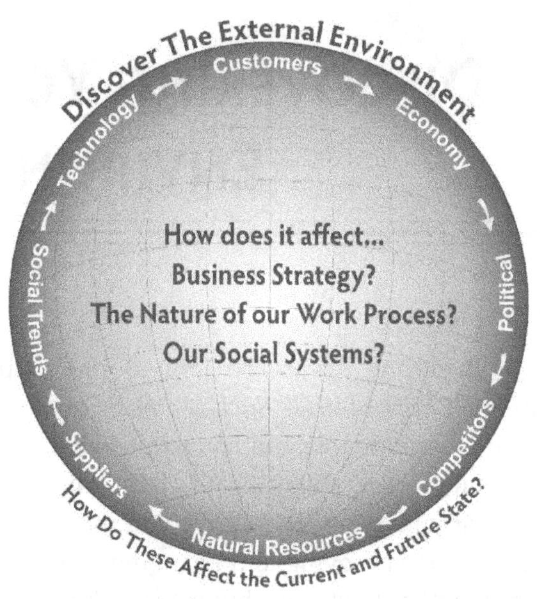

Design your organization and its processes to succeed in not only today's environment, but in tomorrow's environment. This requires intelligence, not merely in the IQ sense, but in the CIA sense. Every national government has an intelligence agency for the purpose of assuring that the government is informed about potential threats and opportunities. Similarly, every company needs to be engaged in intelligence gathering. That does not mean clandestine intelligence. Ninety five of intelligence gathered and processed by intelligence agencies is not covert, but is overt. In other words it is available from public sources. You simply have to be deliberate in seeking it out and utilizing it.

To conduct this assessment of the external environment or the landscape, you will probably need to involve other people beyond the design team members. Sales and marketing is always a good source of intelligence because they are out speaking to customers and learning about their future needs, about the threat of competitors, and even new technologies. Your engineers who design products are probably reading journals and magazines that deal with their particular area of expertise. They are a good source of information on future trends. And, of course, there is our good friend Google, from which you can learn almost anything.

There are three big questions to ask for each the following factors:

- How are we currently responding to the needs or challenges presented by this external influence?
- How will this external force change in the coming years? And,
- What capabilities will we have to develop to perform differently in the future to respond to the threat or opportunity presented by this trend?

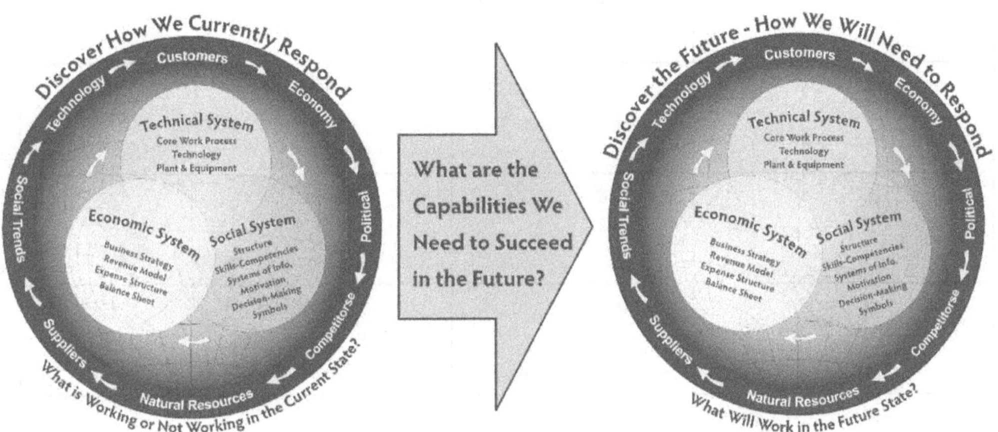

1. CUSTOMERS:

Customers are the most important part of the landscape for any business. Customer expectations and preferences change frequently and they almost always change in the direction of tighter demands, lower cost, and more responsive supply delivery. Listening, sensing, and adapting to the needs of customers is one of the most important capabilities for any business.

- Compared to other competitors, how well are we currently meeting customer requirements?
- What are the key areas in which we need to improve our performance to customer requirements?
- What is the key trend that is affecting our customers, and how will that affect us?
- In one to five years, how will our customer's requirements change?
- What capabilities do we need to meet those changing requirements?

- What are the key impacts this will have on our work process and on our culture?

Key Future Customer Requirements	What Capabilities will we Need?	How will this impact our Technical System?	How will this Impact our Social Systems?

In the next chapter you will find an Interview Guide to be used as a model for you to develop a process of interviewing customers. This is an example for you to adapt to your organization. You may wish to fill out the above after having conducted those interviews. This is an example of the "go-and-see" principle. That is where you must go to understand your customers.

2. Economic Trends:

Economic trends are global, but also within industries. The auto industry, the energy industry and the healthcare industry are all constantly reacting to changes in the larger economy, but also to the economy specific to their industry. Demand for energy may increase the price of crude oil, which is then felt in every aspect of the energy industry. That may have an impact on the auto industry, but may have no impact on the healthcare industry. Knowing the economic trends in your industry will help you design an organization that can adjust to those trends.

- What economic changes are anticipated that will impact your customers?

- What economic changes are anticipated that may impact your suppliers?
- Are there changes expected in the availability and cost of capital that will have an impact on your business?
- Are there any tax law changes that will have an influence?
- Is your customer base becoming more or less affluent, with more or less discretionary money?
- Brainstorm other possible economic changes that may have an impact on your business.

Key Economic Trends	What Capabilities will we Need?	How will this impact our Technical System?	How will this Impact our Social Systems?

3. Political Changes:

Political changes are any changes in government regulation, oversight, programs or tax policy. Many companies have lobbyists in Washington, not only to represent their views to the legislature and the administration, but also to provide intelligence back to the company regarding upcoming legislation. Politics may change regulations and how they are enforced and this can have an impact on your business.

- Are there any political sentiments that lean in the direction of regulation or deregulation that may impact your business? Is there any current legislation that may affect the regulation of your industry?
- Are there any expected changes international relations, trade policies, or the international environment that might impact your business?
- Are there any changes that may impact internal costs such as social security, FICA, insurance, legal costs, etc?
- Are there any political changes possible that may impact your sources of supply or other necessary resources?
- Brainstorm any other political threats and opportunities.

Key Political Trends	What Capabilities will we Need?	How will this impact our Technical System?	How will this Impact our Social Systems?

4. Competitors:

You can learn a great deal from the behavior of your competitors. There is no shame in copying their best practices. If they have discovered a better way, see if you can improve on it.

- Which competitors are increasing market share and what value are they bringing to their customers?
- In which new technologies are your competitors investing, and how may this represent a threat or opportunity?
- What methods of product or service delivery, packaging, or marketing may represent a competitive threat for your competitors?
- What differences in internal culture exist within your competitors, and how may these create an advantage?
- What companies that may not be directly competing with you at this time may be able to meet the same or similar needs of your customers in the future?
- What other competitive threats can you anticipate in the next five years?

Key Competitor Trends	What Capabilities will we Need?	How will this impact our Technical System?	How will this Impact our Social Systems?

5. Natural Resources or Climate:

If you are in the energy business the impact of climate and the natural resource availability is obvious. But, climate is also affecting housing, the vacation industry, the food industry and others. It is likely that this effect will increase in coming years.

- Do long term climate changes have any effect on how your business will be conducted in the coming years?
- What natural resources do you rely on or do your suppliers rely on?
- Will these be as available in the future, or will they be more scares?
- Are there alternative natural resources upon which you may rely in the future and how will affect your organization?

Key Natural Environment Trends	What Capabilities will we Need?	How will this impact our Technical System?	How will this Impact our Social Systems?

6. Suppliers:

Lean manufacturing does not operate within one house. It operates in a long series of houses, each adapting to the needs of the other. Your suppliers may also supply your competitors and you can often gain useful intelligence by listening to how your suppliers are changing to adapt to demands placed on them.

- What trends are your suppliers anticipating in the next five years?
- Do your suppliers anticipate any new technology, material or methods in their business in the coming years?
- What are your suppliers learning from your competitors about their future business, technology, materials or other requirements?

Key Trends Within Our Suppliers	What Capabilities will we Need?	How will this impact our Technical System?	How will this Impact our Social Systems?

7. Social Trends:

Are you marketing to growing and diverse ethnic and social groups? Is your workplace friendly to working mothers? Social trends affect both internal and external relationships. A lack of sensitivity to social changes can lead to the loss of talented employees.

- What changes in the age of the population will impact your organization?
- What changes in the workforce will have an impact on your organization?
- What changes in values or preferences will affect your customers over the next five years?
- What changes in expectations for information, empowerment, and involvement in decisions will impact your organization over the next five years?
- Brainstorm other possible social forces that may have an impact.

Key Social or Demographic Trends	What Capabilities will we Need?	How will this impact our Technical System?	How will this Impact our Social Systems?

8. Technology Developments:

It is a rare company that is not required to adapt to changes in technology, changes that will be adopted by competitors. Whether it is robots in a factory, CRM software, or new software for decision-making or knowledge management, virtually every company lives on a landscape of competitive technologies.

- What technologies are emerging or on the horizon that may impact the competitiveness of your current products or services?
- What technologies may impact the production process, costs, or efficiency in the next five years?
- What technologies may impact your customers in the future?
- What possible technologies are known to your organization which could represent potential for some breakthrough in the capability or your products, their competitive position, or methods of delivery and marketing?
- Brainstorm any other possible technologies that might have an impact on your organization.

Key Technology Trends	What Capabilities will we Need?	How will this impact our Technical System?	How will this Impact our Social Systems?

The external environment is also a system. It includes the pull of market forces and social, political, and economic trends. It includes the chaos caused by new technologies and the often unpredictable behavior of competitors. And, as we have already discussed, it includes the forces of shareholder financial expectations. These forces represent a complex dynamic system. Each of these forces is impacting the other.

Now it is time to identify the most critical external influences on your organization. You may have broken into sub teams to interview subject matter experts to help identify trends or drivers of change. It is possible that you may have as many as fifty different factors to consider. It is not possible for a design team to consider all of these at the same time, so you will need to priorities. One way to do that is to put them all on the wall. Have someone, who gathered the data, describe why each trend is important and how your organization will have to adapt to that change. Then have everyone walk around the room with markers and make dots by the five items that they think are most important. This is a way of gaining consensus. It will probably be apparent that five to ten different items are getting the most votes. Ask the group whether they agree that these items are the key issues and if you have identified the key ways that both the technical and social system will need to change in order to respond successfully to these challenges from the external environment.

It would be a good idea to involve both the steering team and the design team in this exercise. By doing this you will have reached consensus on some critical requirements for the new design.

You can see from this exercise that although you are in the discovery phase, you are actually creating the dream and the design of the future organization.

Summary of Most Critical Future Technical and Social System Requirements			
Critical Changes in the External Environment	**Critical Capabilities we Need to Develop**	**Critical Changes to Our Technical System**	**Critical Changes to our Social System**

CHAPTER 9

DISCOVERING YOUR CUSTOMER'S PRIORITIES

To create a customer focused organization, involve your customers in the process. This is a case of "how you change is the change."

How well do you really know what matters most to your customers? Many companies have customer surveys, records of complaints or other feedback from customers. If you have this data you should examine it carefully. But, there is nothing more insightful than actually sitting down, face-to-face with a customer or a small group of customers to ask them open-ended questions, allowing them to share what is on their mind, and then seeking clarification. When you do this face-to-face you can ask follow-up questions and it is in those follow-up questions that you may find the most insightful information.

CUSTOMER INTERVIEW GUIDE

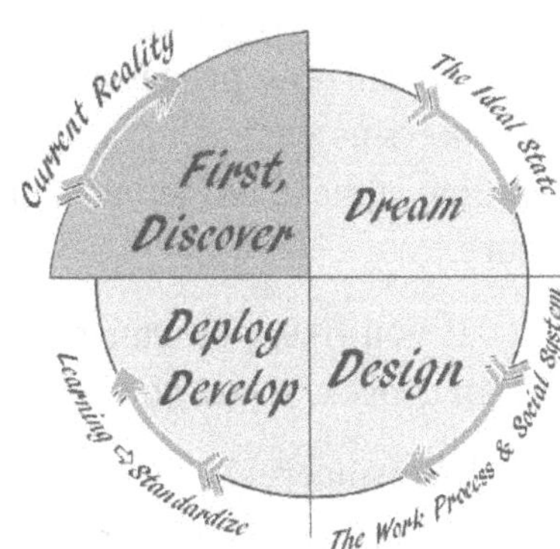

A major university asked for help in designing their Business and Finance Division's services. The customers of the Business and Finance Division are the student body, the faculty and the medical hospital and staff that are associated with the university. The Business and Finance Division includes all IT/IS services, property management, human resource management, security, and financial services.

Using the whole-system architecture process they analyzed the current state of their work process and then decided that they had to engage their customers to identify their critical needs for the future and the cause of their current dissatisfaction. The simple act of conducting these interviews was not merely a preliminary to the change process; it created a major change in perceptions and attitudes. The customers felt that they had not been listened to before and were very appreciative of being asked how they could best be served. This is another example of *"how you change is the change."*

Two members of the design team conducted each interview. One was assigned to be the primary interviewer and asked the initial questions. The second member of the team took the notes and could ask follow-up questions. Immediately after the interview, the two interviewers discussed what they had learned. They asked each other, *"What was the meaning in what we heard?"*

The following is the interview guide we developed for this process. You can take this and modify it to be appropriate to your organization and customers. You will notice that the first question is an "appreciative inquiry" question, asking about what has worked well, to learn from the positive behavior and experiences.

Opening Remarks

Thank them for their time.

Introductory statement:

"As you probably know, the Business and Finance Division has begun a significant program to review our current business processes and design the organization to meet our future customer needs. Our mission is to assess and evaluate current processes and practices by gaining input from all of our customers as well as looking at external benchmarks. We have been asked to examine almost all aspects of our organization to meet your needs in the future.

"If you like, you can find out more about our "design charter" and the design process if you go to the Division website.

"We sincerely appreciate your support and helping us, as our foremost intent is to better serve you."

"My colleague will lead the interview questions, while I take notes, and possibly clarify issues that come up."

Check It Out: Check out their understanding of the statement with something like "Does that make sense?" Or, "Do you have any thoughts or questions about that?"

Questions

1. "Looking back on the past few years, what have been some positive experiences with the Business and Finance Division? What have we done well that has made your work easier or been a help in your work?"
    a. Follow-up: "Is there one person, or one story about what has worked well?"
    b. And, if they still can't think of anything...
    c. Follow-up: "Has anyone else in the organization found any of our work helpful?"
    d. Reflect: "So it sounds like one thing that is important is...
    e. Clarify: "If I understand right it is very helpful when we..."

Finding Meaning: (to be answered by the two interviewers after the interview is complete.)

- The most helpful thing they recognize is:
- The meaning or significance of this for us is:
- The most significant story they told about what we do well was:

2. "What are the most important business and finance services that would help you meet your objectives?
    a. Follow-up: "If you had to do without all of our services except one, which one would that be?"
    b. Reflect: "So, the most value-adding service we provide to you is..."
    c. If they list several, you might say... "So, if I hear you correctly, the three most important things we do are..."

Finding Meaning:

- The most valuable service we provide to them is:
- The meaning or significance of this for us is:

3. "Is there a service that we could provide you that would add more value, to your work?"
   a. Follow-up: "Let's assume that we were going to invest in improving our services. If it was up to you, where would you direct us to spend that investment of time and energy?"
   b. Clarify: "OK, so you would like us to improve..."
   c. Clarify: "From all the things you listed are there a top three things you would like us to improve? Help us prioritize them."

Finding Meaning:

- The most valuable service we provide to them is:
- The meaning or significance of this for us is:

4. "What would be the ideal relationship or the ideal service we could provide to you? If you had a magic wand and could change anything you want, what would that look like?"
   a. Follow-up: "Let's just pretend that you own the University. If you were designing a Business and Finance group, would it look or feel any different than the current Business and Finance Group?"
   b. Clarify: "So you would really like it if we changed the organization to..."
   c. Reflect: "I hear you saying that it would really be an improvement if we..."
   - ***Finding Meaning:***
   - To become the ideal organization in their eyes we would, do what?
   - The meaning or significance of this for us is:
5. "Recognizing that this is just the beginning of a process, we want your guidance on who we should talk to, from whom should we seek input in your organization?"

a. Clarify: "OK, so you think it is important that we talk to the following people..."

b. Reflect: "If I understand right, those who can make the best contribution to this process are ..."

Finding Meaning:

- The guidance they provided means that we should do what?
- Is there any message of significance for us in this message?

6. "We are designing the organization of the future, for five to ten years from now; do you see external things coming down the road, economic, political, technical or social changes, that will impact us and we should be considering in our design."

    a. Follow-up: "What is the most significance technology trend that may influence us?"

    b. "Do you see in major economic changes that we need to take into account?"

    c. "Do you think there will be any political changes that will make a difference?"

    d. "How about social trends. Are there any major social trends that will affect the university or how we help the university?"

    e. Clarify: "So, if I hear you correctly, the most important external trends we should consider are...?"

    f. Clarify: "Do you have any idea how we should respond to these trends?"

Finding Meaning:

- The most significant environmental trends, from their perspective, are:
- The meaning or significance of this for us is:

Prioritizing Customer Requirements

As you survey customer requirements you will discover that there are many of them. There may be dozens depending on the type of product or service you produce. As you work to redesign your process and your organization, you must prioritize and focus. The following ways may help you prioritize requirements and needed capabilities.

Capabilities versus Customer Requirements

It may be useful to make a matrix like the following one. On one dimension there is an assessment of your organization's capability to meet a need. The other is how much it matters to your customers. You could conduct a survey, or in a focus group, ask your customers which of the following factors are most important to their buying decision. Then, for those same factors, how do they evaluate your organization.

For example in a hospital, you might list things like, a) waiting time to process paper work; b) courtesy of staff in admissions; c) cleanliness of the waiting area; d) information provided by staff regarding your care, etc. You could ask them to rate, on a scale of 0-10 which is most important. Then ask

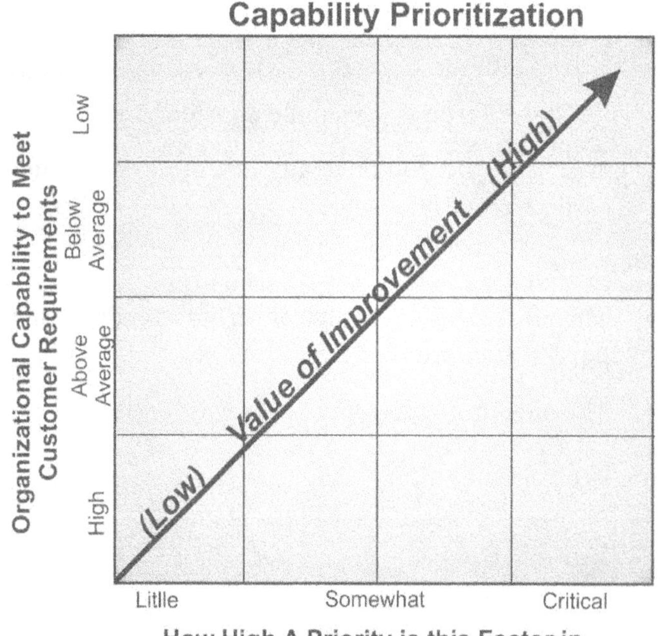

them to rate your performance on those same items.

On this matrix you will see that the capabilities in which you are "high" are at the bottom and those "low" are at the top. That is because you most need to improve those you rated low. On the other axis is how critical this is to your customers. So, those that are most critical, but you perform poorly, are the ones that would appear in the Northeast quadrant and would be the ones you should most focus on improving.

How Many Are Concerned and by How Much

Another analysis is to evaluate the number of customers reporting a concern about an issue versus how big a concern it is. In other words, to take the hospital example again, you could have 90% of customers reporting that they waited too long in the waiting room, but it might be that only 10% would use this as criteria for selecting a hospital to go to for treatment.

This is a good exercise in a focus group. You ask the customers to first make a list of issues that either cause them to be happy or unhappy with the service they receive. Then ask them how important, on a scale of 1-10, it is in their making a decision to use a service or buy a product. Again, those items that are in the Northeast quadrant are the ones you should most focus on improving.

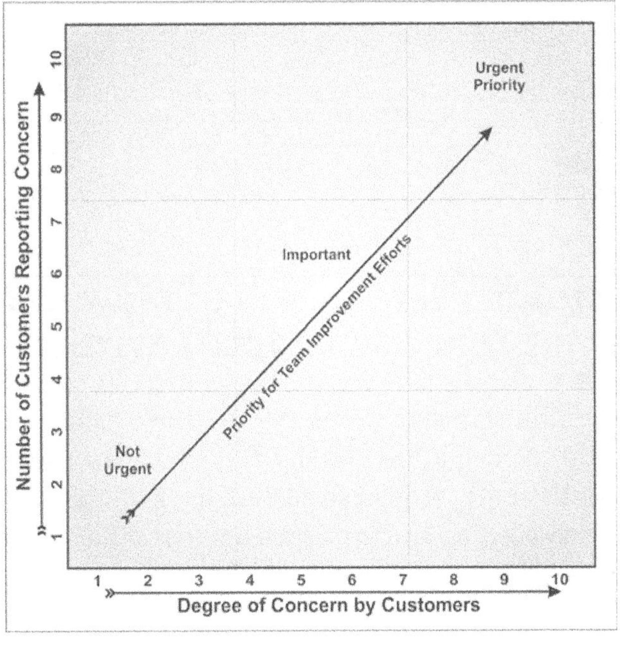

Cost to the Customer/Cost to You

Another analysis is to ask *"how great a cost is a problem to your customer versus how much will it cost you to improve?'* If a quality problem results in a huge cost to your customer, yet would cost little for you to solve, that should be a very high priority. It should be done immediately. On the other hand, if solving another problem would require a large capital investment, and it would have only a small improvement in customer satisfaction; it will be a low priority.

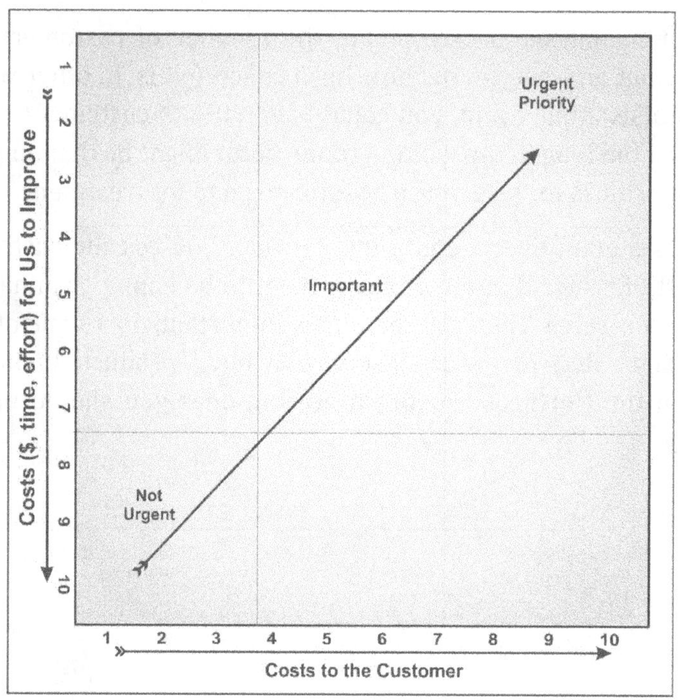

Is the Customer's Satisfaction or Dissatisfaction Caused by the Technical or Social Systems?

If you have prioritized what makes the customer happy or unhappy it may now be worth asking questions about the fundamental causes of their satisfaction or dissatisfaction. When you analyze the work system you will ask more questions about how the process can be improved. But, at this stage, you simply want to use a fishbone diagram and ask whether the problem is caused by the technical system (materials, equipment or the process); or is it caused by people, the social system (information available to employees, their skills, or their motivation)?

To use the hospital example again, if the biggest source of customer complaints is that patients and their families are not informed about stages of treatment, you might ask whether the failure to provide patients with timely information is a result of equipment (the computer system in this case); the work process that has been defined for administrative personnel, nurses or doctors; or is it a lack of motivation or caring on the part of staff? The answer to this question will point you in a direction when it is time to design the improved work process or social system.

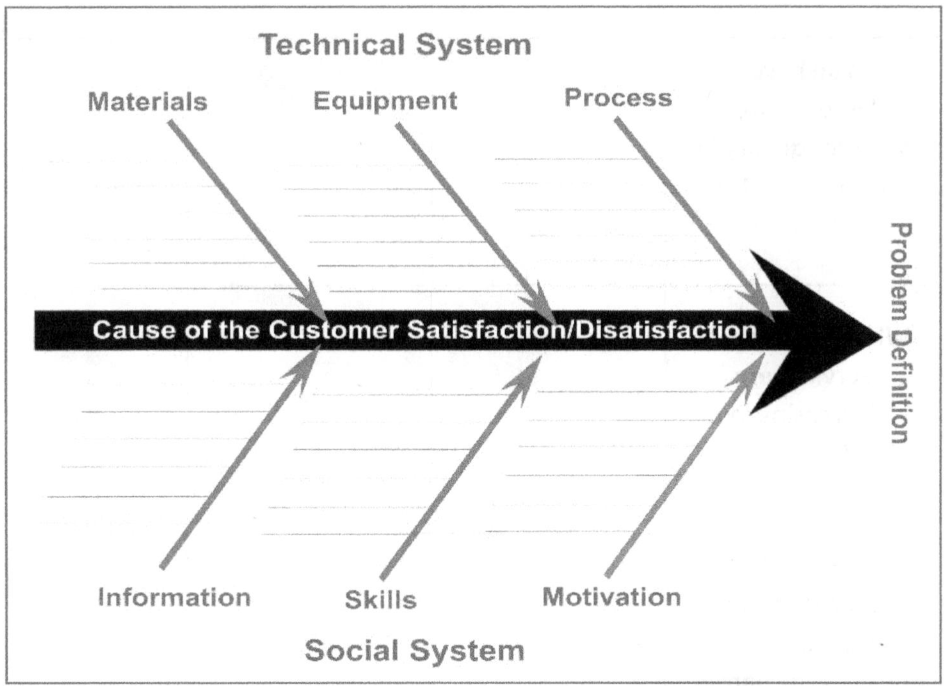

Anticipating Future Customer Requirements

The following table asks you to consider how we meet customer needs and how we will in the future. It is strategically focused. In other words, it asks you to anticipate future customer needs. Your interviews will have provided a basis for this assessment.

Building Future Customer Requirements			
Indicators of Strategic Focus	**Current Customers** (past 3 years)	**Future Customers** (next 3 to 5 years)	**Capabilities We Need to Develop**
Your customers perceive you to have superior technology in which products or services?			
You have demonstrated superior quality in which products or services?			
Which products or services are increasing in demand?			
In which products or services are you most unique, representing barriers to market entry?			
Which products or services represent the greatest financial returns?			

THE SEARCH CONFERENCE

There are several possible ways of gathering information on the current environment. A method that has proven useful in recent years is the search conference methodology first developed by Eric Trist and Fred Emery and later popularized in this country by Marvin Weisbord [57] and Kathie Dannemiller.[58] The primary purpose of this method is to involve as many members of the organization as possible and other stakeholders in the development of the new organization design. Other stakeholders often include customers and suppliers. This provides not only broad input but also increases buy-in to the end product.

There are many ways that the search conference method can be applied. Search or "design conferences" are a way of avoiding the problem of the design team appearing exclusive or working in isolation. There is a fundamental law of change: ***the more people feel that they have contributed to creating the change, the more people will be committed to its success.*** Seek to involve as many members of the organization as possible. The conference method is a great way to do that.

You might consider the following conferences in support of the whole-system architecture process:

1. ***A Work Process Design conference*** to gain input from customers, employees, and managers on the current strengths and deficiencies of the current work process and to define key elements of a future work process.
2. ***Social or Culture Design Conference***: In this conference you might present the basic structure of a future work process and then present questions about the current culture and gain their vision of the future culture or social system.
3. ***An Implementation Conference:*** In this conference you would present the basic work process and social system design and gain input and commitment to the implementation of the design.

---

[57] Marvin Weisbord. *Discovering Common Ground.* San Francisco: Berrett-Koehler, 1992.

[58] Danemiller, K. & Jacobs, R. 1992. Changing the way organizations change: A revolution in common sense. Journal of Applied Behavior Science, 28, 480-498.

By involving many stakeholders in the search conference, the work of the design team is expedited and pressure on them to represent the employees is diminished. A great deal of time can be saved by using the conference method. For example, conference participants (about eighty) in a manufacturing plant produced six variations of an ideal state organization structure and the benefits and risks of each in two and a half hours. The design team was then able to take this input and reach consensus in one hour as to the proposed structure. Because this structure was the result of common thinking developed with a large number of employee members, it had wide acceptance.

In this method, the steering committee still works on the strategy and design boundaries; then provides a charter to the design team and the conference participants. This charter may provide direction regarding growth, future markets, products, and services and some analysis of the competitive environment.

The conference is then organized to work on the vision of the future organization. The conference participants may be selected by the steering team or by invitation to all employees with them self-selecting. A conference may involve fifty to several hundred employees, and several series of conferences may be held to involve a large percent of the employees in the organization. The conference members will include management and employees; and, functions across a business process. It is common for such conferences to include key customers and suppliers.

The conference is led by a trained facilitator who will establish ground rules and assure the opportunity for full participation. When individuals come to the search conference, they do not come as managers, engineers, union members, or shop stewards. They come as members of the community who care about the organization and are committed to its success. The common ground is shared interest in the success of the organization. The purpose is to develop common ground, to develop a shared view of the type of organization that will succeed in the future. The purpose of the conference is not to find and hang the guilty, but to create the vision of the future. This focus must be maintained. The conference should not degenerate into a simple problem-solving exercise or a complaining session.

Conferences can vary, but all successful conferences have eight common characteristics:

1. The whole-system is in the room. By its very nature, conferences involve a large portion of the organization's population, customers,

suppliers, and stakeholders. People are able to talk to each other, have conversations, and make commitments face-to-face.

2. The focus is on the common ground and the future. The conference's focus is not on what is different about everyone in the room, but what they all have in common. What are the challenges facing "us?" What are the opportunities "we" have? How can we change the way "we" do things to improve the business? Rather than rehashing the past, people are asked to make decisions about the future – it is a "future search conference." What are "we" going to make commitments to for the future? Sometimes it is difficult to convince people to let go of the past and focus on the future, but that is the conference's intent.
3. You still need a steering team, charter, and design team. Many of the components of WSA still must be in place when conducting conferences. There needs to be a business case and strategy. The senior leaders need to be on the steering team, write a charter, and be actively involved in the whole process. Many conference designs call for all managers to be at all conferences. You still need a design team or data team that goes to all conferences, summarizes conference outputs, and makes decisions.
4. There is high stakeholder involvement. This means you will include employees, supervisors, managers, corporate staff or functional groups, customers, suppliers, and subject matter experts. The number of participants can range from twenty people to two hundred people in a room at the same time. Over four different sessions, you might include eighty percent of the organization plus outside people. The more people who can put their thumbprint on the design, the more support for the final outcome.
5. People make commitments, not just complain. At the end of each segment and the whole conference process, people are asked to commit to changes. Complaining, finger pointing, and dwelling on the past are discouraged. The goal is for people to focus on the future and create a common understanding of what they have to do to make the organization a success.
6. Conferences are well planned and carefully prepared. You do not bring two hundred people together for a full day without planning and preparing. This includes deciding whom to invite, where to have

it, what activities to use, how to process all the data, what people will have for lunch, etc.

7. There is a great deal of structure. These events are not free-for-alls. Although some consultants bring people together without any structure, we have found it critical to structure people's time during the conference. Having good facilitators, clear agendas, and orderly transitions between topics and activities makes everyone more comfortable and produces better results.
8. It still takes time and commitment. Although at the end of a conference there can be some real change, it still takes time to implement a new process or new organization after the conference is complete.

Code of Conduct

The search conferences will be more rewarding if everyone agrees to:

- **Listen intently** for the value in what others are saying.
- **Speak up**, so others will not have to work to get us to participate.
- **Share the air**, so no one dominates conversations.
- **Be skeptical and sympathetic** simultaneously, to give every idea a chance.
- **Respect each other** by not belittling or dismissing anyone's contribution.
- **Respect the schedule** by showing up on time, including at the end of breaks.
- **Do the work** assigned before, during, and between conference sessions.
- **Stick with it**, even when uncomfortable, exasperated, or exhausted.
- Have fun!

In the Appendix of this book you will find a case study applying the search conference methodology.

CHAPTER 10

DISCOVERING THE CURRENT VALUE STREAM

By this time the reader is probably asking... *"So, when are we going to get to the Dreaming and Designing stages?"* The reality is that you have been doing both if you have worked through the exercises and discovery process to this point. It is impossible, for example, to sit and listen to a customer explain what frustrates them and what they would like from your product or service, and not imagine what could be in the future. You haven't yet been asked to formally construct the dream or design, but all the members of your design team have been doing this in their minds, and perhaps in your shared conversations. That will happen again, as you map your work processes. Hopefully, you have been making notes, or writing things down on a "Parking Lot" of future state design characteristics.

The plan is this...

- You will now map the current state of your work process, your "value-stream." If you are like most design teams, you will immediately connect some of the dissatisfactions of customers and employees with the characteristics of the process.
- From this and the other discovery you have done, you will then develop your "dream" of the ideal

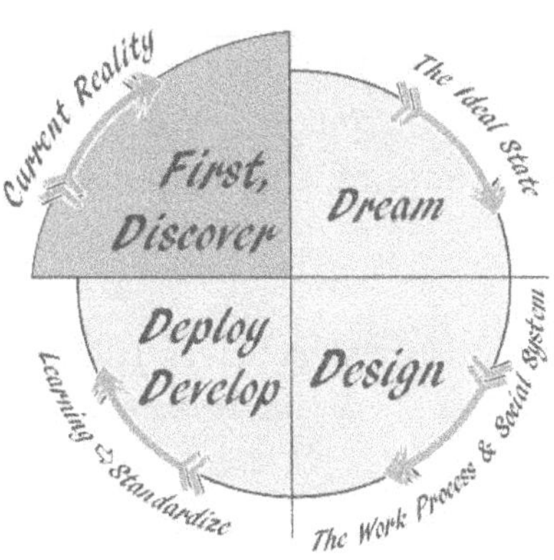

future state – both technical and social.

- Then you will do some more analysis of the work process. You will also be asked to study variances in the process. You will examine and seek to improve cycle time and efficiency by finding and eliminating waste.
- Then, with all that analysis, discovery and dream, you will take a clean sheet of paper and design the ideal future state process.
- Then you will design the social system – the organization of people, job descriptions, and competencies, how decisions are made, and how people are motivated.
- Then you will examine the economic implications of the design you have created. That economic analysis may cause you to re-examine some elements of your design, or it will help you develop the business case for implementing the design.
- Finally, after approval by the steering team, you will develop an implementation plan and start the implementation with an open mind to learning and modification as you go.

Most of these remaining steps will take less time than some of the preceding ones because much of it has already been created in your collective intelligence.

Roots of Process Mapping

Some authors have assumed that value-stream mapping was invented or discovered at Toyota; however, process mapping and analysis has a very long history going back to Frank Gilbreth, considered one of the founders of the field of Industrial Engineering. He presented a paper to the American Society of Manufacturing Engineers in 1921 titled "Process Charts—First Steps in Finding the One Best Way".[59] In more recent times Gary Rummler and Allan Brache[60] promoted the process driven organization and recognized the importance of what they call "managing the white space in the organization

---

[59] Gilbreth, Frank and Lillian (1924), *The Quest of the One Best Way*, Purdue University, Frank and Lillian Gilbreth Papers.

[60] Rummler, Gary A. and Brache, Alan P. *Improving Performance: How to Manage the White Space in the Organization Chart*. Jossey-Basse, San Francisco, 1995.

chart" which are the relationships between people - the players in the process. Their relationship mapping method has now become one of the most useful and popular ways of mapping a process. Value-stream mapping is the same thing, with the addition of measures of value added and/or costs and variances associated with each step.

The technical system or work process is about the horizontal flow of the work, from suppliers to customers, and creating the ideal flow that will add the most value for your customers and contain the least possible waste. The ideal process is so lacking in interruptions that it feels natural - it *flows.*

High performing teams or individuals appear *natural* when their performance flows with seemingly little effort. Athletes experience *flow*, or what they may call, "being in the zone." A musician may say she is in "the groove." Flow for an individual is complete focus, absorption in a task, when all energies move with ease and without interruption. Rather than feeling like great exertion, the work feels natural and exhilarating.

Mihaly Csikszentmihalyi described flow as the psychology of optimal experience. *"It is what the sailor holding a tight course feels when the wind whips through her hair, when the boat lunges through the waves like a colt - sail, hull, wind, and sea humming in a harmony that vibrates in the sailor's veins. It is what the painter feels when the colors on the canvas begin to set up a magnetic tension with each other, and a new thing, a living form, takes shape in front of the astonished creator."*[61]

You have observed flow if you have ever watched a great basketball team run the court on a fast break with each player having perfect confidence in the other, looking one way, and passing the ball another with certainty that the team mate will be there, and three quick passes around and over defenders ends in what looks like an effortless dunk through the hoop. That is a process and that is flow.

Processes at work rarely provide a similar sense of exhilaration. Notice, however, that processes that are exhilarating are without interruption, have an efficiency of no unnecessary steps, those who are engaged in the process are in control, and there is a high level of teamwork and trust.

---

[61] Csikszentmihalyi, Mihaly. Flow: The Psychology of Optimal Experience. New York. Harper Perennial, 1990. p. 3.

Exercise:

Think about these four elements of flow: a) no interruptions; b) no unnecessary steps; c) the players being in control; and, d) teamwork and trust. Do you feel that the process that you perform every day incorporates these elements?

What Inhibits "Flow" in Our Process		
Elements of Flow	What Currently Inhibits Flow?	How Could We Improve Flow?
No Interruptions		
No Unnecessary Steps		
Players in Control		
Teamwork and Trust		

In a high performing organization, the teams and structures are formed around the process to enable that process. Customers pay for the output of the process, not any artificial requirement of vertical approvals or orders issued *up the line*. Teams are formed and designed to optimize the ability of team members to control and manage their process. If you were designing the ideal organization, to create optimum flow in the process, you would design the team structure to optimize each team's capability to manage and improve their process. You would be sure to provide them with all the information they need. You would be sure to provide all necessary tools, skills and knowledge, and the decision-making authority so the team members are empowered to make changes.

Death by Process!

Processes can kill you and sometimes do. I don't know how many coroners' reports have said "Death by Process," but many should have.

My consultants and I were working with a large health care provider in the Midwest and had been given the assignment to "re-engineer" the core process in the organization. Of course, the core process was providing health care solutions to individuals in both clinics and hospitals. A design team was formed to study the core process and develop an improved solution to eliminate many well-known problems. The seriousness of those problems was sometimes buried under the routine of daily work.

The design team, after several months of work analyzing the process and developing a solution, made a presentation to the senior Executive Committee that included the company president. Because they were about to propose some fairly radical changes, they were concerned that they get the executives' attention in a dramatic way. So, they dramatized a patient experience. They role-played a scenario in which one of their members develops an unexplained stomach pain.

Her first stop is to her general practitioner and after filling out forms and sitting for an hour in the waiting room, she is told that she needs to see a specialist and is given a list of several specialists whom she could then call.

Of course, she has taken off from work for her first appointment.

She goes home and gets on the phone. It will be a month before any of the specialists can see her. She makes an appointment.

She shows up a month later at the specialist's office. The specialist immediately tells her that he wants her to take a series of tests and she is referred to a clinic that provides the necessary tests. She calls and makes an appointment for two weeks later.

When she shows up at the clinic, she is informed that she has to get pre-approval from her insurance provider before they can administer these tests.

She goes home and calls the insurance provider.

You get the picture. The story was detailed and frustrating to just listen to, let alone if you had to live through it. The story ends, after months of wrong appointments, delays, and re-routing, in the doctor's office where she finds out that she has cancer and the doctor informs her that treatment could have been much more successful if she had come in sooner. She dies. In effect, *the process* murdered her.

To lighten up the somewhat somber mood in the meeting the leader of the design team said, "Of course that story may be a bit exaggerated. Perhaps we don't kill people, but people do suffer through our system."

With that the president of the company, a doctor and healthcare executive for many years, interrupted and said, "Excuse me, but there is nothing exaggerated about that. That was my mother! That is exactly what happened to my mother."

A long and tense silence followed as everyone tried to figure out how to respond to that revelation. The president broke the silence and said, "Well, let's fix it!" Not surprisingly, they approved implementation of the redesigned process.

Isn't it odd that we often handle packages with more efficiency and care than we handle patients? And that is because package delivery companies have become much more focused on eliminating waste from their processes and assuring that their process meets their customer's requirements.

Processes Are Transformational

Processes exist to transform input to output. The "stuff" that is the input is transformed and that transformation must add value. It must add value greater than the net costs of the transformation process. As the stuff is transformed, there are "state changes" that define the transformation. It is actually these state changes that the customer is paying for. For example, if you are a simple restaurant, you receive input in the form of raw food – vegetables, meat, spices, etc. They arrive from a supplier in one state, but you transform them by your processes of mixing, cooking, etc. That is how you add value.

Every business must be constantly aware of how it adds value. Take book publishing, for example. The technology of printing and the Internet, particularly Amazon, are transforming the publishing business. Publishers add value by changing the state of a manuscript received from an author into a printed book that will appear on the book shelves of your local bookstore. But, the landscape is changing and causing every publisher to rethink how they add value. Now, authors can hire an editor, then a cover designer; get the book printed, converted to an e-book and available on Amazon without the need for a major publisher. Then they can promote it on their own blog and use Google Adwords to gain more publicity. In addition, book store shelves are disappearing. The value proposition of publishers is being transformed due to the changes in technology and the buying and reading habits of their customers.

It will be a good idea to stop here and ask these questions:

- What is the transformation process of our organization for which customers are willing to pay?
- If you follow input to output, what are the state changes that add value?
- Is there a change occurring in the transformations for which customers are willing to pay? In the future, could they go directly to your supplier?
- Are there new or additional transformations, state changes, for which customers may be willing to pay in the future.

These are critical questions as you realize that your system is not only social and technical, but also economic. The "what will they pay for?" question is the most important question for any business.

Mapping Your Process

How we think and feel about process improvement is just as important as any specific technique. Dr. Deming famously said that *"95% of quality problems are in the process, not the person. But 95% of the time we blame the person and fail to improve the process. Then we wonder why we still have the problem."* This is a profound bit of wisdom at the heart of process improvement.

The following are essential attitudes as a team begins to study and improve its processes.

The Attitudes of Process Improvement:

- Most problems are in the process, not the person!
- Don't blame the person - fix the process.
- Every process can be improved – forever!
- Problems are normal – each an opportunity to learn.
- Measurement of processes leads to improvement.
- Every process must have a "process owner" or team responsible for its execution and improvement.
- We "know what we are doing" by knowing the process.

Managers today are many times more aware of their processes than they were twenty years ago. The Toyota Production System is an innovation in process. It is not an innovation in either product or service. It is all about the effectiveness of the process of making cars that led to tremendous competitive advantage for Toyota and other car companies. FEDEX, McDonald's, Facebook and EBay are all examples of companies built on a breakthrough in process innovation. These companies did not create a unique product or service. EBay is essentially a store, a flea market, a way to buy and sell. We have done that for thousands of years. But, it is an innovation in process that makes it easier for millions of people to buy and sell from their home.

Process thinking becomes a way of life. Process thinking is learning to look horizontally through the organization as work flows. Those who are trained in lean processes can walk through a work setting and immediately see piles that signify process delays, interruptions in the form of pallets or in-boxes on the desk, all of which indicate process problems. Think flow!

CORE AND ENABLING PROCESSES

The core process of the organization is that process which serves customers and directly results in payment to your organization. It is largely determined by the money flow. If you are a restaurant, the core process is seating and serving customers and preparing the food. How you do accounting is an enabling process, not a core process. How you train staff, manage information within the organization, are all enabling processes. This does not mean that they are unimportant. In fact, they are essential. But, they are not the core of your purpose as an organization.

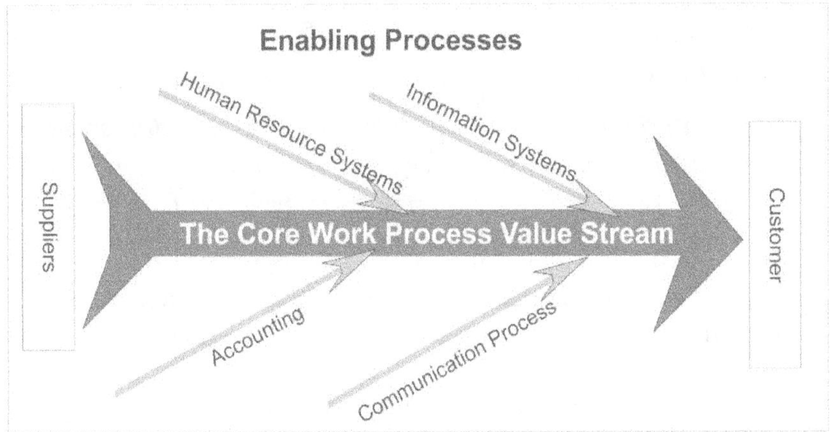

The customers of the core process are those who write checks to the organization. The customers of the enabling processes are those who work in the core process. In other words, if you are an operating manager in a manufacturing plant, the human resource department works for you... not the other way around. The only reason you have a human resource department is to attract, develop and retain the best people to work in the core process.

Why does this distinction matter? As you change the nature of the core process, the enabling processes must change to meet the needs of the core process. In other words, the core process may change to require employees who have more technical skills. Previously, these may not have been an important criteria as HR recruited employees. Just as the core process must adapt to the needs of its customers, those who manage all of the enabling processes must adapt to meet the needs of their customers.

Exercise:

- Define the core work process of your organization. This is where you will start your process mapping.
- What are the enabling processes that enable the core work?
- It is often a good idea to have representatives of these enabling processes serve on the design team as the design team redesigns the core work. At a minimum, you will want to consult with them.

Different Types of Processes Maps

A process is a set of related activities that together result in a desired output for a customer.

A lean process is one in which every step adds value, speed through the process is optimized, there are no interruptions or re-work, and those who work in the process seek continuous improvement.

The set of activities that comprise a process can simply be listed on a sheet of paper. However, we have all heard the saying that a picture is worth a thousand words. It is true. If you have ever downloaded directions on MapQuest, or used a GPS in your car, you received a list of turns and highways. You then also see the map of the suggested route. The map is much more helpful. Human beings are created with a natural talent for visualization. We like to see pictures, and we find it easier to understand a picture than a list of words.

You will have to decide the most useful way to map your process. It will be helpful to look at a number of different process maps and see how each may be useful in different situations.

Macro Maps

Let's start with a very high level map. Think of "macro maps" as looking at your organization from an airplane thirty thousand feet in the air. They give you the big picture.

The following is a macro map of a large manufacturing and marketing company and how the leadership team drew their major processes. Once the team and the CEO agreed that "this is what we do," they restructured the senior team so that the leader of each of these major processes was a member of the leadership team. Following that is a macro map of a university's

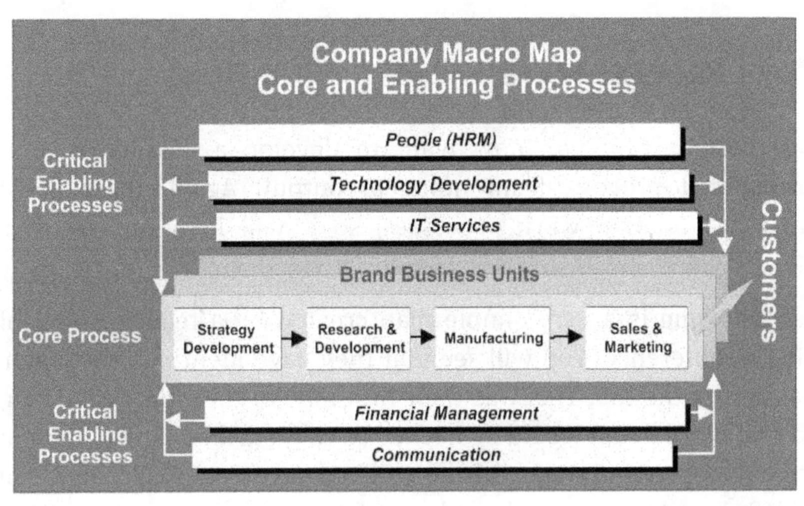

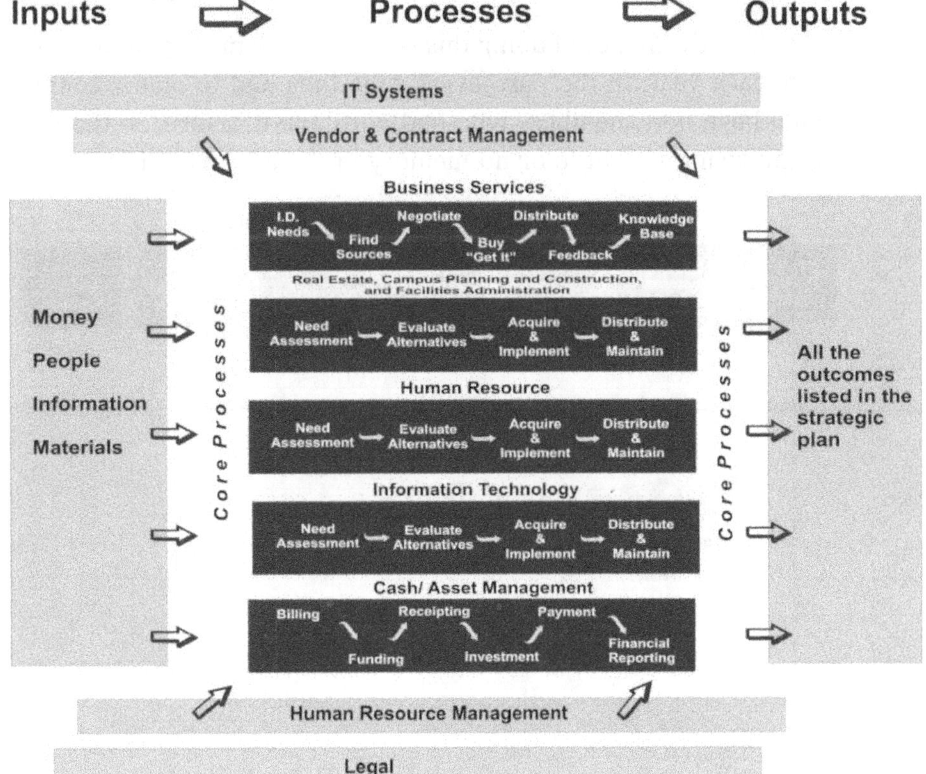

business and finance organization that includes all the enabling processes that support the academic departments, the students, and the hospital.

Now, with your team, develop a thirty thousand foot view of your organization with the major core processes, major enabling processes and critical inputs and outputs.

Work Process Maps

Your design team will now want to develop a detailed map of the transformational process, from input to output. Again, there are many different ways to map work processes, so it will help to look at a few examples.

The following is a very simple map created by a team responsible for managing a conference. You will see that they have identified the major core activities across the top. This was their first map of their process. Then, they decided that more detail would be needed so they "drilled down" and mapped the detailed steps within each of the original seven steps. You can see that under "define customers, needs and goals" they have mapped the five steps for getting that job done. Of course, they did this for each of the seven steps.

One of the advantages of doing this is that this team plans and manages a conference each year. In the past, every time they had to plan a conference, they would have new members who had not done it before. So the learning would begin again with little or no memory of the lessons of previous years.

Now, at the beginning of their planning for the conference they take out the planning map and review the steps from last year. They decided whether these steps still make sense this year, and they assign responsibility for each of the steps. Then, after that conference is completed, they have a learning-reflection meeting. They review what went well and what did not go well. They look at the map again and make changes so the team next year can avoid any mistake they made. In this way, each annual team is able to improve the process and maintain some "corporate memory." This is a form of knowledge management that is often lacking in organizations.

IDENTIFYING THE "VALUE" IN THE PROCESS STREAM

Another name for process mapping is *value stream mapping.* What is the meaning of "value?" Value is created when there is a transformation in the material, information, or other input, and that transformation is necessary to satisfy the customer. Anything that does not add value is waste. Sitting still is waste. Re-doing is waste. Any time spent that is not directly creating the desired transformations is waste. The job of the design team studying a process is to identify exactly which time, materials, motions, etc., are adding value and which are waste.

Value-adding and non-value-adding activity can be identified on your process map by using data boxes. Below you will see an example. These data boxes illustrate three measures of value: CT, the actual cycle time from beginning to the end of that process step; VCT, the value-adding cycle time; and CTVR the ratio of value-adding to total cycle time.

Identifying the actual cycle time and the value-adding time requires discipline, doing your homework. You should not guess. Go and see! Go and

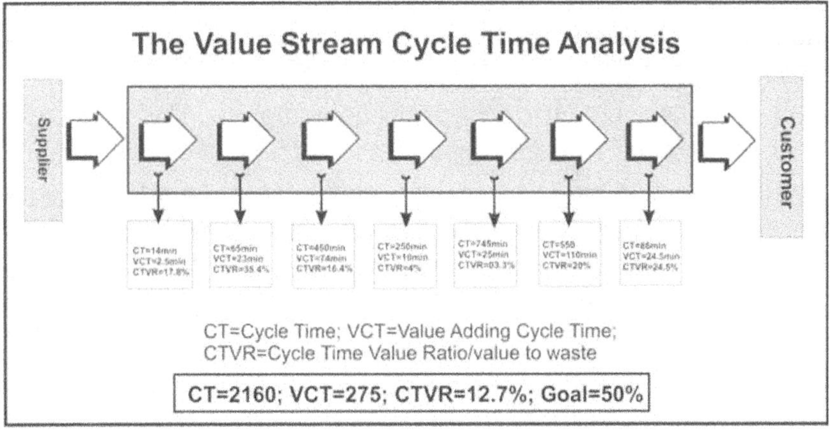

measure! Get the data. Often, it will surprise you.

In this illustration the total and value-adding cycle time of each step has been identified, as well as the totals for the overall process. The percent of value-adding time is 12.7%. This is not an unusual ratio when processes are studied carefully. You will see that this team has set an ambitious goal of getting to 50% value-adding time. This will mean eliminating a lot of non-value-adding activity, delays, re-do loops, or other interruptions in the process.

Which value measures you decide to use when analyzing your process will be dependent on the nature of the work and the output of the work. Beginning with cycle time is one of the best ways to get started.

Common Process or Value Measures

- CT = Cycle Time
- VCT=Value-adding Cycle Time
- CTVR=Ratio of Value-adding to Total Cycle Time
- CO=Change Over Time
- No.O=Number of Separate Operations
- WT=Work Time (actual value-adding work)
- TT=Total Time Worked or Assigned to an Operation
- SC=Scrap
- SCR=Scrap rate (ratio of scrap to total)
- I=Inventory

Another useful question to ask when analyzing processes is, "where are problems found, and where are they caused?" It is normal that problems are caused in one place, but discovered in another place. This almost always means that they are caused "upstream" and found "downstream." For example, imagine that you are making chairs. One department cuts and prepares legs for assembly. A "downstream" department does the actual assembly. It is important that the legs are exactly the same length. Hopefully, those who are cutting the legs are conducting their own self-inspection. However, it will not be surprising if those who are assembling the chair find that some of the legs are irregular and cause the chair to wobble. In such cases

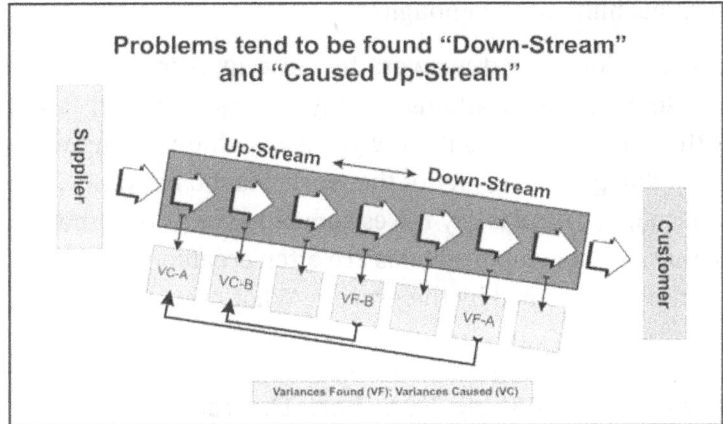

it is important that there be a clear feedback loop established whereby the assembly team can immediately provide feedback upstream to the team that caused the problem. This feedback loop should be almost instantaneous to avoid the production of off-specification parts. Any delay in this feedback loop will increase waste of materials and time.

Relationship Maps

Here is a very simple map. This is a process with which we are all familiar. It is a simple work process: making a meal. If you are a good cook you know that the order in which you do things is very important. For example, if you are going to make a spaghetti dinner you don't start your preparations by sticking the pasta in a pot of cold water, and then thinking about how to prepare the sauce. You begin preparing the sauce long before putting water on to boil for the spaghetti. Order is important in most work processes. It is one of the reasons why you should map your processes. Problems often occur because the order is wrong.

While this process map is useful, it is also lacking a lot of very helpful information. Who is doing what? Why is one person doing something rather than other people? Does one person bare too much responsibility or not enough?

It is much easier to find answers to these questions in a "relationship map." The following map contains exactly the same steps; it is the same process, as the previous one. But, now you have who is doing what. You can see that Dad is doing the majority of the work. Maybe he wants it this way, or maybe he doesn't, but it certainly raises some questions that should be asked. You can see that relationship problems are often created by how we do things. The relationships are defined by the process. What problems do you think this

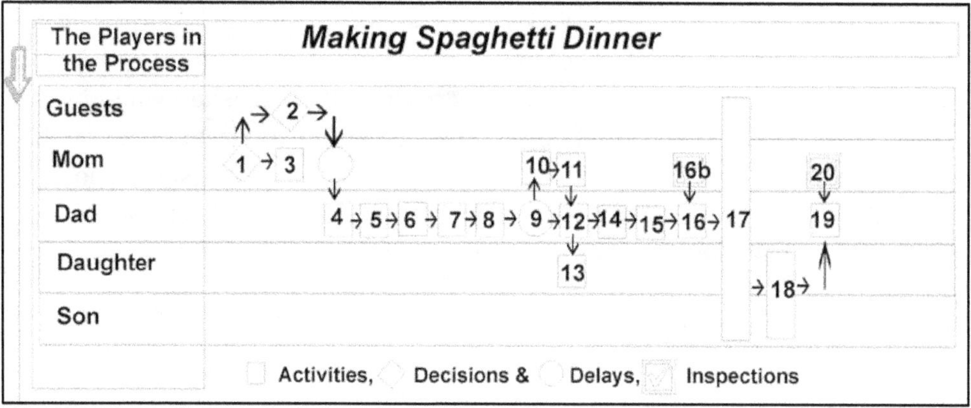

process might lead to? You might try reversing the roles of Mom and Dad. Do you like it better or worse that way? Why?

Turn Processes into Flow: Steps in Redesign

Here are some simple steps to follow to create a process map. These nine steps have generally proven to be a logical sequence to follow when mapping and improving processes.

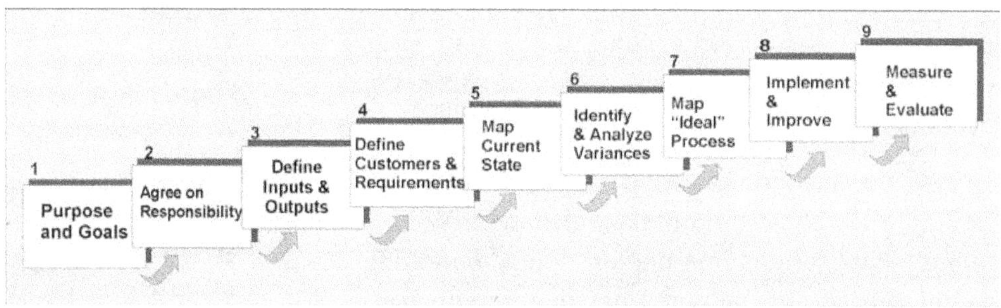

1. Clarify Purpose and Goals

The purpose and goals of every process should be clear. Review them here. The purpose should make clear why the process is important and to whom. The goals should not be detailed scorecard goals, but the general goal of the process.

2. Agree on Responsibility

Is it clear which team owns this process? Are the process owners in the room? Do teams understand what their responsibility is for this process? These are important considerations in design both the process and the organization that surrounds the process. One of the goals of redesign should be to make this very clear and to enable those teams to manage and continuously improve those processes.

3. Define Inputs & Outputs

If you have completed the work in the previous chapters, you have already done much the necessary work to be ready to work on process improvement. You should have answers to the following questions

- What are the inputs to your work process (include materials, information, capital, people)? What are the requirements for each of these inputs?
- Who are the suppliers who provide input? What capabilities are needed on the part of suppliers in order to meet these requirements?
- What are the feedback loops from your team to your suppliers, and how do they function (speed, quality of information)?
- What are the outputs of your work system?
- Given the above, what are the requirements for your work process?
- What are the feedback loops that inform us of customer satisfaction, and how do they function (speed, quality of information)?

4. Define customer Requirement

If you followed the guidance in the previous chapters, you have this. It is helpful to just put this on a flip chart so the team can see and refer to these requirements as they begin mapping the process.

5. Map the Current State

It is a mistake to start mapping how things should be done in the future until you have mapped how things are done today. This is the "current state" of the process.

It is often true that even those doing the job don't know how the whole process gets done. People tend to only understand their very narrow piece of the process. You can't analyze how things can be improved or study the causes of variances if you don't know how things are currently done. This is why it is important that design team members are recruited from all major areas of the process.

There is a discipline to mapping the current state and that is the discipline of remaining "fact-based." Years ago there was a TV and previously a radio show, called Dragnet. The lead character was named Sergeant Friday. Sergeant Friday would always interview witnesses and they would start telling stories and he would bring them back by saying "I want the facts, nothing but the facts." The design team should follow the advice of Sergeant Friday.

It may be helpful to imagine a meeting in which a team is going to map their process. It is very helpful to have Post-It-Notes, especially the 3x5 kind. Inevitably, you will be moving these around as you remember steps that were forgotten or realize you have the order wrong. Have the team members write down steps in the process and put those on the wall. It is very helpful to have a roll paper that you can spread across the wall. Give yourself lots of room.

Let's go through how that meeting might flow:

1. First, let's check to see that we have the right people in the room. Are the team members in this room the "world's greatest experts" in this process? Is there anyone else we should invite to participate in mapping the process?

2. Now let's define the process. Do we agree on the process boundaries? Where does this process begin and where does it end?

3. Now we will make a list of the inputs and outputs and customer requirements for this process. We will also make a list of any other specifications for the output of this process.

4. Now let's map the current state steps in the process. Let's start this by brainstorming without worrying about whether we have the steps in exactly the right order

5. Some process steps are work activities; some are decisions. If you can, use a different color for these. Or you can indicate in some way that these are symbols. Agree on another kind of note for delays.

6. Give everyone a chance to get all of the steps up on the wall and then ask, "Who are the Players in the process?" Make a note for each individual who participates in the work of this process. Now put these players in a vertical column to the left of your paper. If you can, draw a horizontal line across the paper, representing the occasions when that player may be involved.

7. Now order the steps. Arrange each of the work steps and decisions on your map going from left to right. They should be in chronological order. If two things are happening at the same time, they can be on top of each other. If they happen after one another, then they should be to the right of the previous step.

8. Ask yourself how these happen in time. Are there delays between steps? If these delays are for any significant amount of time, put a post-it-note up for that delay.

9. Now create a timeline from left to right. It may be that the process is not the same every time. Take a typical process cycle for the sake of your studying the process. On the left, when the process begins, put a zero at the beginning of your timeline. Then, at the end of the process put the amount of time a typical cycle takes, whether it is one hour or one month. Then, try to put time marks from left to right as the steps occur. This will give you some idea where the delays are occurring and how much time is involved in each step of the process. This may raise some questions when you analyze the process for speed or cycle time improvement.

10. This is probably enough work for one meeting. Getting to this point may have taken one to several hours. When a team is assigned to work on a complex process that flows through the organization, just mapping the current state may involve many meetings over a period of weeks. It may also be necessary to go and interview other people who are working in the process in order to have knowledge of those steps.
11. It is sometimes desirable at this point to invite others into the meeting, perhaps some managers, perhaps members of other teams and ask them if they agree that this is how things currently work. They may have some insights that your team may have missed.
12. It will probably be in another meeting that you begin to analyze the variances in the process. Below is an introduction to the analysis of variances. This will be explored in more detail in the following chapter.

Chapter 11

Dreaming the Ideal Future

You have done enough discovery - you are ready to burst! And, you work in the system and you have your own experience to guide you in defining the ideal future system. It's time to create the dream!

You may remember that when you began the discovery process it was recommended that you create a "Future State Wall" where you put Post-it-Notes with ideas for the future technical and social system of the organization. So... you probably already have many dozens of ideas.

It is important that the design team recognize the value in thinking about the "ideal" versus the "practical." It is common for people to say, even to themselves, "Well, it would be great if we could have that decision made immediately by the people on the line; but, they don't have the knowledge or skills to make that decision, so that won't work." They then give up on the idea and do not allow it to be considered. A better response is to say "It would be ideal if they could make that decision, and in order for them to do that we will need to provide them with training and information that will allow them to make good decisions." This is thinking about the whole-system rather than fragments of the system. Every ideal state element has dependencies. This is the nature of all human systems.

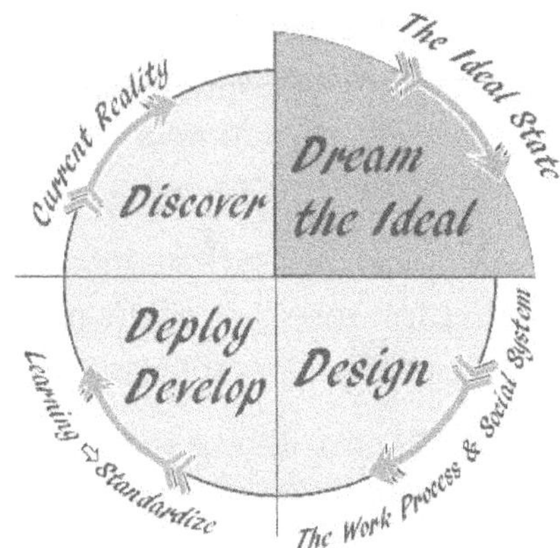

When you imagine the ideal process you may find that it requires new technology, new skills, new decision-making processes, or new organization structure to enable that new element of a design. While some of these may at first seem impossible obstacles, it often turns that they are not impossible and simply require an investment that needs to be evaluated relative to its potential positive impact.

Brainstorm the Ideal Future

Here is a simple way to brainstorm, organize your ideas, and reach consensus on a vision for the future organization.

1. First, you have a wall filled with Post-it-Notes that are ideas for the future technical and social systems. Ask the team to go to the wall and silently (that's the hard part) organize them into affinity groups. In other words, there may be several notes concerning teamwork that they should organize in a cluster. Or, there may be several notes regarding reducing the time required for the process. Simply organize them into general categories. You aren't making any decisions now, just reviewing the ideas you already came up with.

2. Then simply ask the team to sit silently for fifteen to twenty minutes and think. Think about all the information you received from customers, about changes in the market, about capabilities you need to develop to succeed in the future. Ask them to review their notes, review flip charts that may be on the wall, post-it-notes, etc. Then ask them this question: *"From the perspective of the customer, what will the ideal product or service look like, feel like, and how will it be delivered to them in order for them to consider you the supplier of choice in two to three years?"*
3. Then ask each member of the team to share their vision of this ideal from the customer's point of view. Ask the group NOT to judge, criticize or attempt to evaluate these perspectives.
4. Then ask the group to identify the most common elements from each individual's presentations. It is likely that a consensus view of the

customer's desires will emerge. If not, it is OK to have more than one consensus view. In other words, it will be either this or that. It is likely that those two scenarios will have a great deal in common.

5. Then ask the team to again think individually, and silently, about the implications this customer's requirements will have for your work process, the technical system. Ask them to review all the post-it-notes that were placed on the wall concerning the future technical system and ask them to look at the process map you developed that describes your current state. Ask them to describe, not in great detail, the three to five key changes that will have to occur in how we do our work to enable us to meet the customer's needs.

6. Again, ask the group to individually share their ideas about the future work process, without any judging of the ideas. Identify the most common elements in from their individual sharing. You can do this by writing each person's ideas on a flip chart and then identifying those that are repeated.

7. Ask the group if they have considered the use of current or likely future technology in their description of this future state. Ask them to discuss how technology will impact their future delivery of your product or service.

8. Ask if there is a consensus in terms how the future work process will not to operate, what it will need to accomplish. Please note that you are not attempting to redesign the process in any detail at this point. You are just saying "It will need to accomplish this..."

9. Now that you have an agreed upon general idea about the customer requirements and the performance of the work process, do the same exercise for the social system. Ask the team this question: *"In order for us to meet the customer's needs, and for us to successfully perform the new work process; and, for us to be the employer of choice in our field, what changes will we have to make in how we do the following?"*

    a. Organize people.

    b. Make decisions.

    c. Train and develop people.

    d. Communicate within teams and across teams.

    e. Manage people and recognize performance.

   f. Any other ideas regarding the social system.

10. Again, ask the group to share their ideas, without judgment, consider all the idea you have put on the wall, and again seek to reach consensus on the key ideas for your future social system. Remember that you are not designing or deciding on any details yet, you are merely creating a dream.
11. At this point it will be a good idea if everyone takes out the charter that they were given by the steering team. Read the principles, purpose, and boundaries. Does our dream fulfill the intent of the charter? Does the charter suggest any additional elements that are missing from our dream?
12. Finally, ask this question concerning the economic system. Realizing that they have not yet analyzed this is any way, do they see any implications in the above dream for the income and expenses of the organization? The purpose of this question is simply to initiate their thinking about this subject.
13. You should now have four sets of ideas: a) a view of the future customer requirements; b) a view of the future work process; c) a view of the future social system; and d) a view of the future economic system. Put these side by side. Ask the group if there is general alignment between them. In other words, to achieve the customer view, does that match the future work process and the future social system?
14. You now have a dream of the future state.

Dreaming of The Ideal Home Care Nursing Team

(As an alternative to the previous guidance, this is an exercise that worked well with the HomeCare design team. You may be able to adapt these instructions to your own team.)

You and your team members are living five years from this date. We have come a long way in the past five years. The organization and your team has matured into a very high performing and self-managing team. Your clients are delighted with the service you provide.

However, the world has also become more competitive. All home care agencies have improved their level of service and reduced their costs. Your funder is going to simplify their life by dealing with only one primary care team in each geographic area. This will reduce their administrative costs. Of course, they want to work with that one team that will provide absolutely the best possible care, the smoothest administrative and communication processes, and the quickest response to their communications and problems.

In a few hours you are going to meet with that funding agency's representatives. Your job is to convince them that you will be the best possible team they could work with, fulfilling all of their requirements.

- Why will you be the team that can provide the best possible home nursing care?
- How will you make life easy for the funder?
- Describe how you will handle all communications with the funder.
- Describe why you will be the most professionally competent team.
- What will it feel like to work on this team?
- Are there different roles and responsibilities on your team? Describe them.

Soon, you will be interviewed by your funder. Be prepared to describe why you will be the winning team.

After the first half hour of discussion, you are free to communicate with any other team. You will have a total of one and a half hours to develop and describe your "ideal state."

Presentation to Steering Team

If you have not done so yet, this is a good point at which to have a presentation to the steering team. You will want to share with them all of your discovery and you will want to share your dream with them. It will be important to ask them not to judge the dream in terms of details or exactly how it is going to work. That is what you will now design. But ask them if they have any questions about what you have discovered and ask them if they have anything they would like to add to the dream.

CHAPTER 12

DESIGNING THE WORK SYSTEM: VARIANCE ANALYSIS

Now that you have created your dream and your current state map you are probably anxious to start mapping the details of your future work process. However, there are two additional types of analysis that are worth doing before mapping the future. These will help you refine your dream. These are an analysis of variances and a search for waste in your process. Both will help you design the leanest possible process.

As you go through both of these analyses you will be asking, "So, if this is a cause of a variance or waste, then how can we change the process to eliminate that variance or waste?" Answering this will help define the future process. It might even cause you to revise your dream. Remember that this process is not entirely linear. In other words, there are no rigid silos between the 4D's of this process. It is normal to modify your dream as you are designing, and as you are designing you may recognize the need for additional discovery.

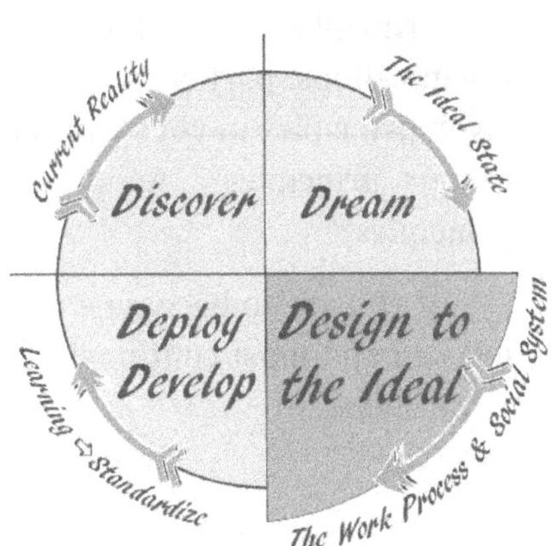

WHAT IS A VARIANCE?

A variance is a problem. It is something that varies from either the standard of performance or from the performance that meets the customer's expectations. The purpose of this chapter is to analyze your work process to discover the causes of variances and design those out of the process.

Let's define the different types of variances:

Type 1 Variance: Statistical Variation

If you know your data (we'll talk more about that) you will see that there is standard deviation and statistical variability in every process. Then, there is some cause of abnormal variability, or what Dr. Deming called a "special cause." This is a quality problem and we need to identify its cause so we can design those causes out of the process.

Type 2 Variance: Cost

The process may be in statistical control and may be meeting the customer's requirements. However, the cost of the operation may be excessive. If there is a lower cost way to do something, the current costs versus the potential lower cost, is a variance.

Type 3 Variance: Variance from Customer Requirements

Your process may be in control, in fact it may be performing within a very tight range of variability, but that performance is not what the customer wants. You could serve a meal in exactly the same way every day in a restaurant, but the majority of customers may not like it. So, it is not a quality problem in the sense of variability, but it is a quality problem in that it doesn't meet customer requirements.

Type 4 Variance: From Your Principles

Principles or values make a great difference in the design of organizations, particularly in the design of the social system. You have been given principles in your charter. It is worth asking "Does our process conform to our principles?" And, if not, "how can we align our process to our principles?"

If you are to become a truly lean organization you must become process focused and must continually seek to reduce or eliminate each of these types of variances.

Statistical Variability and Variances

Statistical variation is the variability around a mean for any performance. There is always some variation around a mean. The question is when is that a problem?

To understand variability it will help to understand a simple example. You may have a gun that you aim at a target. Let's assume that you are one hundred meters away from that target. Let's also assume that there is no wind and the gun is in a vice-grip so it will not move. Will every bullet land in exactly the same spot, assuming that the gun itself is perfectly stable? No, the bullets will not all fall in the same place. If you fire fifty shots from the gun, you will see a pattern. That pattern illustrates the statistical variation resulting from this system. This pattern describes system performance. There is always variability around a mean. The average bullet may fall at or very close to the target, but the pattern will be in a circle around that point. Depending on the gun, (and how far back you are) the pattern may be a few centimeters wide or a few meters. This pattern will describe the capability of this system in its current state.

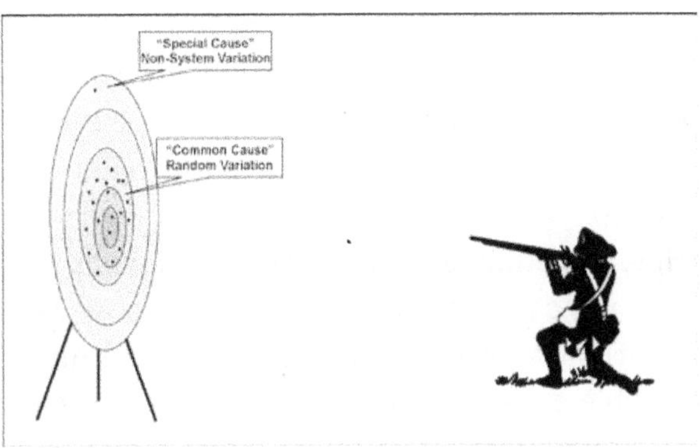

Knowing *system capability* and normal *system performance* is important knowledge for anyone managing any system.

Common and Special Causes of Variation

Dr. Deming described the important distinction between what he called *common cause* and *special cause* of variation. In the example of the bullets hitting a target, if you fire fifty or one hundred shots, you will see that all of the shots fall within some circle. This variation from the mean, the center of the circle, is *common cause*. It is explained by the nature of the system.

Within the normal performance of this system, the only explanation for each variation is simple randomness. There is always random variability around a mean. If you want to reduce this variation you will have to change the system. You could add a longer barrel on the gun, for example, and that would reduce the variation.

This is an important understanding because if you know what normal performance for a system is, you won't blame the person operating within that system. Blaming individuals is useless. The system has to be redesigned.

But, there is another kind of variation and this is not the result of the inherent properties of the system. A *special cause* is the result of something "being wrong" in the operation of the system. In other words, if the circle on the target is normally a radius of twelve centimeters, this is "system" performance. However, if suddenly a bullet falls two meters away from the center, you know that this is not normal for this system. You only know this because you already have data on system performance. You immediately say "Hey, something is wrong here!" And what you mean is that "Hey, this is not a common cause; this is a special cause of variation." This is caused by some abnormality in the system or abnormal input. Now you can brainstorm the possible causes of this defect. The cause may be a bad bullet. Or something may have knocked and moved the gun. The gun may be getting dirty. There may be many possible reasons for a special cause.

The important point of this distinction is that you will do different things depending on whether the variation is a special or common cause variation. If you seek to improve the normal variation produced by a system, common cause, you will have to redesign that system. On the other hand, if you are witnessing a special cause, you would be making a serious mistake to redesign the system. This would cause even more variation. You need to track down the reason you have experienced a special cause.

Costs of Variability

There is a cost to variation. For example, when you drive to work each day it may take an average of thirty minutes to make the drive from home to work. But, it is rarely exactly thirty minutes. It may vary ten minutes on either side. If the weather and traffic are good, you may get to work in twenty minutes. But if there is an accident, it could take a lot more than thirty minutes. Let us assume that you live in an area where there is a lot of road construction and there tend to be a lot of accidents. When there is no traffic and no construction, the process of driving from home to work is "interruption free." But, in your situation, during a normal drive to work, there is a fair likelihood of an interruption, something that will cause a deviation from the mean.

Now let's also assume that there are some consequences for being either late or early. Your team cannot start work until you get there. If one person is late by thirty minutes, that is the equivalent of all ten members of the team being late. The consequence is that there are three hundred minutes of lost work time. Being on time is so important that it is a factor in your performance reviews. If you are late too many times, that may result in not achieving a merit increase in pay. This is a risk that you do not want to take. On the other hand, if you are thirty minutes early, the door is locked and you can't enter. This means standing out in the cold. These are the costs of variation in the process. Variation almost always has costs even if we fail to see or understand them. We often behave on the assumption of variability in a process and we therefore consider it "just the way things are."

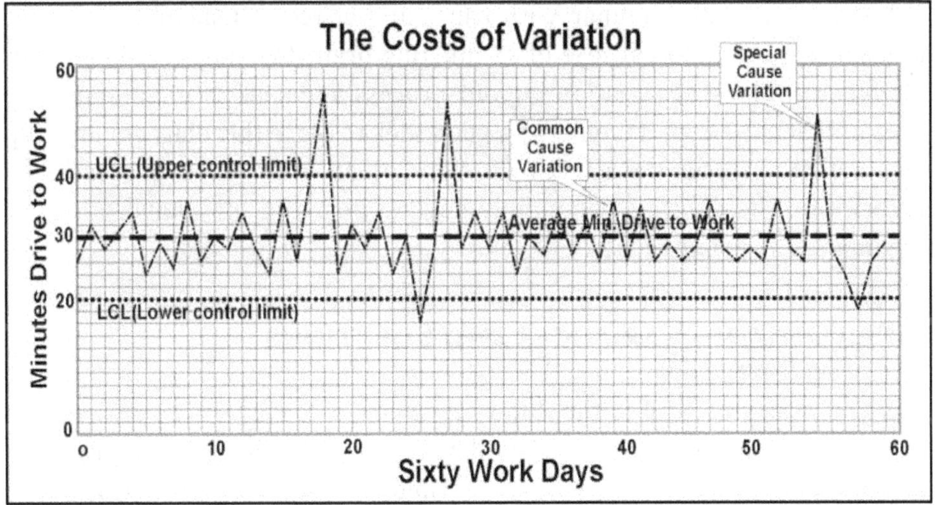

If you look at the above graph, you can see this variation illustrated. You have measured the time it takes you to drive to work for sixty days. The average is thirty minutes, but on three occasions it took about fifty minutes. On two occasions it took less than twenty minutes. Now that you know about the consequences of extreme variation, would you alter your behavior?

Now think about your own work process. Look at your most important three or four measures of performance. Do you know how these measures vary from day-to-day? Make a graph of this variation? What are the costs of this variation? What are the causes?

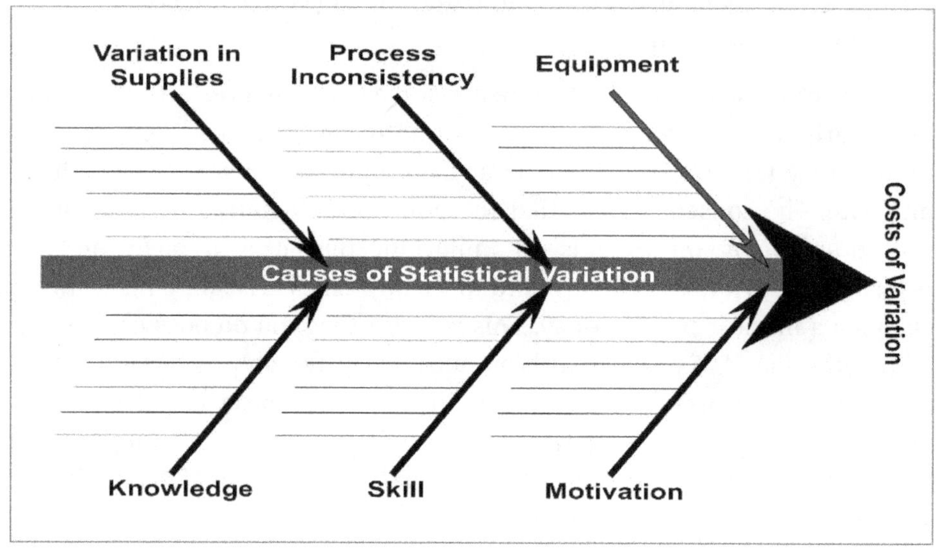

You are probably familiar with cause-and-effect or fishbone diagrams. These serve the simple purpose of stimulating brainstorming. It is important that your team look at variation in your process and seek to understand the causes of that variation. It would be a good idea to place this diagram on a flip chart and brainstorm the causes of variation in your work process. The categories on the diagram are simply suggestions. You may have other, or more important, major causes.

Prioritizing Variances and Solutions

If you brainstorm all of the different causes of variation in performance resulting from your work process it will be helpful to categorize and prioritize them. Some variances are not design problems. They may be performance problems within the system. In other words, they may be daily management problems that are best solved through continuous improvement, feedback or training. Some problems, on the other hand, are the result of the nature of the system.

For example, you may experience poor operating efficiency on a line in a manufacturing facility. This could be because of the way the line is designed, or the way people are assigned work, or trained. These are all system characteristics. On the other hand, the problem may result from those working on the line failing to follow standard work. That may be a result of the lack of feedback from their manager or from the team failing to discuss and monitor standard work. That is a daily management problem that the team should work on continuously improving, but it is not an issue for redesigning the system.

It may help to brainstorm all the causes of variation in the process and put them on this chart. Are they technical or social system issues? And is the problem one of performance within the system, or is it the design of the system?

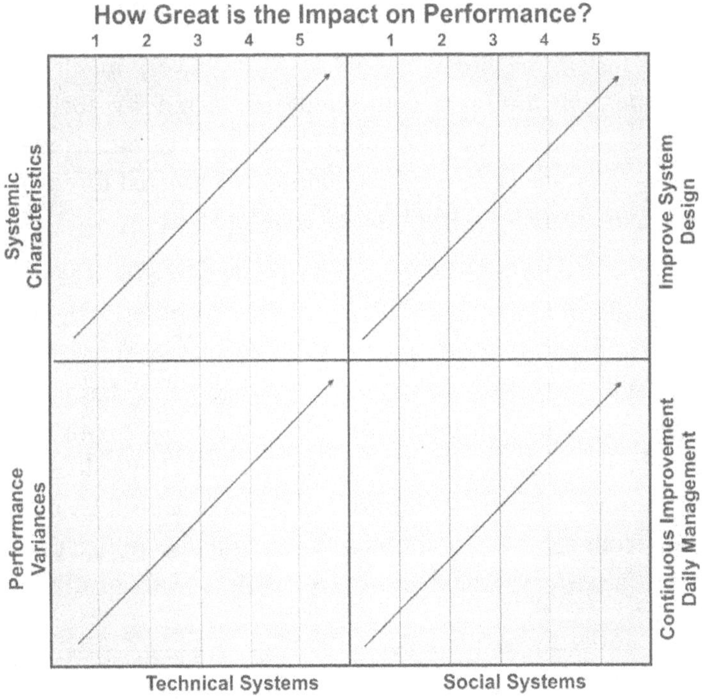

VARIATION WITHIN HUMAN PERFORMANCE

Each human being is a system with our own variations. We don't feel the same each day and we don't perform the same each day. To some degree the cause of that variation is simply the way the human system is designed. However, variation is often a result of interaction with uncontrollable events in the environment. Imagine a football team. Even if the team played the same opponent with the same players every game, there would still be some variation in performance. The quarterback would not throw the same number of completed passes each game. And, in the real world, every opponent is different, with different defensive schemes, and this will cause variation in the play of the quarterback. You can think of the job of the defense as doing everything they can to create "variances" in the play of the quarterback. The environment in which the quarterback is playing will cause variation in his performance.

Much of our work is like this, continually adjusting to the external environment to maintain consistent performance. The trick is to learn what forces are influencing performance, seek to control those we can control, and adjust to those we cannot control.

Selling is also a human performance process that is very much under the control of the individual, but also continually impacted by forces in the environment. A great manager is a student of the larger system, as well as his or her own system. They are continually adjusting to external forces in order to optimize human performance within the internal system.

In the chart below you will see the annual performance for a team of new car salesmen in a group of auto dealerships. This is a "cumulative" graph. That means that each data point is added to the previous data points, so it never goes down. You will see that for the year the sales team will sell approximately one thousand automobiles. That does not mean that each month they will sell exactly one twelfth of this number. If they sold exactly the same amount each month, all end-of-month sales points would be on the line that is on the slope from zero to one thousand. You will also notice that within each month there is a pattern. Sales vary from the first week of the month to

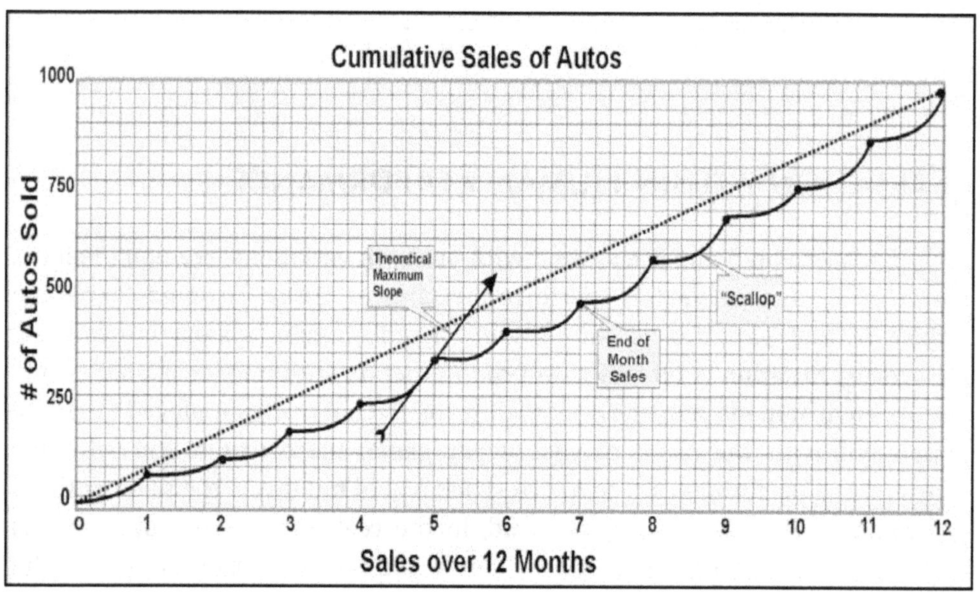

the last week. In fact, in every case, the last week of the month has much stronger sales than the first week of the month. If you were the manager of this organization, it would probably benefit you to know why there is this variation in performance. What do you think is causing this end of month increase in sales?

You will also notice that if you take the maximum slope that occurs during the last week of the month and project this line, it is a significantly greater rate of performance than the average performance for the year. Imagine the increase in total sales that could be gained if you could achieve that same rate of sales every week of the year.

This performance is the result of the *schedule of reinforcement* – when and how positive reinforcement is delivered following behavior. The curve of performance within each month is what is known as a "scallop." It is very familiar to experimental psychologists who study the science of human behavior. The sales people in this organization are very clearly on what is called a fixed-interval schedule of reinforcement. What this simply means is the rewards are delivered at the end of each month, a fixed interval. After the end of each month, these salespeople experience what is known as a *post-reinforcement-pause.* These sales people receive a monthly bonus check for their sales during the previous month. They receive this on the first day of the month. They do what most people do: as the potential reward approaches, they work harder to get that reward. We have all done this. It is the same as cramming the night before for the test in school. Congress passes the largest number of bills just before they achieve the reward of going home at the end of the session.

If you are a customer, what does this tell you about when is the best time to buy a car? When are you likely to get the best deal? You may not be surprised to know that it is during the last few days of the month. The incentive system conditions the sales people, and the sales people condition the customers to buy at the end of the month.

Understanding this pattern of variability and its cause can be extremely valuable to the organization. How could the reward system be modified to reduce the variability and increase the total sales? The answer is in shifting from a fixed-interval (once a month on the last day of the month) reinforcement schedule, to one that varies and has the element of surprise, like all gambling that maintains strong and consistent rates of behavior. In other words, you could shift the positive reinforcement from a fixed to a *variable interval* or *variable ratio* schedule of reinforcement.

- What are processes and performance in which the variation is more the result of human motivation?
- If you plot that performance on a graph, what variation will you see?
- What are the causes of this variation?
- How could you change the consequences, the schedule of reinforcement, to reduce variability and increase total performance?

Variance from Your Principles

You may be familiar with the work of the late Stephen Covey who wrote *7 Habits of Highly Effective People* and *Principle Centered Leadership*. Both emphasized the importance that principles play in personal success and in the success of organizations. Every organization and every process has been designed, intentionally or unintentionally, based on the principles of the designer. For many organizations those principles are contrary to the principles of lean management. The organization may have been designed on the principle of high control rather than high trust. Inherent in a design based on control, rather than trust, are levels of management and management activity that is not only waste, but serves to destroy morale and empowerment. The design of organizations defines who will make what decision and that definition is based on a belief about the competence and motives of employees. All of this needs to be reconsidered.

Principles may be stated and aspirational, or they may be actualized in our behavior and operational. It is good to have stated principles to which you aspire, but it is much better to put them into practice in the way you do your work, manage, and deal with the people around you. To bring your processes into conformance to your principles is to operationalize or actualize those principles.

To actualize your principles is not an easy matter. The United States, at the formation of the country, stated principles such as "the right to life, liberty and the pursuit of happiness" and the principle of equality before the law. However, the mere statement of those principles did not make them instantly the way of life for many who were born and lived in this country. A great deal of blood was shed to bring us closer to realizing those principles.

When you have mapped out your current process make a list of principles or values that are either stated in the charter or which you know to be the aspirational values of your organization. Then, and this sounds simple, but isn't... walk each principle through the process and ask yourself the following questions:

- If this principle were the only thing that mattered, is this the way we would do this work?
- To whom is this principle most important (usually the customer or employees)? Through their eyes and their experience with this process, are we conforming to this principle?
- How would we change this process to most ideally conform to this principle?

Do this for each principle. You will identify variances from your principles and you will come up with possible changes to your process that will bring you closer to your principles.

CHAPTER 13

DESIGNING THE WORK SYSTEM: ELIMINATING WASTE

The purpose of this chapter is to eliminate all non-value-adding activity, materials, time or costs from your processes. Eliminating waste has been a cornerstone of the Toyota Production System and whether in manufacturing, in service delivery, or in management processes, we should continually be looking for and eliminating waste.

Many companies have cut costs, which too often simply means cutting people. They cut people and they leave the waste. The waste is in the process, not the person. If you eliminate the waste in the process, you can then redeploy the person and other assets to "value-adding" work and thereby increase value to customers. Company after company has gone out of business cutting costs, which results in worse products, worse service, fearful employees who lose their creativity, and the inevitable loss of customers. You stay in business by maximizing value to customers.

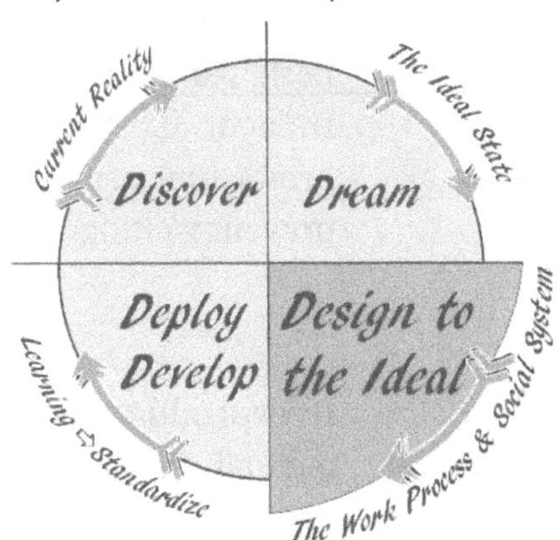

WHAT IS WASTE?

Any activity that does not directly contribute to providing excellent service delivery or producing your product is waste.

The founders of lean manufacturing,

Taiichi Ohno and Dr. Shigeo Shingo, focused on seven types of waste. You will want to search for each of these in your process.

1. **Inventory:** Any "piles" are waste. Anything that is standing still and not in motion is waste, whether it is in a warehouse or in bins or on pallets in the production area. Inventory consumes space (waste), requires employees to move and manage (waste), inventory requires accounting (waste), and instead of having one mistake that is caught immediately, you will have a large pile of defects… big waste! Just-in-time is the process of arranging the supply chain and production process so that each input arrives at the process just-in-time, and each output goes directly to the next stage of the process, just-in-time.

2. **Motion:** Motion is a key variable addressed by industrial engineering. Teams in lean processes constantly study their motions to determine how motions can be eliminated or made easier.

3. **Transportation:** If steps in the process are separated by physical space, forklifts, trucks, dollies, or other mechanisms of transportation are required. All of this is waste. The production process should be designed to minimize transportation.

4. **Defects:** Every defective product or part is waste. The time, effort, and supply that went into producing it are waste. Re-working errors is necessary, but waste is not, because if it had been done right the first time, the re-work would not be needed. It is the job of the team to study and eliminate waste.

5. **Waiting time:** Kanban and other methods in lean production are designed to eliminate waiting time. People should be flexible, trained, and assigned to move from one job to another in a production area so they can smooth the flow of production to prevent waiting.

6. **Overproduction:** Overproduction produces the need for storage and all the related activities of moving and storing work in process.

7. **Processing:** These are inefficiencies within a process – things done the wrong way, lack of training, etc.

How do the seven forms of waste appear in your organization? They are generally described in terms of making a product. But think creatively and try to identify examples of each of these forms of waste in the service delivery or other processes at your organization.

Cycle Time Reduction

One of the most effective ways to eliminate waste is to focus on cycle time. Cycle time is the actual time from a beginning of a process to its completion. This is always different from the time that value-adding work is being performance. The moment materials standstill or a patient waits in a waiting room, or a report sits in an inbox, time is being added to the cycle time that is non-value-adding.

Case Study:

A few years ago I was coaching the senior management team of a major oil company in Houston, Texas. In addition to coaching teams, we had been asked to help them design their deep-water exploration and production operation in the Gulf of Mexico. In discussing the goals for this project it was reported that the cycle time, from the time they leased property from the U.S. Government, to the time that oil actually flowed through a pipeline to market, was approximately eight years. Of course, it varied depending on the depth of water, the complexity of the drilling process and other factors. However, eight years was considered normal. To understand the importance of this you must know that the oil company paid for the lease at the time they signed a contract and made no money in return until the oil was flowing. In other words, capital was sitting still for eight years while they went through the process of exploration, designing a production rig, etc. The amount of money involved was in the tens or hundreds of millions of dollars.

I worked with the senior management team as a steering team and we wrote a charter for a design team. In that charter we agreed to give the design team a goal that would challenge them to speed the cycle time. We gave them the goal of designing the process to be completed in less than four years. The first reaction was that this was probably impossible.

When someone says that a goal is impossible, what they usually mean is that the goal is impossible the *way we do things today*. That means that you can't get there by just working harder or faster. You have to reinvent how you do things.

We formed a design team and began mapping the current state work process. This was a very complex process involving economic analysis, geological analysis, 3D seismic research, engineering of drilling and then production rigs, and several other major sub-processes. For each of the sub-processes there was a separate team of experts who were responsible for that sub-process. When they finished their work, they handed it off to the next team. If you asked why there were delays, each team had a different answer and that answer was usually the preceding team. If you asked who owned the project from womb-to-tomb, from beginning to end, no one knew the answer to that question.

As the design team did their work of seeking to eliminate all non-value-adding steps, eliminating causes of variation and rework, they realized that part of the problem with the process was the sense of ownership from beginning-to-end. Part of the redesign had to be the structure of people around the process and their motivation and decision-making responsibility. In other words, the social system had to be changed to support the new work process.

The final design included an *asset team* who owned the property as a business and whose responsibility it was to achieve a return on investment for the property and for the exploration and production process. This team was like the parents and each of the specialty teams were like the teachers, doctors, or other specialists you send your children to. Previously the project had no parents and that was one of the major causes of waste. These parents, or the asset team, was led by a manager and included representatives from the different areas of specialized knowledge such as geologists, engineers, and financial experts. Their job was to manage the project through each step and assure that any cause of delay or rework was eliminated. This team became the permanent continuous improvement team for that project. They also managed the project as a business and were evaluated as a team for the performance of the property.

To make a long story short, the redesigned process and organization has resulted in a reduction of cycle time by more than 50%. The economic impact of that reduction has been huge.

There are several lessons you can take from this case that you may be able to apply to your own process and your own efforts to eliminate waste:

- Cycle time goals and reduction can be a powerful way to eliminate waste.
- Eliminating waste can be encouraged by setting a breakthrough goal for cutting cycle-time in half, or some other significant goal.
- Eliminating waste and speeding cycle time very often involved not only removing technical steps from a process, but changing the system of organization, decision-making and motivation around that process.

ELIMINATE MANAGEMENT WASTE

Much management activity is waste. This waste is just as destructive, or more so, than waste among front-line employees.

What does this waste look like? I have identified six forms of management waste. Feel free to add to the list.

Management Waste # 1: Escalating Decisions

Sucking decisions up the ladder due to the lack of empowerment, education and encouragement at lower levels is a major form of management created waste. Much of it is what Dr. Deming used to call "tampering" in the work of others. If often occurs because managers are unclear as to how they are actually supposed to add value. Management thinks they are busy because they are doing other people's work and they do this because they have not structured the organization, established the training and systems to create competent problem-solving and decisions at lower levels.

Management Waste #2: Contradictory Models

When management displays contradictory models in their own behavior they reinforce the wrong behavior. If you want to teach your children not to smoke, drink or swear, but you walk around the house smoking, drinking and swearing, your efforts are going to be little more than wasted energy. Management, leaders, must model the behavior they desire of others. The failure to do so cripples any change effort. Millions of dollars in consulting and training have become waste because management didn't walk the talk.

Management Waste #3: Failing to Manage Their Own Work

There are processes that are owned by the senior management team. Every team, at every level, should have a SIPOC that defines input, output, and value-adding processes owned by that team. They don't own any process? Then it is possible that the entire team unnecessary. Many management teams do not know what their processes are, and reinvent them annually manner. Developing strategy is a senior management value-adding process. Where is the map that visualizes how they develop strategy? When they did it last year, did they study the process and what did they learn? Unfortunately, too many management teams are not themselves engaged in continuous improvement. Therefore, they don't understand it and do not set the model.

Management Waste #4: Failure of Decision-Making

I have coached dozens of senior management teams. One would think, logically, that the higher you go in the company, the more skilled would be the decision makers and decision-making process. The value of decisions made at the top, should be of greatest value. Errors made at the top are the most expensive. The truth is that in most companies, the decision-making process at the top is not better than it is at lower levels.

Many years ago I was doing a redesign of a major financial organization on Wall Street. The only room the design team could find to meet in was the Board Room. Very expensive furniture, huge table, mahogany paneled walls, etc. After a day or two the design team had half the wall area covered with flip chart sheets. In stormed the official keeper of the room with steam spurting out of his ears. He yelled, "Take that down immediately! No one has ever put anything on these walls!" I asked, "Really? No one has ever brainstormed or put flip charts on the walls in here?" "Absolutely Not!" He yelled back. Poor fellow. He had never seen a room in which people were actually solving problems, brainstorming, reaching consensus, developing action plans, etc. It tells you a lot about how senior management teams fail to employ disciplined decision processes.

Management Waste #5: Wasted Space and Resources

That board room was used once a quarter. It sat empty and unused most of the time. The new Chairman of Chrysler has closed down the entire executive floor of the Chrysler building and he now sits at a desk in an open office area with engineers designing cars. According to him, the entire executive suite of offices was a way that executives removed themselves from the actual and important work of the organization. Now executives sit where real work is being done.

Why do managers need larger offices as they move up the ladder? Do they have bigger computers or more books? What is that about? It is about waste. It is the waste of ego. The time spent at resorts doing annual strategic planning that could be done in their own conference room is also waste. Apply the same disciplined standards of waste and resource utilization at the executive and management level as you apply to the factory floor.

Management Waste #6: The failure of trust

An effective management team, like any team, is a social system built on trust. It has embedded social capital. That trust enables members to share, to ask questions, to offer suggestions, and to listen well to each other. On most management teams there is a failure of trust among its members that inhibits their ability to solve problems and make effective decisions.

The solution to these forms of waste is training, coaching and feedback. Managers need hands on help in order to change their habits. This is why the coaching model, the *Sensei*, is so important in how Toyota develops their managers.

CHAPTER 14

DESIGNING KNOWLEDGE WORK

In the 1940's the percent of workers employed in manufacturing in the United States was above 35%. After World War II it began its long decline. Today it is approximately 9% of the total workforce in the United States.[62] Recent reports of an alleged manufacturing renaissance in the U.S. have only resulted in a leveling of the decline, but no actual gain in manufacturing employment. That means that 91% of all employed people in the United States work in services, healthcare or other work that we loosely call *knowledge work*. It is remarkable how much of the discussion and examples of lean management are still focused on manufacturing.

From my own experience working in food services, sales, healthcare, energy and engineering organizations, I have no doubt that most of the same methods we have learned from the Toyota Production System can be applied to all of these other fields. However, there are also additional methods that should be considered when designing how groups of people arrive at a shared product that is a service or knowledge.

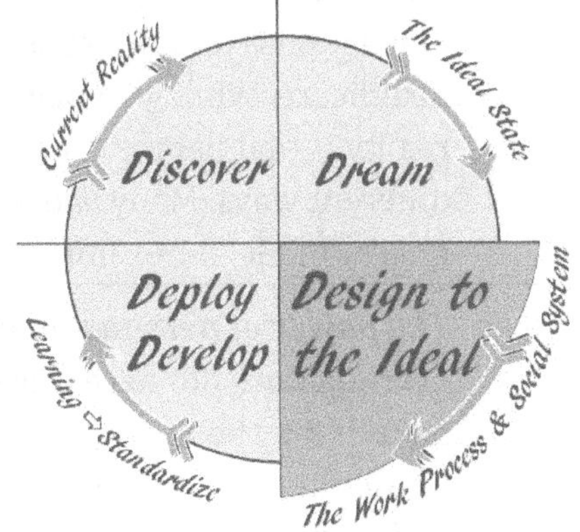

Much of the important work done in our modern organizations is very different than following the linear flow of an automotive assembly line. The

[62] 2013 research by the St. Louis Federal Reserve and reported in Slate Magazine, Moneybox on 2013/07/25.

wonderful thing about an assembly line is that you can see the work in progress. You can measure it based on what you are seeing. You can see that it gets done the same way each time, so there is standardization of the tasks. This is not true in genuine knowledge work and much of the most value-adding work which occurs in our organizations. Knowledge work tends to be non-linear, contrary to the assembly line. Non-linear human interaction, deliberations among people, is what now produces the product of work.

What is the difference between work that occurs around making things and knowledge work? Consider two examples. One might be when a company decides to go to market with a new and innovative product. Another might be an experience you or a loved one has had. You feel a pain or lump, and you call your doctor and he recommends a series of tests. The tests are received and the tumor is malignant. Now decisions need to be made. Here are some of the ways both of these cases are different from a manufacturing process:

- ***Each case is unique***. Each product development and product launch is unique in its market, the product characteristics, and the launching process itself. Each patient's experience is unique to that patient and the patient is the primary decision maker who is in control of her body. For the patient, emotions may play as great a role as the facts.
- ***Different players have different interests.*** On an assembly line you can assume that all of the associates on the line are working to the same goals and purpose. This cannot always be assumed in knowledge work. The researcher who developed the product has one set of interests. The vice president of marketing has another and the finance manager has another set of interests. The same is true in the case of healthcare. While you may think that everyone has the same goals, the reality is that people care about different factors in the decision in different ways. Many cancer patients will trade length of life for quality of life, for example.
- ***The power of persuasion matters.*** How much you know about a decision does not necessarily equate with how much influence you have. It may be that another person has great powers of persuasion. Or another person has a history that makes her very well respected and therefore has great influence although she may know little about the decision at hand. Intimacy with the patient may prove more important than knowledge. a

- ***Decision-making may not be transparent.*** Do you really know how decisions get made? When you watch a car going down an assembly line you can study the process and figure out which part goes on in which order and why. Do you really know why the CEO decided not to launch that new product? Do you know who called him the night before the decision while he was at home and told him about something a competitor was doing, information the CEO didn't share with anyone else.

  When that patient decided not to follow-up with chemo-therapy for her tumor, do you know whether that was a purely rational decision, or was it based on her feelings about what happened when her mother had breast cancer? Or, perhaps it was based on some article she read in a health or nutrition magazine. And, why did she discount the oncologist's advice? He had thirty-years of training, experience and research in exactly this type of decision.

  These decision processes are non-linear.

- ***Influence boundaries have dissolved.*** In the "good old days" you could say, "OK, we need to decide whether to expand the capacity of this production line. Here are the criteria and here are the people who should be involved, let's get them in the room and let's decide." What you just did was to create clear boundaries for whom and how the decision was to be made. Can you do that with the cancer patient, or with the decision to launch a new product?

  What happens today, with the Internet, Google Search and every form of social networking creates a very different process of deliberation. The patient hears her diagnosis and she goes on Facebook. She announces to her five hundred "friends" that she has just been diagnosed with breast cancer. In minutes, she receives dozens of good wishes, prayers, and stories about someone who went to Mexico to an organic health spa where they were on an all vegan diet and their cancer disappeared to the amazement of the "traditional" doctors. She does a Google search on alternative cancer treatments and dozens of sites come up offering a dozen different treatments with incredible claims and all dismissing traditional medicine as ineffective. Ultimately, she, the patient, is the "decider" and there are virtually no boundaries on the information she can receive and she has little ability to evaluate their legitimacy. The flow of information is chaos, or complexity, at best.

- ***Self-organizing sub-groups form with no central control.*** In a manufacturing environment you know which groups, teams or committees are formed and what authority they have. In a company that develops gaming software there are formal teams to work on designated products. But it is almost certain that coalitions or affinity groups will self-organize to discuss, work on, imagine and begin developing ideas with no central control. And, the most important thing is that the smart executive will recognize that this is a good thing, not a bad thing. These are what we used to call "skunk works" but they may form and disappear in one week as the participants lose interest. Or, they may continue for years until they have fully developed something. And, there is probably a great deal of wisdom in the self-empowered decision-making. If they lose interest it is probably because the idea reached a dead-end and wasn't that great an idea.
- ***High non-linear connectivity***. LinkedIn is just one example of the non-linear creativity of today's knowledge neural network. This author is on LinkedIn discussion forums on Socio-Technical Systems, Toyota Production System, Lean in Healthcare, Culture Change in organizations and a dozen others. Someone in the STS forum posts information on a theory or research on deliberation analysis, for example, and the next day I am seeing a discussion in the Lean Healthcare forum about solving problems regarding decisions around patient care. I immediately connected those two comments and someone from Australia asks me for a reference to the research, which I provide, and they then bring that to a meeting of their hospital staff in Perth. Within twenty-four hours a global conversation just happened, that involved people from four or five different professions, on four or five continents, with no one in control. It was completely "non-linear," self-organized, out-of-control and with no boundaries. But, in the end, it may have very well served an important need.

Knowledge or Deliberation Systems

It is possible to map out a linear process for a lot of knowledge work. However, that linear map can fool you because around that linear map there may be a non-linear "swarm system" surrounding it which may be the more important process.

These types of systems, like the human body, weather patterns, and the free economy, may appear chaotic but are actually governed by organizing principles. Deliberation analysis can help you see these patterns and decide if they are the right ones for the future. To analyze and design knowledge-based work and organizations it is important to understand something about complex, non-linear systems.

Let's look at a beehive. It is a perfectly ordered little corporation, incredibly efficient, reliable, hard-working, and designed to utilize its resources in the most efficient way. And how is this order maintained? How are decisions made and executed? It was once believed that the queen bee sat atop a traditional hierarchy issuing decisions to be executed by worker bees. This has been disproved, and we now know that the queen is a mere servant to the hive. The swarm of bees is able to make momentous decisions with no apparent hierarchy of decision-makers. Deciding to pack up and move, leave and create an entirely new hive, is a decision requiring the concurrent obedience of twenty to thirty thousand swarming workers - a good size corporation.

Kevin Kelly, an editor of *Wired Magazine* and a beekeeper himself, gives the following description of how a hive makes the momentous decision to abandon its hive and, in a swarm, move to a new location:

> *"When a swarm pours itself out through the front slot of the hive, the queen bee can only follow. The queen's daughters manage the election of where and when the swarm should settle. A half-dozen anonymous workers scout ahead to check possible hive locations in hollow trees or wall cavities. They report back to the resting swarm by dancing on its contracting surface. During the report, the more theatrically a scout dances, the better the site she is championing. Deputy bees then check out the competing sites according to the intensity of the dances, and will concur with the scout by joining in the scout's twirling. That induces more followers to check out the lead prospects and join the ruckus when they return by leaping into the performance of their choice."*[63]

Without order from above, order is created by the swarm. But it is not order created by the hierarchy of authority, decisions made, decisions executed, and measurement reported. Rather it is the order of patterns, laws, shapes, tendencies, or the transparent order of complex, non-hierarchical

---

[63] Kelly, Kevin. *Out of Control*. Reading, MA, Addison-Wesley Publishing Company, 1994. P. 7.

systems. The order is in the specific behavior and habits of the organization's members. When the queen is moved and the swarm follows, it does so in perfect unison. Each bee flaps its wings and emits an odor of rose from a gland under its wing. The odor is passed on to the worker behind saying, "The queen went this way, follow this way," and all thirty thousand give and receive the same message, one to the next. What a perfectly designed system, free of any bureaucracy or centralized control!

When the transparent order of complex systems is understood, we accept and appreciate the natural process. One of the best examples of complex systems is the functioning of our own free economy, free of the hand of the bureaucrat's order, but subject to its own natural laws.

In the early days of the cold war thaw, Russian bureaucrats came to the United States and attempted to understand our system of free markets. They wanted to know "Who decides who can start a new company?" And the answer of, "Anyone who wants to," fell on disbelieving ears. "This is too important. Someone must approve this." "Who decides who gets how much capital? Which committee makes this decision?" The answer that anyone can give capital and anyone can ask others for capital again fell on disbelieving ears. To the mind programmed to expect predictable order, the chaos of a free economy contains too many inefficiencies and failures. The true answer is that the entrepreneurial bee that performs the best dance gets the money!

Deliberations Analysis

How do you assess and improve the quality of decisions or deliberations amongst a group of people, whether those people are formed formally or they "swarm" informally? This is the challenge for designing organizations with high knowledge content. There are two ways to begin that analysis and improvement: the first is to analyze participation in the process and the second is to analyze the quality and content of those deliberations.

Participation Analysis

Who participates makes a great deal of difference in the outcome of any decision. It has been well demonstrated that participation in goal setting and decision-making is a major determinant of motivation to achieve goals.[64] Low participation results in low motivation toward a goal. [65] Therefore, understanding and analyzing participation becomes an important aspect of designing an effective system.

One simple way of thinking about participation is to think about *Who Knows? Who Cares*? *Who Acts*? And, *Who Decides*?

It is logical that people who have knowledge of a situation would be participants in the decision-making process. In the example of the woman who discovers that she has a cancerous tumor you can think of all the people who would have relevant knowledge. Obviously the patient, the husband may have some relevant knowledge. And, the oncologist, a nurse, a radiology oncologist, and her general physician would all be "Players in the Process" who have knowledge. Those are the obvious and more transparent players. However, the Facebook friend who sends her information on the vegan clinic in Mexico is also a player in the process and is at least attempting to influence her decisions. You can rate on a scale of 1-10 for example, how much relevant knowledge you think each player has. One would assume that the oncologist and radiation oncologist would have a very high level of knowledge. The husband will have some background knowledge, but not expert knowledge, so you would rate him lower in that category.

Then ask, "Who cares?" It is often the case that there are people who care a great deal about a matter, although they may have little knowledge. For example, let's assume that this patient has three grown children. They care deeply about their mother and what happens in regard to her treatment, despite having no particular expertise. Their level of caring may give them a place at the table, so to speak, when it comes to deciding on a course of action because of the degree to which they care about the outcome.

In a work setting it is often wise to involve employees in a deliberation process simply because the outcome will affect them and because they care. It is a reason to engage people in the whole-system design process, whether just asking for their input or having them actively participate.

---

[64] Locke, E. A., Shaw, K.N., Saari, L.M. & Latham, G.P. 1981. Goal-setting and task performance 1969-1980. *Psychological Bulletin*, 90: 125-152.

[65] Latham, G.P., Mitchell, T.R., & Dossett, D. L. 1978. Importance of participative goal setting and anticipated rewards on goal difficulty and job performance. *Journal of Applied Psychology*, 63: 163-171.

Asking "Who acts?" is important because those who must implement a decision are more likely to be committed to a course of action if they are involved and if their views are considered before a decision is made. They are also likely to have substantive knowledge about the effects of a decision.

Then identify who actually makes the decision. When asking who decides, ask yourself whether the decision is a *command, consultative* or *consensus* decision. In a following chapter we will give guidance for designing the social system, including the style of decision-making for each decision. In the case of our cancer patient it is most likely that the decision will be a consultative one, with the patient being the primary decision-maker, while others are serving in a consulting or advising role. In the case of the new product decision there may be a formal decision-making group who will decide whether a new product will be launched or not. In that case you may have as many as ten people making the actual decision.

In using the following form you may use a 1 to 10 scale and have the design team, or a group who are more familiar with a particular decision process, rate the degree of knowledge, participation, and other factors as the deliberation process is currently carried out. Then ask yourself if this is the optimal decision process. If not, why not?

- Are there people who should participate but who don't?
- Are there players who should participate more or less?
- Are there players in the process who are participating but don't care? Are there some who care, but don't participate?
- Are players with little knowledge participating too much?
- Are there players with a great deal of knowledge who don't participate enough and who are not participating in the final decision-making?

Based on these questions put a 1 to10 rating for the desired future state of this type of deliberation. In this way you can see how a deliberation process should be changed in the future based on who is participating and how they are participating.

Deliberation Analysis *Participation Analysis*				
Players in the Process	Who Knows	Who Cares	Who Acts	Who Decides
	Current / Desired	Current / Desired	Current / Desired	Current / Desired

Qualitative Analysis

In addition to analyzing the participation you may also wish to analyze the qualitative nature of the deliberation process. The difficulty in deliberation processes is often not who sits at the table, but the way they behave when they do participate.

The following form, like the previous one, asks you to evaluate the current state of deliberations and the desired future state.

Frequency

Frequency of participating is not necessarily a qualitative measure, but if someone who has little knowledge, is not respected by others, offers no evidence or justification for their comments, yet participates at the highest rate relative to others, there is something wrong with that process. Frequency does not equal influence. A well respected person with thoughtful comments may have great influence while speaking little. If the person who is most respected participates the least, however, you may wish to increase that person's participation. Again, you can rate each of these factors on a 1 to 10 scale or use any other scale you wish.

Respect

The degree to which someone is respected is the degree to which his or her opinion will be valued and taken into account. If ten people are involved in making a decision, about whether to launch a new product, for example, you could have those ten people evaluate the deliberations amongst them by having them evaluate every other member. You would want to do this confidentially, have them fill out this form and have a neutral facilitator compute the results. How much do they respect the participation of each other member? If a member has low respect by others, even though that person may be knowledgeable, it will be worth counseling that person on how they may increase the respect they gain from others. That respect is most likely conditioned by the next three factors.

Justification

The worst way to participate in a deliberation is to say what many children hear from their mothers or fathers: "Do it just because I said so!" That is offering an opinion or decision with no evidence to justify the opinion or decision. In healthy deliberations, members of the group offer justification for their opinions. They may offer anecdotes which may justify their opinion. Or, they may have actual empirical data to offer as proof that a course of action is likely to produce a desired outcome. The degree to which they offer justification they are making a useful contribution to the deliberations.

Integration

Deliberative groups most often have someone who serves in a formal facilitating role. However, all group members can serve to facilitate the conversation. Listening well to others is a critical skill that is essential to group progress. If one is a truly good listener, you integrate the opinions or evidence of another with what has been previously said. For example, "In other words, I hear you saying that your quality of life after surgery, chemo-therapy and radiation is extremely important to you. So, you are trying to weigh that against what you say are the advantages offered by this nutritional program at the health spa. And, I am sure you are also weighing the data that is available on the success rates of those who complete the recommended therapy."

A statement like this one acknowledges the concerns of the patient and her family and also brings her to the point of taking into consideration the actual data available on cure rates for cancer patients undergoing different therapies. This integration of concerns helps the patient think about the issues in an effective manner and increases the likelihood that the patient will give consideration to the facts. It is more effective than saying something like "Well you know those health spas where they feed you nuts and leaves and claim it cures cancer is just bunk! There is no research to support that at all." This kind of adversarial or opposition statement puts the poor patient in the position of having to sort through research and opinions on her own, when she most likely does not have the skill or training to do this. Making statements that integrate issues or concerns, helps the deliberations arrive at successful conclusion.

Unifies

Integration helps create unity of thought. If a group is trying to reach a consensus on whether or not to launch a new product, the most helpful comments may not be from those offering pros and cons evidence or justification, but from the person who is able to find points of unity and agreement and focus the members on those points. It is often true that deliberations become consumed in disagreements over some point of evidence or concern, even when that issue is not central to the decision that must be made. So, a comment like "I understand that we have different views on one thing; but, it sounds like we are in agreement on these three other issues, and don't you feel those are sufficient for us to decide to move forward?" This comment is intended to help the group put things in perspective, rather than arguing for a particular point of view. This comment is unifying for the common good.

You may be able to think of other qualitative factors, but these are ones that will certainly impact the speed and quality of deliberations. Again you can observe a deliberation process and then rate the current state for each player in the process and indicate a desired future state.

Deliberation Analysis *Qualitative Analysis*					
Players in the Process	Frequency of Participation	Respected by Others	Justification Evidence	Integration Listens	Unifies Common Good
	Current / Desired	Current / Desired	Current / Desired	Current / Desired	Current / Desired

Summary of Knowledge Work Analysis

A lot of different issues or ways of looking at knowledge work have been presented in this chapter. It may be helpful to summarize the advice on how to approach analyzing and improving knowledge work.

1. ***Map the Process:*** Start by doing what you would do for more traditional work. In mapping and analyzing the flow in the traditional linear fashion you are likely to find a number of ways the process can be improved.
    - Value-stream, process flow, or relationship map for the current state. Map any simultaneous processes and show how they connect.
    - Identify major customers and their requirements.
    - Complete a cycle time analysis and include these numbers on the maps.
    - Analyze waste in the process. Look at both the seven traditional forms of waste and the six management forms of waste to see if these point to possible improvements.
    - Analyze the process for key variances and causes.
    - Mark any decision or deliberation points.
2. ***Do a Deliberation Analysis***
    - Use either the forms covered previously in this chapter for *Deliberation Analysis.*
    - Identify ways that both the participation and quality of deliberation can be improved.
3. ***Create a Map or Description of the Future State***
    - Using the variance or deliberation analysis to redesign the way work should be done in the future. Specify who should be involved; what tools, equipment and technology will be needed; and other requirements for the new process.

CHAPTER 15

DESIGNING THE IDEAL SYSTEM OF WORK

By this time you are more than ready to start designing the future work system. You have done a lot of analysis and you should have dozens of ideas to incorporate into your new design.

It will be very helpful if you have a large conference room to use as you develop your new design. On one side of the room you will want to have the current state process map on the wall and all of your analysis. On the opposite wall, roll out a fresh role of paper on which to start putting Post-it-Notes with which you will construct the new design

Before you begin to design the new system, review the following items:

- **The Design Charter:** Remember that you want to design a new system that is based on a vision of the future, not merely an analysis of what is wrong with the current state. Review your principles, and remember that it is your job to make these principles come alive in the new design.

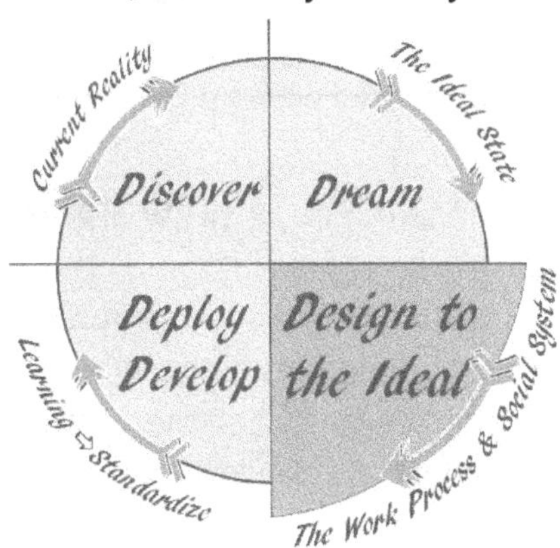

- **Internal and External Environment:** When you analyzed both the internal and external environments you were identifying factors that would impact the future design of your work as well as your social systems. You should review those requirements and needed capabilities now.

- **Customer Requirements:** What is the primary thing you are trying to achieve for your customers? Is the primary objective to increase speed? Or is the main objective to eliminate a particular variance? Create a future work flow that can adapt as customers and products change.
- **Variances and Waste:** Review the variances and the causes or location of waste in your process. You will design to eliminate these variances or control them at their source. Make sure you design in the equipment, tools, and resources necessary to make the work processes function properly.
- **Review Deliberation Analysis:** Your analysis of knowledge work, particularly your deliberation analysis may be a significant source of guidance for designing the future process.
- **Input from Others:** Review all the comments, suggestions, and ideas from your interviews. Include information from search conferences if you had any.

Design to the Dream

Your design is now going to follow your dream. It is important to think "idealistically" when you do your first future state design. There is a danger in being practical. If you are practical, suggestions for change will be met with, "Well, we can't do that because of this...." Usually this is because people are still thinking about the current way work is done or the present human systems. If the discussion about what can be improved is a "practical" discussion, it is likely that little or nothing can be changed. You must be impractical. Focus on the future.

Map Your New Process

It is best to start with a relationship map, identifying the players in the process, and only those who are required to perform the essential work that meets the needs of the customer. Begin where the input is received from suppliers, and review every step in the process. Do not worry about *who* will do what in the future state. Do not try to fix the human systems. Just focus on the work system, work processes, technology, equipment, etc.

As you are mapping the future state, ask yourselves the following questions:

1. **Are we eliminating waste?** Any unnecessary step is waste. Anything standing or waiting is waste. Any time spent on unnecessary activities is wasted time. Eliminate everything that is not necessary.
2. **How can the process be changed to eliminate or control variances?** You have analyzed the causes of variances, and you have proposed solutions. Now design those into the new system.
3. **Can we change the process to increase individual control or empowerment?** Design work for intelligent people and you will find that you have intelligent people working. They will act intelligently when intelligence is called for.
4. **How can we eliminate frustration?** Variances often occur because employees do not feel that it is their job to control quality or to change the process to achieve results. They have learned this from a system designed to minimize their input. Redesign the system to create control. When designing the social systems, you will create the incentives to motivate employees to control well.
5. **How can we eliminate interruptions?** A quality process is an interruption-free process.

You may ask how long it will take to design the future work process. That all depends on the nature of the process, how complex it is, and how revolutionary are the changes you are making. Some design teams can develop a new process in a day or two, and some have taken weeks. Processes vary enormously in their complexity.

Design Testing for Robustness

Think about the difference between a house of cards, and a robust design. A house of cards may look good if no wind blows or the earth doesn't shake. In other words, it works if nothing goes wrong. But, the earth does shake and the wind does blow! Your design has to be robust. It must be able to withstand all of the things that could happen – the loss of electricity; the snow storm; the computer failure, and anything else you can think of that may go wrong.

Once you have developed a potential future workflow, you will want to test it. One easy way to test it is to bring a focus group of people who do this work into the design team's meeting room, and go through how you visualize the design working. If you can act it out in a skit that is better. Then ask for reactions. Ask them to be critical, find things that won't work or that will be obstacles to implementation. They may point out required training, or they may point out work that will have to be eliminated in order for this new design to work. That is all useful.

It is likely that when you present this to your steering team they will ask some of these "robustness" questions, and they should. And, the design team should have answers to what happens if or when something goes wrong. This is not being critical; it is simply recognizing that a good design can withstand the wind blowing.

Present to the Steering Team

Once you have developed a proposed future work process, you should present your dream and your design to your steering team. Make clear that you are asking them for their honest reactions, and that you expect them to ask "what-if?" questions that will help you strengthen the design.

When you make your presentation be clear about what you have not yet designed, the social system and all that it involves. But, as the social system should be built to enable the work system, you would like a general approval to move forward at this point. They do not need to give you a final approval. But, if you wait until the social system and the implementation plan are done, it is likely that you will completely overwhelm the steering team with too much information. That does not produce a good reaction. By sharing the idealized work system at this point, you will hopefully create enthusiasm and anticipation for the work yet to be done.

CHAPTER 16

DESIGNING THE IDEAL SOCIAL SYSTEM

First, think about the nature of social systems that impact performance.

Buurtzorg ("neighbourhood care") was formed by one nurse, in one location, who created a team of nurses on his own initiative. Buurtzorg is an innovative approach to delivering home health care in the Netherlands. It originated in 2006 from nursing staff's dissatisfied with traditional home care organisations. Their complaints were the bureaucratic duties, working in isolation from other care providers, and above all, neglect of their professional development.

The organisational model of Buurtzorg is to have care delivered by small self-managing teams consisting of a maximum of twelve professional care givers, and to keep organisational costs as low as possible. Also, Buurtzorg aims to deliver care to a client for as short a period as possible, by involving and reinforcing the client's resources.

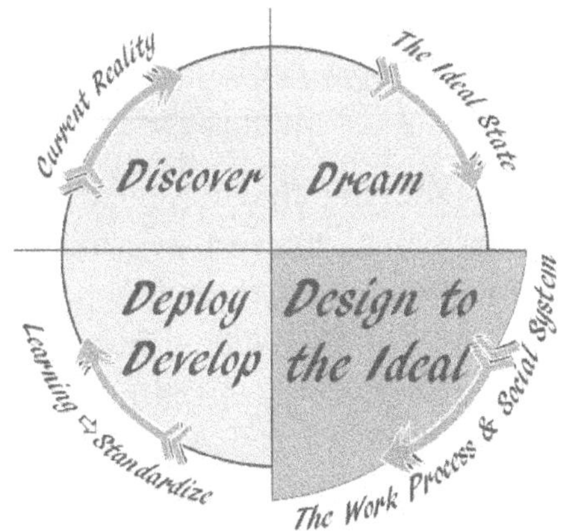

By mid-2010, teams were active in 250 locations nationwide. So far, data on patients' satisfaction show that it is extremely high. Also satisfaction of staff and of co-working doctors is very high. At the same time indications are that Buurtzorg home care is only about half as expensive as usual home care.

- Buurtzorg ranks number 1 amongst all home care organizations in user satisfaction according to results of the mandatory national quality of care assessment in the Netherlands.
- In 2011, Buurtzorg has been chosen for the award as the best employer of the Netherlands in organizations of more than 1,000 employees. With now more than 4,000 employees Buurtzorg scored (on a scale from 1-10) 9.5 for involvement, 9.1 for low turnover of employees, and 8.7 for staff satisfaction.
- A significant result is the enormous decrease of cost: the consultancy agency Ernst and Young have calculated that Buurtzorg seems to be less than half as expensive as usual home care.

Now... just think. This was begun in 2006 by one nurse and one team. It is the result of self-organization by professionals. By 2011 they employed 4,000, were providing service at half the cost and had the highest employee satisfaction.

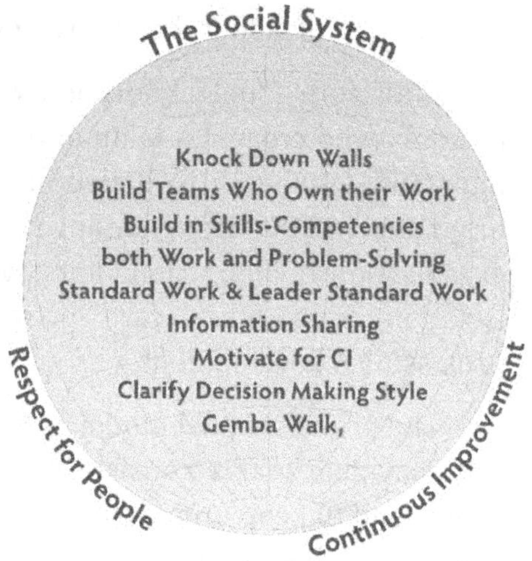

This did not begin with lean management or analyzing waste in the work process. It began because Jos de Blok, a nurse himself, recognized that the working conditions and relationships of nurses were unsatisfying and felt there had to be a better way. So, he formed one team of nurses to be responsible for one geographic area, and it took off from there. The organization began, not because of financial or business interests, but because employees desired a better social system.

The Social System
Knock Down Walls
Build Teams Who Own their Work
Build in Skills-Competencies
both Work and Problem-Solving
Standard Work & Leader Standard Work
Information Sharing
Motivate for CI
Clarify Decision Making Style
Gemba Walk,
Respect for People
Continuous Improvement

You can first design the ideal work process and then form the best possible social system around that work with the idea of enabling the performance of the work process. This is the way it is usually done. But, Buurtzorg proves that innovation can begin with the idea of a better social system. Sometimes the need to redesign is driven by social system needs. Even Toyota has had to redesign its system around the needs of the people who work in the system.

"Shoichiro Toyoda, chairman of the corporation since 1992, has in a recent article used the term 'new production system' when summing up various issues that the corporation is facing: In the production shops ... [we need to consider] the development of a 'new production system' that is responsive to the reduction in the number of skilled persons and other changes in the quality of the workforce and that is responsive to a production formation that has taken on international proportions. [We also need] to consider production shops where it is possible to feel attraction towards manufacturing and a sense of fulfillment in connection with manufacturing, and there is a need to secure personnel within middle- and long range technologies (Toyoda, 1993, his italics)."[66]

"As far as 'team work' is concerned, it is the group leader who organizes the task rotation in his group, taking into account the skill level of his workers. Through the task rotation a worker now learns all tasks in his group to become a professional worker in this segment. He can also move to another work group after having learned all tasks in his original group, in so far as he wishes to obtain a wider skill, and if his leader permits it. The groups in the assembly area include at least one woman, who receives the same salary as men of the same age, at least to start with (salaries will later vary, not by gender, but due to hierarchical position and Sateï). This is possible because the factory has become an acceptable place even for young women to work."[67]

So, what are these two cases telling you about your social system and work system? In both cases the social system was built around self-directed teams in which responsibility and self-control were maximized. As yourself this, also: In the United States we a romantic attachment to the idea of the family farm. Why? What is it about the family farm or the small craft shop of early America that we find so appealing? And, how does that translate to your own organization's social system?

---

[66] "Recent developments at Toyota Motor Corporation: The emergence of a "Neo-Toyotaism'?" by Terje Gronning. In Enriching Production: Perspectives on Volvo's Uddevalla Plant as an Alternative to lean production. p.408.

[67] "*Humanization of the production system and work at Toyota Motor Co and Toyota Motor Kyushu.*" By Koichi Shimizu, In Enriching Production: Perspectives on Volvo's Uddevalla Plant as an Alternative to lean production. Sandberg, Ake, Editor, Digital Edition, Stockholm. 2007. P. 398.

WHAT IS THE SOCIAL SYSTEM?

The social system is everything that affects what people do, think and feel. It is how they are hired, trained, promoted, evaluated, organized, motivated and everything else that influences how they will behave.

You have already assessed the assets and liabilities of your culture – the spiritual, social, human, innovation and financial capital. When you mapped your work process and discovered variances, waste, and the need to improve deliberations, you were discovering how your culture works to affect the work process. It is now time to design the ideal social system for your organization.

An easy way to think about the social system is to think about six S's – *Structure, Systems, Skills, Style, Symbols* and *Stories*. Let's briefly define each and then get about designing them.

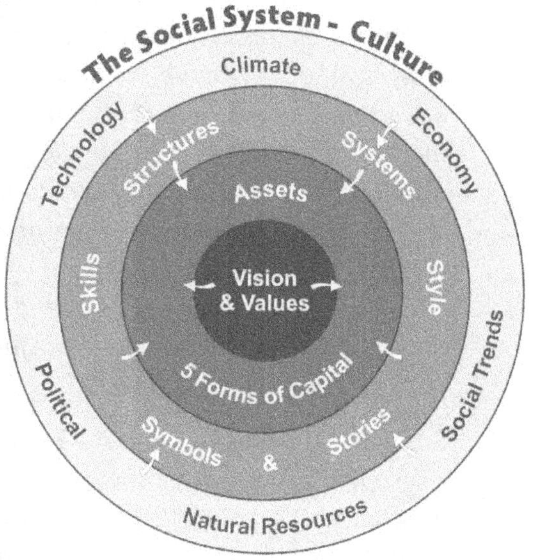

Structure: Every grouping of people within the organization is a form of structure. All divisions, horizontal and vertical, and all groupings in teams, work cells, or other groups, represent structure. The family farm, the tribe, and the team are all social structures.

Systems: Systems include every system that impacts human behavior. This includes all information systems that provide knowledge or feedback; it includes all human resource systems, training, assessment, recognition and motivation systems.

Skills: Skills includes all competencies required to do every job. Skills can generally be divided into the technical skills of doing the work and the social skills of teamwork, facilitating, coaching, problem-solving and decision-making.

Style: Style includes the patterns of communication and decision-making. When you did deliberation analysis you were analysing the style of communications. There is also a style of decision-making, from autocratic to participative.

Symbols: Every culture creates symbols to reinforce the bonding within groups, to create association with the organization, and to distinguish status within the group.

Stories: The history of culture, whether in organizations or in the larger society, is the history of storytelling from Adam and Eve to Greek mythology. Leaders in companies are also story tellers, telling stories to reinforce the values that promote the common good of the organization. Stories are not something you will design, but you do hope to create new stories that will serve as cultural models.

PRINCIPLES OF SOCIAL SYSTEM DESIGN

The following principles have proven helpful to design teams as they design the human systems.

1. **Design from the Bottom-Up and Around the Work:** Too often organizations are designed from the top down. The CEO hires a consultant and he starts with some macro theory and soon the organization is designed to meet the needs of executives and not the needs of those doing the value-adding work.

   The principle of whole-system architecture that should be the first principle of organization design is this: *The only reason organizations exist is to facilitate the work that adds value to customers.* Design to optimize this work. The design of organization structure should begin on the frontline, where the work is done, to create the structure that will optimize the performance of those doing the work.

   James P. Womack and his associates at MIT spent five years and five million dollars studying the differences between auto assembly plants in the U.S., Japan, and Europe to identify the key differences in the systems that were the cause of different levels of quality and productivity.

   "What are the truly important organizational features of a lean plant - the specific aspects of plant operations that account for up to half of the overall performance differences among plants across the world? The truly lean plant has two key organizational features: It transfers the maximum number of tasks and responsibilities to those workers actually adding value to the car on the line, and it has in place a system for detecting defects that quickly traces every problem, once discovered, to

its ultimate cause....So in the end, it is the dynamic work team that emerges as the heart of the lean factory."[68]

Just as the family unit is the bedrock structure of every society, the first learning organization; the work group or team is the foundation structure of every organization. It is where learning and innovation will occur. It is the structure that will have the greatest impact on daily performance. Get this right and other things become easy.

2. **Minimize Walls, Divisions, Hand-offs, and Levels.** Each of these represents an interruption in workflow and a possible source of variance. Each division creates work for managers and tends to diminish the work of those creating value for customers. Where walls or divisions are necessary make the walls as "porous" as possible so the work can flow easily and quickly, and learning can occur easily, through those walls.
3. **Make Chairs, Not Legs.** To the degree possible design the organization so employees can have pride and joy in their work. Pride and joy come from "whole" work – making an entire piece of furniture, for example, not a piece that has no use by itself. Pride of ownership comes from completing a whole work process resulting in a complete product. Craftsman made complete chairs. People will make furniture, whole furniture, as a hobby. No one goes home on Saturday and makes legs. In mass production hourly factory workers were organized into leg, seat, back, and assembly departments. This destroyed their pride and ownership, and it destroyed the quality of products. Create teams to increase intimacy with the product and pride of ownership.
4. **Each Level of the Organization Must Add Value That is Unique.** The first level of teams is responsible for doing and managing the day-to-day work process. The next level is responsible for managing and coordinating the decision-making and process boundaries of teams. The top management team is concerned with strategy and the overall performance of the organization. Be clear about the value-adding work of each team or level. If they do no value-adding work they are waste.

---

[68] Womack, J.P., Jones, D.T. and Roos D. *The Machine that Changed the World.* New York. Free Press, 1990. P. 99.

5. **Design Competencies for Future Performance:** People perform, not organizations. There is no such thing as a competent organization; there are only competent people. Different types of performance require different competencies, and the design team must design the structure and systems that will build and reinforce required competencies.
6. **Design for Continuous Learning:** Design feedback loops and shared learning mechanisms to ensure continuous improvement. The design team should ask how they will maximize learning, not only within teams, but across teams and across organizational units.
7. **Create an Intelligent Network:** Design your organization for the realities of the Internet age, social networks, and networked learning. Create collective intelligence through formal and informal networks, interaction, and communication systems. Design in virtual meeting platforms and processes when appropriate. All deliberations will not be face-to-face.
8. **Reinforce Superior Performance:** People perform when it matters. Make performance matter. Design the systems to recognize and reinforce superior performance. Design multiple systems of reinforcement.
9. **Design Symbols to Reinforce Values and Behavior:** Change necessary symbols to support the new culture, work system, and human system. New symbols indicate a new culture.
10. **Design the House, but not Where the Furniture Goes:** There is always a question as to how much detail to go. A good way of thinking about it is to think about an architect designing a house. He has to decide where the walls go. He has to decide where the kitchen and bathrooms will be. And, he has to layout where electricity, plumbing and cables will flow through the walls. But, he doesn't have to decide what carpet will go in or what color the walls will be. And, he definitely does not have to decide what furniture, or where the furniture will be placed. Of course, you will then ask "What is furniture and what are walls?" That is something you will have to decide as you do your design work. But simply asking the question will help your team to not waste time debating where the furniture goes.

STRUCTURE

Initially, you are only going to think about one question: *How can we best group people around the work that serves customers at the first level of the organization?* What is "best?" Best is that structure that will most closely conform to the ten principles previously stated. There are a hundred other questions that may occur to you. But first, just think about this one question.

DESIGN FROM THE BOTTOM-UP

Form that first level structure to follow and enable the workflow. It does help to visualize structure. But, try to avoid the usual boxes from top to bottom connected by straight lines. That is not how the real world works. The reality of things is much more interconnected and circular. Design reality.

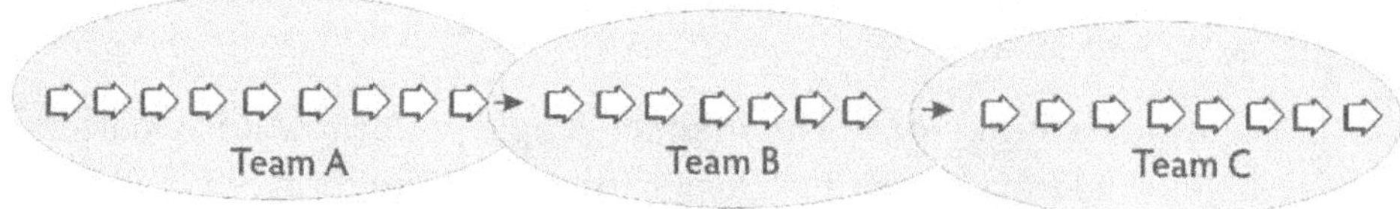

Core Work Teams Follow the Process

The first illustration represents a team structure built around a linear process, as in a manufacturing facility. The second represents a non-linear process built around servicing clients in a health care organization. Ask yourself why the circles overlap. What does it mean that some people seem to be on two or even three teams? Perhaps it is because they have a particular expertise that is needed by more than one team, but not on a full time basis.

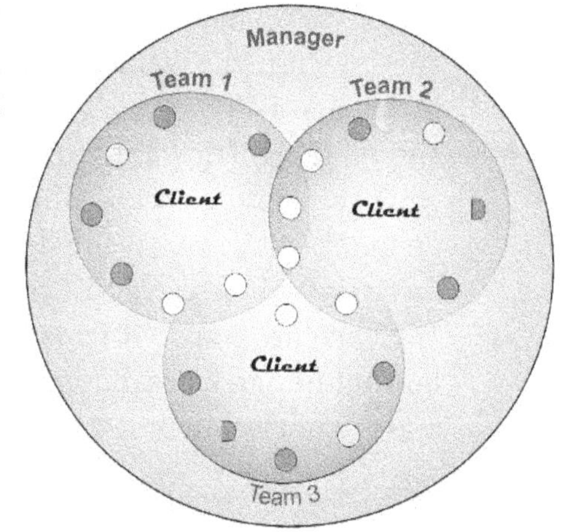

In deciding on your structure ask yourself the following questions:

1. Where are team members located and what structure will most allow them to help each other, share learning, and make decisions together? Co-location is ideal; close is desirable.
2. In order to create a *whole-*

product, or to provide service to a *whole-person* what are all the different skills needed on a team? Does your structure provide for multi-skilled team members who can rotate among jobs and engage in load-leveling?

3. How large will a team be? The best size is between 5 and 15 and around the middle of that is ideal. With fewer there is insufficient diversity of opinion and skill; with more it becomes more difficult to share and make decisions.
4. Have you designed the team for maximum self-direction? In the end, there is no such thing as a completely self-managed team – it is a relative concept. Design to maximize control and decision-making within the team. The degree to which you do this you will require less management, less external motivation, and you will minimize control problems because control will be exerted from within the team.
5. Can you identify added functions within the team to increase its self-management? In other words, should there be a team leader to facilitate meetings and decisions within the team? This would be a member of the team, not someone "above" the team. Are there other functions, such as maintenance, communications, equipment set-up, or reporting that might be assigned to one person on the team? And, should these positions be rotated, elected, or permanently assigned?

Once you have formed your base teams you then have to decide how they will be grouped into larger teams to share learning and resources on a larger scale. You now have to decide whether you are grouping teams by location, proximity to one another, or are you grouping them by affinity in skills or knowledge? Here you may decide to have two types of teams, a work or service delivery team, and an affinity or knowledge based team. It is becoming

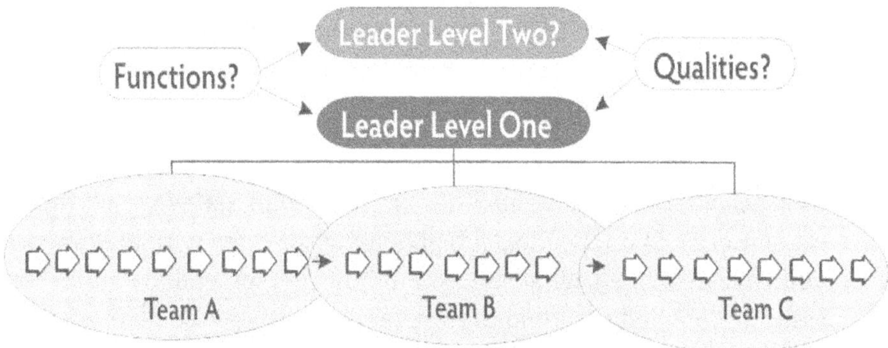

increasingly normal for people to serve on more than one team, with each team being formed to accomplish a different function. For example, engineers may be organized into "home room" teams based on their competence or speciality; but they are then assigned to projects that have multiple specialties formed to build a building or engineer an oil drilling platform, for example.

Design Leader Functions that Add Value... Only!

As you group teams you are immediately defining the job of the next level, the person or people who are going to help these teams in their development and functioning. Do not design in waste! Design only those functions that will add value to the process and the teams who are creating value for the customer.

Here are a few rules that may help:

1. ***Strong recommendation!*** As you design the structure do not use any current titles, such as supervisor or manager. The moment you use the old titles the members of the design team will immediately think of the individuals who fill the current jobs and their current functions. They will not be thinking creatively. So, use *Leader Level One* just as a working title when design that job. You do not know anyone in that job because it doesn't exist yet. Then use *Leader Level Two* for the next level.

2. When you are designing the new leader level one job, ask yourselves this question: *"What help does the team need to optimize its performance?"* You will design the functioning of the team to maximize its ability to control and manage itself. But, it will need some help. It will need coaching. It will need help gaining access to resources. It will need some coordination with other teams and functions. Be very specific in defining the exact functions of this job with the purpose of helping the team perform. Theoretically, if the team needed no help, you would not need any leaders or managers above the team at all.

3. Once you have designed the functions of the first level leader's job then ask yourself, "What qualities are needed in that person?" In other words, to do the ideal job of helping the team with the functions you have described, what style should this person employ and what skills or knowledge should they have?

4. Then ask, "Given the scope of our design and the nature of the teams we have formed, how many leader level one's do we need and how should they be formed into a team of leaders at this level to share learning and support one another?" Keep in mind, that if you have done a good job of designing teams that can maximize their own self-management; you will need far fewer managers than in a traditional organization. It is very typical for this position to provide leadership and coordination to three to five teams.

As you are grouping teams into larger teams, either by location or function it may help to examine the following diagrams that are all actual designs done by previous design teams.

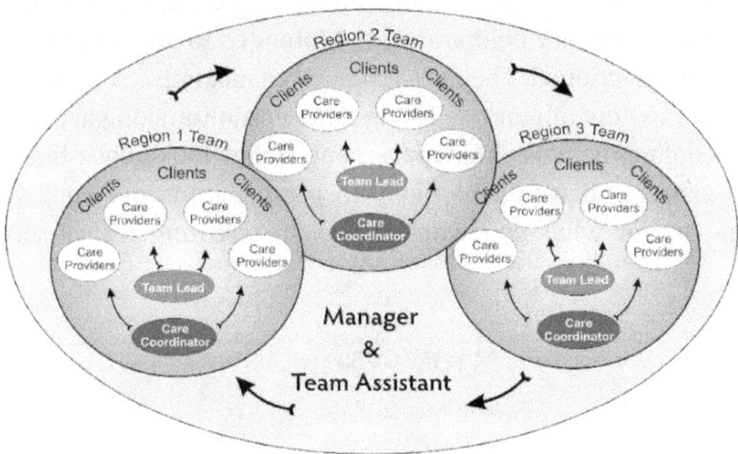

The illustration above shows how HomeCare service providers were first formed into "primary care teams" to provide service in a geographic area, and were then grouped into a larger geographic area, a district, with a district manager.

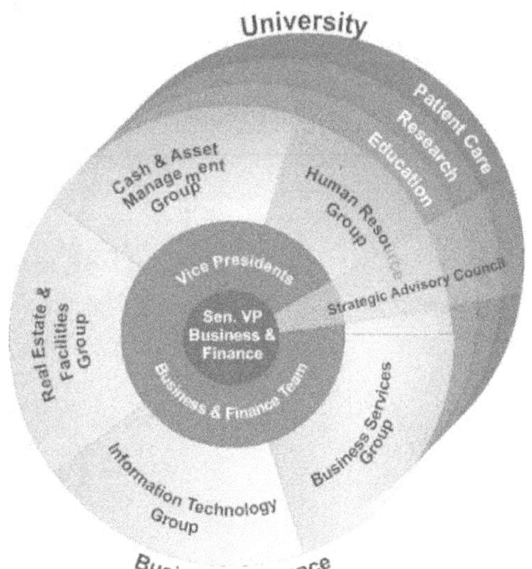

The second describes the organization of a University's Business and Finance organization that serves the needs of educators and students, a research organization, and a hospital. You will see that the senior vice president of this organization is in the middle and his team is comprised of the leaders of each of the major functional areas. The "Strategic Advisory Council" was made up of individuals from each of the three areas served by the human resources group, for example. You can think of this as a board of customers.

In the next diagram you can see a more detailed illustration of the more specific functions within each of these department teams.

You may ask, "Why don't these organization charts look like normal organization charts with the leader at the top and the boxes cascading downward and connected by straight lines leading up the top? Isn't that how organization charts are "supposed to" be drawn? The reason they are drawn this way is two-fold: First, the traditional organization charts never described how things actually worked anyway! These more closely describe how people are intended to behave and relate to one another. Second, it is intended that these organizations are very deliberately not intended to function the way the old organizations functioned. They are intended to maximize responsibility of teams, increase the flow of work, learning and decision-making across teams, and they all redefine the work of management. If they looked just like the old organization charts you would be likely to get the same old behavior and mindset. That is not what you want if you are creating transformational change!

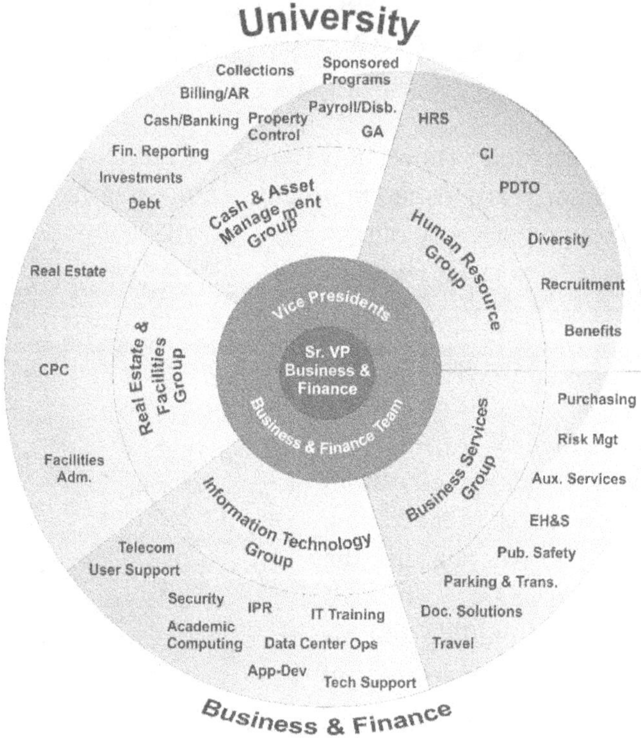

Design the Structure of Knowledge Networks

Every organization is a network of individuals with different types of competencies. In addition to the structure that surrounds the day-to-day work tasks these can be a structure that networks individuals who will benefit from sharing knowledge, ideas and problem-solving. If you are in a hospital you will have X-Ray technicians who work in several different departments. In a manufacturing facility you will have individuals who work on teams and have an interest in quality management or equipment repair. How can these people learn from each other and help each other?

Knowledge networks can be informal, just as you may be a member of a photography club or a parenting organization. We self-organize groups for hundreds of different reasons. Most often these are for knowledge sharing and problem-solving. Today on LinkedIn and other websites you can find discussion forums or "knowledge networks" on virtually any subject. In an organization that depends on knowledge sharing and problem-solving for continuous improvement, these networks should be built into your organization design and self-organization should be encouraged.

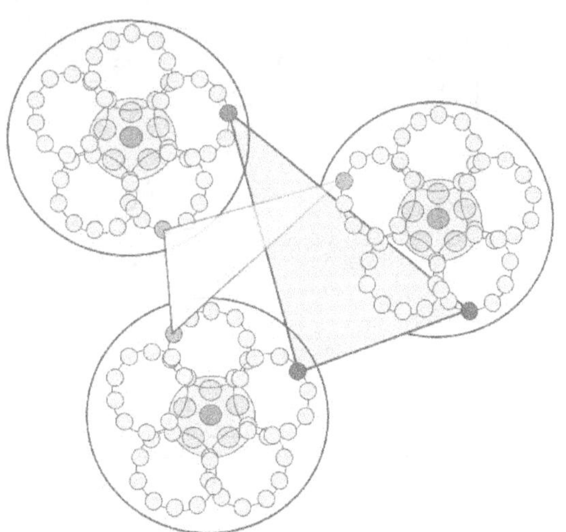

If you look at this diagram you see one organization's attempt to illustrate the formation of teams, clusters of teams, and then subject matter experts on teams who are formed into expert teams or knowledge networks.

Now try to apply this idea to your own organization and ask the following:

- What knowledge experts reside on teams that are in different locations and would benefit from sharing their knowledge across teams?
- How best could they network? Can they have lunch meetings? Can they have an on-line discussion forum?
- Who would serve as a convener or facilitator of these groups?

DESIGNING ENABLING SYSTEMS

Once you have created the basic structure of your teams that will do the value-adding work of the organization, you now have an obligation to do everything you can to enable and empower those teams. There are dozens of ways to sub-optimize a team's performance with systems that are misaligned. For example, imagine that you have formed teams, yet the old system of piece rate pay remains unchanged. What effect will this have on the performance of the team? What if the team received no or little information on its performance as a team? What if new team members are hired and put into the team without any involvement of the team? Each of these and dozens of other system misalignment problems can sub-optimize the performance of the team. Let's look at each of these systems and how they may serve to optimize performance of the teams.

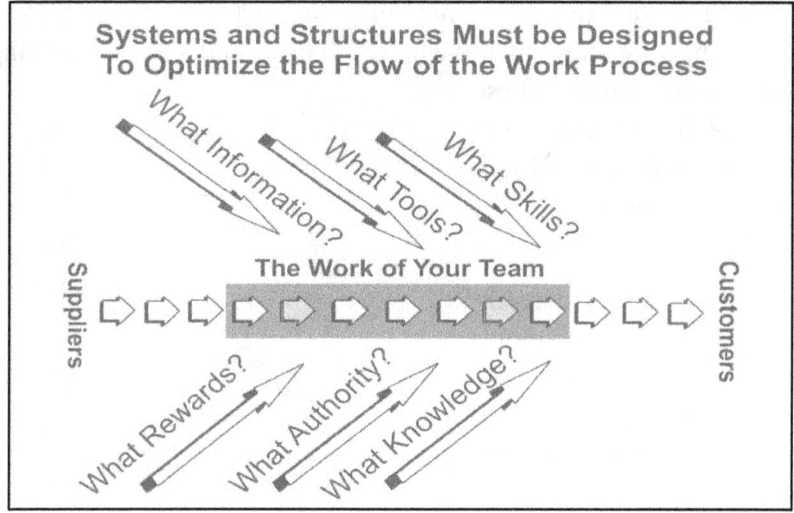

INFORMATION SYSTEMS

When you think of the word "team" you think of scorekeeping. Every sport is fun to watch or participate in because of scorekeeping. It is the feeling that you can control or impact the score of your team that results in motivation. If the scoreboard at a basketball game was covered up, how entertaining would it be, and how would that change the behavior of the players on the court? It wouldn't be much fun to watch or play. Work is no different and that is why so often work isn't much fun. It doesn't need to be that way!

One design team used a chart like the following to map out the information that would flow to individuals and to the each team. This defined the information they felt was critical, where the information would come from, and how it would be delivered.

What Scores are Need For...		**How will Scores be Provided and used?**	
Personal Performance	**Team Performance**	**Where does it come from**	**How is it delivered?**

You don't need to design a complete information system, but you do need to design the critical elements that will affect team performance. This is a set of information system requirements. Remember that the teams doing the real work of the organization are the customers of the information systems. Here are some things to take into consideration:

Immediacy: The more immediate the feedback, the more effective it will be in motivating performance. If the score appeared on the scoreboard at a football or basketball game five minutes after the score was made, it would lose most of its motivational effect. List the key performance variables and figure out how to make them as immediate as possible.

Visual Display: Good scorekeeping is not in someone's file drawer or buried in a computer spreadsheet. Get it up on the wall!!! Make it BIG! Make it COLORFUL! And Graph it! A list of numbers is not one tenth as effective as a graph. Everyone reacts to a graph going up (good) or down (bad), even if we don't understand what it is. Every team should have its own scoreboard with its three to five key data variables graphed.

Keep the data up-to-date: Immediacy and importance is lost if the data display is allowed to get days, weeks or months (I'd shoot myself!) out-of-date. It will be viewed as unimportant if it is not up-to-date.

Create a Balanced Scorecard: The scorecard for a first level team may not need to be as balanced as the senior management team's scorecard, but it should include measures that are both quantity (rate of production) and quality (meeting customer requirements, defects, rework, etc.). If it is possible, include financial numbers that will make the team feel more like they are running a business. Consider the ideas of open-book management[69] in which teams have an actual profit-and-loss statement with revenue and expenses. It makes playing the business game much more enjoyable. It is also helpful to have developmental or training measures on their balanced scorecard.

Plan a Daily Huddle and/or Weekly Team Meeting: It is not enough to simply visualize the data, although that is critical. You must also discuss it. In many manufacturing settings every team meets in a pre-shift huddle every day. They meet around the data display board and discuss their scorecard. There are simple questions that should be asked every day in every huddle:

- Did performance improve or decline yesterday?
- Why did it improve or decline?
- What did we learn from this?
- What do we need to do differently based on what we have learned?
- Is there anything we should do differently, any experiment or improvement, we should try today?

These simple questions are essential following the idea of Plan, Do, Check, Act, that are the essential model of continuous improvement practiced in lean management. And, the PDCA cycle is dependent on having the right information, at the right time, in the right place.

Assign Responsibility: Someone on the team must be responsible for assuring that the right information gets to the right people, and to assure that the visual display is kept up-to-date. Whose job is this?

Reward and Recognition Systems

Your design charter probably created expectations for reward and recognition systems. Certainly you cannot increase everyone's compensation to the level they would like, nor can you can create a lottery to give away large sums of money, as fun as that might be. What you do have to do is ask the question *"What will make performance matter to the team members?"*

---

[69] Case, John. *The Open-Book Experience*. Reading, MA, Addison-Wesley. 1998.

Keep in mind that positive reinforcement is not only money or material things. It is more often social recognition. We all care about being recognized by our peers and by our superiors. Even having someone bring in pizza for lunch when we meet our goals can be an effective form of recognition. The most effective positive reinforcement is most often the sincere expression of appreciation by those you work for. While every manager should practice the admonition to *Catch Someone Doing Something Good Today*, that principle should also be designed into the systems of the organization.

If you think that your team, or your profession is "above it" when it comes to recognition, one short story might help. This author was coaching the senior management team of one of the world's largest oil companies. The team was going through a training process and with each training module the team members were to complete *deliverables* with their teams. In other words, when they went through the training module on the balanced scorecard, for example, they were to develop a balanced scorecard, both on the senior team and each subordinate team. I found that some of the members of the senior team were lagging behind. I made a chart with the names of each of the team members and boxes to the right for each deliverable completed. For those team members who had completed a deliverable I put a gold star. Yes! A gold star just like the ones you might give to your five year old child for brushing their teeth and cleaning their room. It is hard to describe exactly the effect this had. But, it was the first thing the team members looked at when they walked into the room, and they were quick to point out to everyone else when they were ahead of their fellow team members, and they would sometimes argue that "Yes I did complete that" when they weren't recognized. They always wanted their gold star and wanted to be recognized for doing their tasks.

Simple and visual recognition works for most people – of any age and any compensation level!

There are literally a thousand ways that you can establish a system of reward or recognition for achieving desired performance by your teams. But, it is important to allow the team members to decide specific goals and specific reinforcing events for achieving those goals. Some design teams have proposed a monthly budget for recognition so that each team can decide on their own how to celebrate achievements.

Make it fun!

Positive Reinforcement and the 4 to 1 Rule

Toyota practices Four-to-One.[70] What does it mean and where does it come from?

I'll let you in on a little management history. In 1973 I joined Aubrey Daniels and Fran Tarkenton in Atlanta where they had just started Behavioral Systems, Inc. The company was focused on spreading the use of positive reinforcement in industry. Around that time a behavioral psychologist named Dr. Ogden Lindsley did research in classrooms to determine what ratio of positive to negative comments by teachers resulted in the highest rate of learning by students. The answer: 3.57 to 1. Since we expected that no one would remember 3.57 to 1 (although this author has for some strange reason), we rounded it off to 4 to 1. Our training and consultants promoted the 4 to 1 principle.

For several years we worked in southern textile mills teaching supervisors to *"Catch Someone Doing Something Good Today,"* and we had them record their own interactions with employees. How many of those interactions were positive and how many were negative? How many were recognizing good behavior and how many were criticizing bad behavior? Initially, most supervisors found that they were more likely to be 1 to 4, rather than 4 to 1, in other words, four times more negative than positive.

Every parent should know that punishing bad behavior may suppress that behavior, but if you don't reward the opposite good behavior the child is likely to misbehave in another way. You must define the desired alternative behavior and reward that behavior. We do what pays off in a positive way. You get what you reward! If you want good performance you must positively reinforce good behavior.

Adam Grant, who teaches organizational behavior at the Wharton Business School, has conducted research that demonstrates how employees, even in relatively mundane jobs, may be motivated by altruism – the desire to do good for others:

> *"Over the years, Grant has followed up that study with other experiments testing his theories about pro-social motivation — the desire to help others, independent of easily foreseeable payback. In one study,*

---

[70] Liker, Jeffrey K. and Hoseus, Michael. Toyota Culture. New York, McGraw-Hill, 2008, p. 403.

Grant put up two different signs at hand-washing stations in a hospital. One reminded doctors and nurses, "Hand hygiene prevents you from catching diseases"; another read, "Hand hygiene prevents patients from catching diseases." Grant measured the amount of soap used at each station. Doctors and nurses at the station where the sign referred to their patients used 45 percent more soap or hand sanitizer.

"These studies, two of Grant's best known, focus on typically worthy beneficiaries: needy students and vulnerable patients. But some of his other research makes the case that pro-social behavior is as applicable in corporate America as it is in a hospital or a university. "Think of it this way," he said. "In corporate America, people do sometimes feel that the work they do isn't meaningful. And contributing to co-workers can be a substitute for that."[71]

Adam Grant's experiments demonstrate that workers will be motivated to do well by their fellow workers. But that shouldn't be news to us. Approval by our team members and being of service to our team members is often more important than recognition from above. Everyone who has played on a sports team, at any level, has experienced the power of peer approval.

Intrinsic and Extrinsic Reinforcement

There are several different ways to understand the different types of consequences that impact behavior. One way is to understand that some motivation comes intrinsically from the work itself. Making chairs is more intrinsically reinforcing than making legs. If you enjoy playing the piano or playing tennis, it isn't work. You don't need to be paid for this activity because it is intrinsically reinforcing. In almost every job there are elements of intrinsic reinforcement. The ability to exert control and improve performance is intrinsically reinforcing, while feeling out of control is not intrinsically reinforcing. The relationships with team members can make our work more intrinsically reinforcing. Novelty, changing tasks and learning new tasks, makes more work enjoyable.

Much of the work that needs to get done in this world is not sufficiently intrinsically motivating and requires extrinsic motivation. Extrinsic reinforcement includes our compensation – both salary or wage, and bonuses.

---

[71] New York Times Magazine, March 31, 2013. *Is Giving the Secret to Getting Ahead?*

But, ordering pizza for your team because they achieved some performance goal, or taking them out to dinner, or an award of some type, is all extrinsic reinforcement even though the event, the social aspect, is most likely more reinforcing than the pizza itself.

Consider some of the activities that are critical to your work and consider what intrinsic and extrinsic reinforcement strengthens or maintains these activities.

Work Tasks or Behavior	Intrinsic Reinforcement	Extrinsic Reinforcement

One design team found the following simple table helpful in brainstorming and deciding on reward and recognition for the teams.

Health Care Team		
Individual Performance	Team Performance	Reinforcement

Discipline Systems

This is a topic we would all probably rather avoid. However, no matter how well you design your system you will still have to deal with the imperfections of human behavior. Inevitably, there will be behavior problems by team members. It is not necessary to develop an elaborate system of discipline. However, your design team does need to make some basic decisions about how performance problems will be handled.

Generally, team members are comfortable recognizing desirable behavior but then referring discipline issues to the first level manager. Some companies have developed a peer review discipline system, *a jury of your peers,* but not just by the direct team members. The way this is done is that there is a jury drawn from a larger body of employees, and the jury will hear the case and decides on discipline within some predetermined guidelines.

The System of Hiring

Hiring is something in which most frontline employees do not participate. However, most employees are not on teams that have been designed to have a high level of self-management. This is a change that can symbolize a more mature level of responsibility for the team.

When hiring new employees it is generally more clear which work skills are required rather than which social skills will contribute to the success of the team. More often those hiring know that they need someone who can operate certain equipment, is familiar with a certain language, or has specific technical experience. But do they know how to identify someone who will be a good team player or be good at problem-solving?

The design team may define a general procedure for hiring and may suggest that a sub-group be appointed to develop the details of the process along with human resource professionals. Human resource professionals can assure that the legal implications of the hiring process are taken into account. Equal employment practices must be considered. Valid testing and evaluation procedures must be developed. Whoever does the interviewing must have a way of determining if the candidate has the required work and social skills to succeed in the new work environment.

Those who design the hiring process would do well to consider carefully the expectations that are set. Imagine in one case that you tell applicants you are hiring hourly "workers" to work in the finishing department of a plant. In a second case you tell applicants that you are hiring "team members" or "associates" who will be responsible for the quality of products delivered to a specific set of customers, and who will be responsible for managing and improving the process that satisfies those customers. You are actually hiring for the same job. However, the ideas communicated about that job are entirely different. Expectations are easy to set at the beginning and hard to change later on.

Brainstorm and agree on a list of technical skills and social or people skills that will be required for the entry level job. This will be part of the competency model for that job.

Skills: Develop a Competency Model

For each position you will want to develop a competency model. You will want to develop one that applies to all team members and for the team leader, coach or coordinator, and for any additional jobs that are critical to your design. The competency model describes what an individual will need to know and be able to do – knowing and doing – knowledge and skills; these are the essential competencies. And, for both knowing and doing you may divide these into either technical competencies or social skills.

There will be some skills that should be a requirement prior to team membership. For example, a team member may need to know how to perform certain functions that are the entry-level work of team members. From that point there is a hierarchy of desirability, from those skills that are needed often and which someone on the team must possess; those that would be good for everyone to possess; to those skills that would be nice for someone to have but are not essential.

You may also decide that there are some skills that can best be shared across several teams. For example in healthcare, nursing teams may not possess every possible nursing specialty, but those specialities (i.e. ambulatory care, palliative care, or neonatal care) might exist within a larger cluster, and be available to all the teams in that cluster, as needed.

The chart on the next page can be used to brainstorm and decide which competencies are needed by team members.

Team Member Competency Chart		
Priority	**Technical Skills**	**People Skills**
Required for Team Membership		
All Members Should Work Toward Developing		
Most Members Should Develop These Skills		
Some Members Should Develop		
Would Be Beneficial but Not Necessary		

Style of Decision-making

A true lean culture is one in which decision-making at the lowest level is maximized, decisions are made quickly, and consensus decision-making is valued. When teams are empowered and clear in their responsibility they are capable of making many decisions on-the-spot and speeding improvement. The design team should develop a prescription for which types of decisions will be made by which individual or group, and what style of decision-making should be employed for each. This is an important component of defining the future culture.

Sometimes rapid decision-making is best. However, sometime taking more time to reach consensus among a large number of people is a worthwhile investment.

The Consensus Principle at Honda

One day I received a phone call from the Executive Vice President of Honda America Manufacturing, Scott Whitlock. In my book, *American Spirit*, which they were using, I promoted *The Consensus Principle* as one of the keys to high performing companies. The VP asked me "Larry, what percent of the people do we need to have a consensus."

I had no idea what he was talking about, so I asked, "Well, how many people do you have?"

He replied that they had about ten thousand people. A bit surprised that he was trying to get a consensus from ten thousand people, I then asked, "Well, what is the decision on which you are trying to get consensus?"

"The drug policy" he replied.

Still a bit surprised, I then asked, "Well how many people are in agreement now?" He said that more than eighty-seven percent were in agreement.

I then told him that I thought that was pretty good considering the number of people and nature of the question. But, that didn't satisfy him. He said that they were going to go through another round of involving the associates to reach consensus.

Honda is one of the world's best organizations. I am not saying that a 100% of employees need to agree on this or any other policy. However, this demonstrates their commitment to the principle of consensus. This doesn't mean that all decisions should be consensus, even on a team. Some decisions are better made as "command" or "consultative" decisions.

Many of the conflicts involve a failure to clarify the decision process. If team members think they are going to make a decision, and a manager then makes the decision alone, they will be upset even if they agree with the decision. Disunity results from differing expectations and feeling betrayed that an agreement isn't being followed.

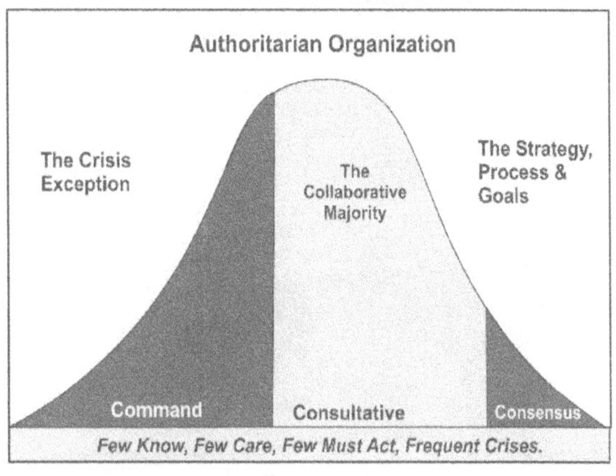

It is not true that team members want to be involved in making every decision, but they do want input, and they want to know how decisions are made. Clarify the decision process reduces conflicts and clarifies expectations.

Here is a quick primer on assigning decision responsibility: Consider three types of decisions: *Command, consultative* and *consensus.* The criteria for deciding which to use are *who knows, who cares, who acts, when must it be made?* The answer to these questions will determine which style of decision-making is most appropriate.

Command Decisions

Command decisions are those made by an individual. Individual command authority is not merely a left over dinosaur of the Roman Legions. Of course, command worked well on the battlefield where quick decisions were required and obedience won battles. Even today, if the building is burning down, if the machine is spitting smoke and oil, if the customer calls and is furious that he got the wrong material delivered – is the right answer to call a meeting? Definitely not! These are decisions in which speed is more important than reaching consensus. These decisions are best left to individuals who are on-the-spot and have expert knowledge.

Speed and expert knowledge are two reasons for command to be the preferred decision style. In the operating room, with the patient cut open and the cardiologist holding a heart in his hand that has just stopped beating – do you want him to call a meeting to achieve a consensus decision? Not if it's your heart! Of course, you want him to use his expert knowledge and make a decision, fast! The greater the degree of knowledge an individual has compared to others on a team, the more likely a command decision is appropriate. The greater the required speed, the more likely it is that command decision-making is appropriate. Command is what you do in crisis.

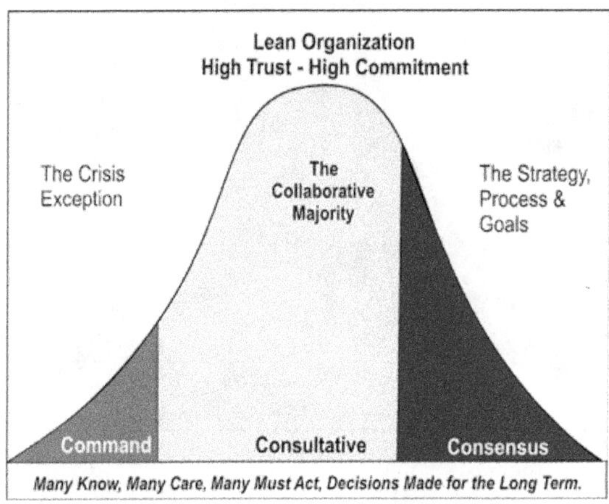

An organization in which command decision-making is predominant is an organization that lives in frequent crisis. This raises serious questions about the ability of the leaders to plan, engage in systematic action, and develop the people below them. If the predominant style is command, it may be an organization dominated by personalities whose egos prevent them from letting go of decisions and trusting others. Predominance of command decision-making reflects low trust and will soon de-motivate employees.

Consultative or Shared Decisions

Consultative decisions involve selective involvement by those who know, care, or must act. The majority of decisions in most organizations tend to be consultative.

If the customer calls and was shipped the wrong order, you may say, "I am very sorry about that. Let me look into it and call you back within an hour. We will definitely solve the problem." The customer will likely say "fine." The customer does not want to be told it will be taken up at the weekly meeting. And it is likely that you personally do not have sufficient information to know what to do to solve the problem. What you are likely to do is gather the two or three people who have knowledge, who may have some investment in this decision (they care), and who may have to take action to solve the problem. You can do this quickly. You will give them the facts and ask them what they think should be done to meet this customer's needs now. You are not trying to solve a systemic or process problem. You are just trying to fix this problem now. You are consulting with associates, but you are going to make a decision quickly, rather than turn the decision over to the team. This is consultative decision-making.

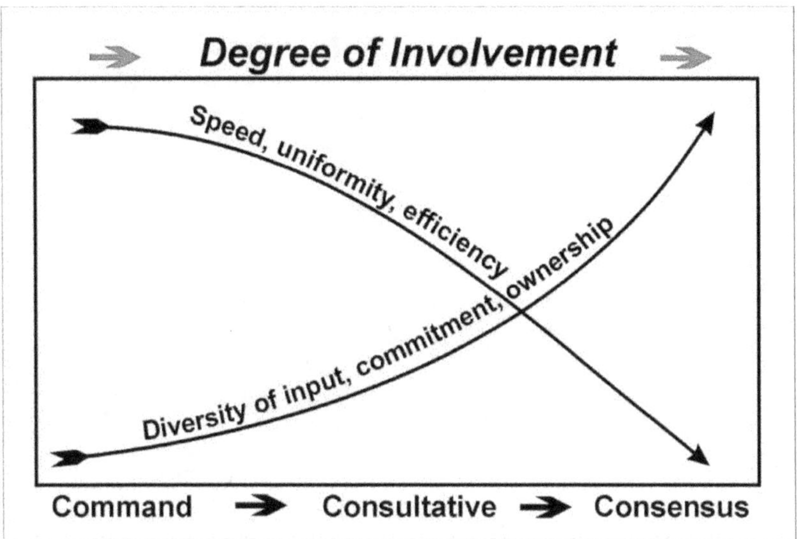

CONSENSUS DECISIONS

Consensus decisions are true team decisions where you turn over the decision to the group. The decision is then owned by the group. Consensus decisions involve a cost – the cost of time, energy, and the risk that you may not like the decision.

When do you employ consensus decision-making? First, when the conditions of speed and individual expertise are not the most important factors. You employ consensus when the quality of the decision, commitment, and unified action are most important; when the "who knows, who cares and who must act" includes the group.

Consensus is generally worth the investment for those decisions that involve long-term goals, and how we do things, our ongoing processes. All members of the group have an investment in the goals of the group, and the "how" and "why" we do our work. Involvement in these types of decisions gains commitment, gains the wisdom of the group, and provides for shared learning.

Ask your team which decisions should be command, consultative or consensus for each team you have designed. This will create clarity and have the group focus on those things that add most value. The time and energy of teams is often wasted with trivial and inappropriate decisions. Use common sense.

Decision-Making Worksheet

Command Decisions

Command decisions are those made by one individual who has been given authority to make that decision. Best when the priority is speed and conformity to the decision such as in a fire drill or crisis mode.

Consultative Decisions

Those controlled by one person who consults with others who have knowledge or who must be committed to the decision. Use when time is important and when the decision is not sufficiently important to justify an entire team meeting.

Consensus Decisions

Decisions made by the entire team as a group. Use for those decisions that are important to all team members, need the commitment of entire team, and provide important learning for team members.

Symbols that Bond

When you think about symbols you may at first think that these are trivial or unnecessary. However, think about great teams. Think about culture. Are you a fan of any sports team? Do you have a hat, a jacket, a t-shirt or anything else with the team's name or mascot? Are you religious? Is a cross important, a Star of David, or other religious symbol? How about your country's flag? Is that important and why does a country need a flag anyway? They aren't that trivial, are they?

All cultures create symbols to reinforce the values of the culture and to bond together its members. This has been true since the earliest tribes hunted for antelope on the Serengeti plains. It probably doesn't matter exactly why this is true; it is one of those things that is "natural" for human beings. Symbols unite people and motivate them to sacrifice for their group.

What symbols can be created for your teams or your company that will reinforce their unity and commitment? A change in symbols can symbolize a change in culture.

We employ all sorts of symbols in ritualistic fashion, and like the inhabitants of other cultures, we give little thought to their origin or their impact on behavior. We have separate parking and entrances for managers. Why? Is it to send a message that managers are different, superior to, and more important than others? Why do we want to send this message? The president of Honda America Manufacturing sits in his "office," a large room with dozens of other identical desks and with other employees all dressed like him, in a white smock-like uniform. Can he not afford a private office? Does he not understand that familiarity breeds contempt and, therefore, he should not mingle so closely with his employees? Honda performs quite well despite this violation of the traditions of American corporate culture. Honda regards the principles of "unity" and "consensus" very seriously. They train their managers in these principles, and have they designed their culture to promote the spirit of unity and consensus. The new CEO of Chrysler has closed down the entire floor of the Chrysler building that was the executive suite and his own office is a shared office in an open space in an engineering department. He is now close to the Gemba.

Symbols are generally not important unto themselves. Whether the president of Honda has a private office or not, or whether there are reserved parking places for managers, has little impact on the bottom line of the company. It is the bonding, the social capital, created by symbols that are important.

Changing symbols can be among the most important decisions a design team makes. While many perceive these as unimportant, they communicate powerful messages of change to the organization. The greater population of employees are often looking for some symbolic changes to demonstrate a real change in the culture of the organization.

Stories that Define Our Identify

Like symbols, it may at first seem silly to think about story telling as part of an organization design process. However, if you think seriously about culture you will recognize that every culture has stories, and leaders tell stories, that define the valued behavior within that culture. From the story of David and Goliath, to Shakespeare, Mark Twain, and George Washington cutting down the apple tree, we have been telling stories that convey not only our history, but our values.

When we say that someone is a hero or heroine, why do we honor them with this status? Of course, it is because they have acted with courage to defend something important to us and telling their story serves the purpose of encouraging others to behave in a similar manner.

Now think about the culture that you are trying to create. Are there heroes or heroines within your organization that have acted in a manner that exemplifies what you are trying to achieve. This is what some may call "*appreciative inquiry*," in which you seek positive stories and role models to use as examples of what can be done and what should be done, models of desired behavior. Surely, you can think of one.

And, you may wish to write a story. Yes, I know you aren't a novelist. But, sometimes a design team will actually write a short play. The first act of the play is "How We Treat Customer's Today," and they act out the process and the social relationships that exist around that process. Then there is a second act, in which it is "NewCorp" the redesigned organization, and they act out the customer experience and the social relationships as customers will experience when the new design is implemented.

Try your hand at making up a story of the old and the new. Make up a story of the prototypical hero of the new culture and new process. How would that hero behave? How would they demonstrate the values that you have embedded in your design? Have some fun with it.

Social System Final Check-Up:

Has the Design Team Answered the Following Questions?

1. Have we embedded our values and principles in the new design?
2. Have you defined the performance metrics that are the responsibility of each team?
3. Where will teams be physically located and have you maximized co-location for bonding and information sharing?
4. How many teams will be needed?
5. How many team members should there be on each team?
6. What process will be each team own and be responsible for?
7. What administrative and reporting responsibilities will the team have?
8. What support will the design team need from other teams?
9. What decisions about the work process should the team have authority to make?
10. What people decisions should the team have authority to make?
11. What are the decision-making boundaries for each front-line team? What decisions affecting the front-line teams should be made at the next level in the structure?
12. What are the technical and support responsibilities of the first level of management?
13. In addition to the primary work process teams, have you created knowledge networks to share expertise and learning across teams?
14. What are the decision-making boundaries of the first level of management?
15. What style of decision-making will be used for each decision and who will make it?
16. What are the key performance indicators for each team? How will teams measure their performance?

17. What support teams are needed to complete the full structure? How do they fit into the structure?
18. How will teams give feedback to their suppliers?
19. How will teams get feedback from their customers?
20. How will information get from top management to front-line teams and vice versa?
21. How will information be communicated from one department to another or from one site to another?
22. How will new employees be hired?
23. What will new employee orientation consist of? Who will conduct it?
24. How will employees transfer from one team to another? What role will seniority play? How will new team members be oriented to the team?
25. How will team members' performance be appraised? By whom? How frequently? How will performance feedback be given to individual team members?
26. For what will performance appraisals be used?
27. What is the process for disciplining a team member? How will fairness be ensured?
28. How will team members be trained? Who will do the training? How will success at learning new skills be determined? Will there be certification? How will the system provide for ongoing training?
29. How will employees be compensated? Will they be paid for knowledge, skills, or performance? How will the system work? Who determines when a team member's compensation should be increased?
30. What social recognition or other rewards will there be for achieving improved performance?
31. Where will the team's data be visually displayed?
32. For what planning will teams be responsible?
33. How will success be reinforced for individuals? For teams? For departments? For sites?
34. What symbols will identify the teams and bond them to one another?

CHAPTER 17

DESIGNING THE FUTURE ECONOMIC SYSTEM

All organizations are economic systems. Ignoring the economic realities of the organization is like ignoring gravity. Sooner or later we will have to conform to economic laws just as we will have to conform to the laws of physics. All businesses, hospitals, charities, and universities are economic systems. Money comes in and money goes out. If the system is to be sustainable, sooner or later, the amount of money coming in must balance the amount of money going out. Any redesign should seek to achieve that balance.

The purpose of this chapter is not to redesign your accounting system. It is to help the design team construct a business case, an economic analysis, to support the new design. It is possible that it will result in some reconsideration of the design to assure that there is a business case for the new design.

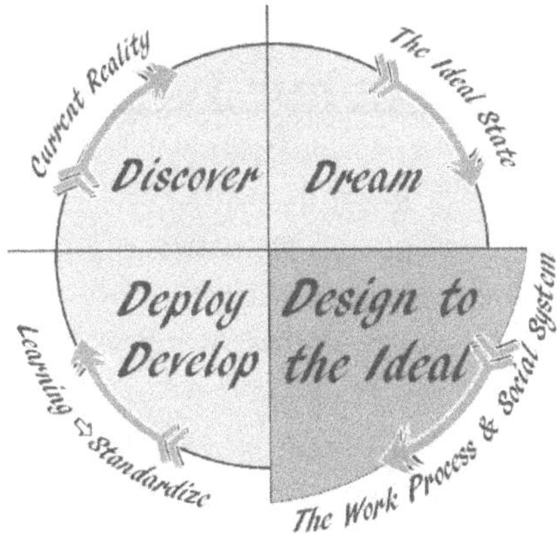

You are going to present your design to your steering committee, the senior managers of the organization. Those senior managers have a responsibility for its economic success. While they will be happy to hear that you have eliminated waste, reduced quality problems, and built a culture that will be more attractive to employees, they will want to know that you have considered and improved the

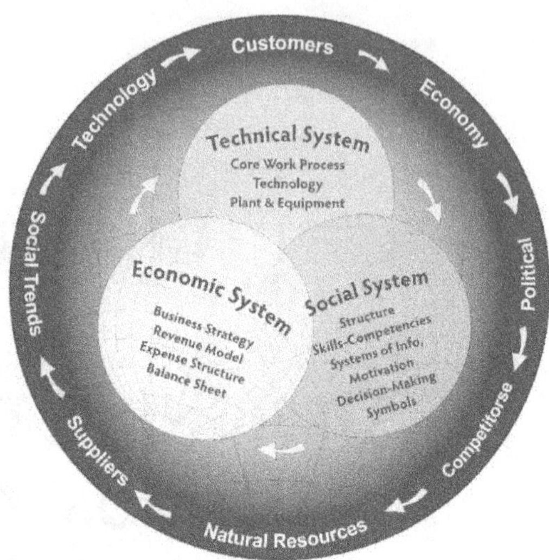

financial performance of the organization.

Having sat through many design team presentations to steering teams, let me make a simple suggestion. In your opening statements to the steering team, without going into details, let them know that you have created a design that will reduce costs and/or increased revenue. Tell them that you will explain the details and how you will achieve that result. By doing this you are demonstrating empathy for their concerns and they will be much more receptive to every other aspect of the design.

In constructing your business case and analyzing the economic system, it is possible that on your design team you may not have sufficient expertise. What many design teams have done successfully is form a sub-team of two or three design team members who are more knowledgeable in financial matters and they may engage one or two key financial managers to help them with the financial analysis. If you have consulted with key financial managers and you make this clear in your presentation to the steering team, it will be well received.

Every type of industry or organization constructs its financial statements in a somewhat different manner. Language is used differently. If you are the finance manager of a manufacturing company, as skilled as you may be, if you are studying the financial statements of an international bank for the first time, you can be certain that you will likely be confused. Therefore, it is impossible to recommend how to do this analysis in any detailed way without knowing the business of the reader. However, the simple description that follows of the nature of the economic system of any organization could be useful for members of the design team who have little experience with financial statements.

The Flow of Money

Your organization, in addition to transforming materials from incoming supply to outgoing end product, is also transforming money. It is transforming the value of input to the value of output. In the end, the value of output must exceed the value of input.

Money is consumed in two basic ways by any organization. First, there are the ***operating costs***: salaries, insurance, supplies, rent, energy, travel, etc. Second, there are the ***capital costs*** that include the costs of a building, land, equipment and debt.

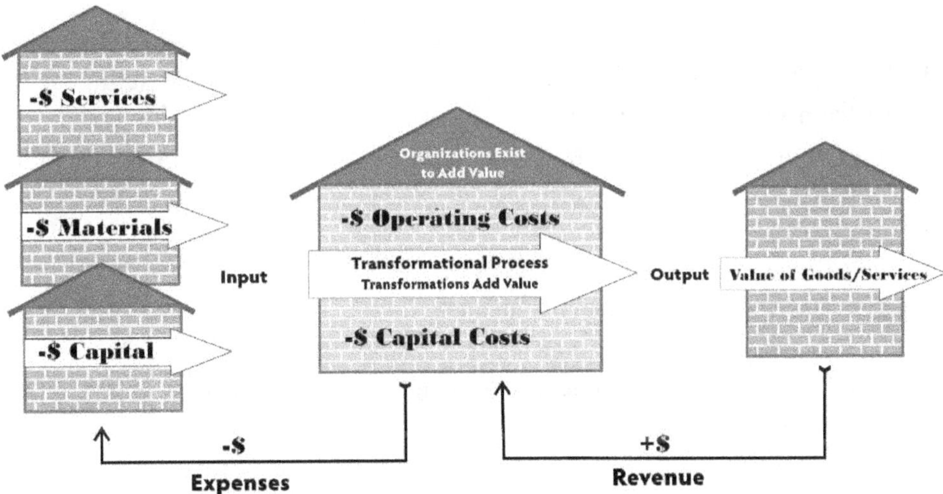

All of the operating costs come and go. Like the operating costs of your household, you pay for utilities, food and clothing. But these don't have lasting value. Buying a home is different. Presumably, that home or land has lasting value. It is not simply consumed the way food is. Therefore, it is capital. Operating costs are expenses that are listed on the income statement (or profit and loss statement); while capital assets and liabilities are listed on the balance sheet.

You can generally find three types of input to any organization. The first is the ***cost of capital*** that is invested in the business; the second is the cost of ***material supplies*** that are required; and the third is the cost of ***services*** that must be purchased by the organization. Imagine that you and two friends are going to open a restaurant. You are either going to buy or rent property. You are going to have to purchase a significant amount of equipment for the kitchen and furniture for the dining room. This requires capital. You either will draw this capital from savings or borrow it from a bank, friend or relative. These are your capital expenses.

Once the restaurant is open, you will have ***operating expenses***. This will include the costs of meat and vegetables, salaries for cooks and waiters, the energy bill, advertising costs, and insurance.

The revenue you receive from your customers is generally the only source of money to offset your operating expenses. If you are a charity, this revenue may be donations. If the revenue does not equal the expenses, you will then have to borrow more money, increasing the capital and the costs of capital. The more you borrow, the harder it becomes to be profitable because you have to pay the costs of capital.

This then is the simple view of the economic system of any organization. It isn't complicated, although the language of accounting can make it appear to be very complicated. In essence, it is no more complicated than economic system of your household, with income and expenses, and capital assets that you have acquired. Let's now consider how your design may have improved economic performance.

Improving Operating Costs

Lean production or management focuses a great deal on eliminating waste. You have studied and hopefully eliminated waste. Less in process inventory, less time required to accomplish the flow through from input to output, less space requirements, all result in reduced operating expenses. The following are questions to ask, or issues to investigate, that will create the business case for your design.

Inventory

Inventory is a form of "working capital" money that has been spent, but is not returning any revenue. If you have a manufacturing plant with a million dollars' worth of inventory, often comprised of buffers between operations or stored in the warehouse, it is a form of waste. It is not value-adding because it is not in motion. When you studied waste in your system and mapped your process you looked for opportunities to eliminate "piles," things standing still and not moving.

One way to measure potential gain is simply to add up the entire current inventory in the warehouse and work-in-progress and estimate a current dollar amount for that inventory. You aren't likely to be precise in this, but a general estimate will probably be useful. Then you will have to estimate the reduction in inventory and work-in-process in your new design. Perhaps you can create something like the following:

Inventory Cost Analysis			
	Current State	**Future State**	**Savings**
Warehouse Inventory			
Work-In-Progress			
Net			

Productivity Gains

In most businesses there are productivity measures that are tracked and generally equate to financial performance. For example, in the airline industry there are two key productivity numbers: Load factor and yield. Load factor is the percentage of available seats that are filled; yield is the dollars of income per sold seat. If those two numbers are improving they will positively impact the bottom line. In the auto assembly plants that have been the focus of lean, the most common productivity number is hours required to assemble a vehicle or hours per car. At Honda and Toyota it has been in the range of 11-14 hours per car; ten or twenty years ago in the U.S. auto companies it was 22-24 hours per car. In home health care, a measure used is visits per-full time equivalent care provider. In general, if a nurse is making ten home visits a day rather than six or seven, the revenue will increase in relation to expenses.

You should find out what the key productivity numbers are in your industry and establish baseline data and projected improvement in those measures.

Productivity can be directly related to people or to assets. For example, in the airline industry you can understand that there are huge capital costs, primarily airplanes. An airplane sitting empty it is a huge expense with no return on the investment. If it is making ten flights a day and with all the seats filled, it would obviously represent a greater return on the capital invested. In the home health care example, there are relatively few capital costs, but people costs are a high percentage of monthly expenses. There the focus is more on the productivity of people.

Productivity of space is another area where you may find gains. In a manufacturing facility there is a cost of space. This cost may be either a capital (balance sheet) cost or it may be rent, a monthly operating expense. In either case the revenue generated per square foot of space is a measure that should improve when transitioning from a traditional manufacturing environment to a lean manufacturing environment. If there are no interruptions in the process, there is less work-in-process, there is less space utilized. Therefore, the productivity of space utilization will improve.

Cycle time is a critical measure of productivity in many organizations. This writer was involved in a major redesign of a large unit of a major oil company that did deep water exploration and production. The average cycle time from the time land was leased to the time oil actually flowed out of that property was eight years. Amazingly, the redesigned process reduced that time to less than four years. There are many ways to compute the savings in that process. But, the easiest way was the time value of money. The lease of property was a cash outlay and it was many millions of dollars. If you have five hundred thousand dollars of leases (a conservative number) and that sits for eight years, depending on the interest rates, you can compute the time value of that money. By reducing the cycle time from eight years to four years they gained a very large savings.

Return on People

Conversion to a lean process and lean culture will improve the value of each person in the operation. If you have eliminated waste and reduced variances and therefore rework or rejected materials, the value-adding work of each individual will improve. To take a simple example, in the auto assembly plant, if every third car had to be reworked in some way, and if that rework required two person/hours per reworked car, and if the auto assembly plant assembled 1000 cars a day, you would be reworking 333 cars

X two hours = 666 hours per day. If you know the average total compensation per employee per hour you can multiply that by 666. Compensation costs might be $25 per hour on average. Therefore, the daily costs of the quality variances that caused the rework would be (666 X $25) = $16,650 per day! Multiply that time by the total days of operation per year and you have a huge amount of wasted money! If you can eliminate this you have increased the value-added by those working in that plant by that amount. You can view it as reducing an expense or increase the value-added. On the bottom line it is the same number.

That may be an extreme example, but the point is that you can compute the dollar value of quality variances that cause rework, and if your design has eliminated causes of rework, you can estimate a dollar savings. You therefore can estimate the improvement in the value added by your employees.

There are other ways of computing a reduction in expenses or an improved return on people. The more your business is based on people, rather than things, the more it is a service business; the more significant are the saving from improved culture and treatment of people.

It is a generally accepted rule that when an employee leaves an organization, the replacement cost associated with recruitment, training and other costs equals 150% of their annual compensation. Even Toyota at one point was experiencing a 25% turnover of new employees in their manufacturing plants in Japan. This caused them to redesign their social system.

In healthcare, like other service industries, the value and costs associated with people is their most significant costs. This concern was the basis of the development of the Magnet Healthcare concept intended to retain nurses. It has long been understood that there is a relationship between job satisfaction and retention of staff. A study of nursing work environments highlighted the relationship between the work environment of nurses and their trust in the management of their organization.

"The results of this study support the proposition that features of nursing work environments such as autonomy, control over the practice environment, and collaboration with physicians have an impact on staff nurses trust in management and ultimately influence nurses' job satisfaction and their assessment of patient care quality. The results suggest that both trust in management and emotional exhaustion are important mediators of job satisfaction and perceptions of quality. These findings highlight the importance

of creating environments which empower nurses to accomplish their work and generate positive feelings about their work and its effects on patient outcomes."[72]

In other words, the ability of health care workers to exert control on their environment is directly related to trust, satisfaction and the quality of care. This is exactly consistent with the idea that workers in a manufacturing setting, when respected for their work, given the control and ability to improve their work, will produce better cars or any other product. This is an essential philosophy of the Toyota Production System, or lean manufacturing.

If you have done a good job of redesigning the social system you should experience lower turnover and therefore lower costs.

You may also be able to predict some increase in productivity per team, based on the logic of teams taking responsibility for managing their own performance. If you can establish a pilot team to demonstrate this gain, and then perfect that model before gaining commitment to deploy it in the rest of the organization, it will help to present the business case.

Another possible saving can be in the area of human resource utilization. In many companies individuals with high value-adding skills spend much of their time doing work of lower value. One aircraft manufacturer found that engineers were actually doing engineering only five percent of the time. Shifting less value-adding work to lower paid administrative personnel or to interns, or to those working virtually in remote locations can off-load work to save time of the more expensive and specialized staff.

Research by McKinsey Global Institute suggests that by 2020 the worldwide shortage of highly skilled, college-educated workers could reach 38 million to 40 million, or 13% of demand.[73] The United Kingdom's National Health Service took a close look at the entire "patient journey" through its system, including the locations were patients receive care, the practices that have the best patient outcomes, and the skills required to deliver high quality care. By doing this they found numerous opportunities to redefine jobs to ensure that highly paid professional care providers could focus more on doing

---

[72] *"Impact of Magnet Hospital Characteristics on Nurses' Perceptions of Trust, Burnout, Quality of Care, and Work Satisfaction."* Heather K. Spence Laschinger, Judith Shamian, Donna Thomson. Nursing Economics, Vol.19/No. 5. October, 2001.

[73] *Redesigning Knowledge Work*, Martin Dewhurst, Bryan Hancock, and Diana Ellsworthy. Harvard Business Review, January-February 2013.

what they do well, and reducing the burden of less value-adding administrative and other work.

The economic value gained can be estimated by, for example, seeing that your work redesign will reduce eight hours a week of doctor's time spent in lower value-adding work. If you reassign this work to a lower paid individual, then compute compensation differentials between the higher and lower paid person, you can then multiply that on an annualized basis, and by the total number of persons involved.

Costs of Management

In most whole-system designs you create some version of self-directed teams. If you have done a good job of designing those teams they will need less management or supervision. It is important to redefine the role of managers so they spend their time doing value-adding work and not tampering in the work of the teams.

It is not uncommon to remove one or two layers of management from the hierarchy. If this is done, it is a very significant savings. If you are unclear about this go back and read the case of Buurtzorg or research this organization. It is a great example of the efficiencies that can be gained by pushing decision-making and self-management into the teams.

You should be able to present a table like the previous one but for people related costs. It might look something like this:

Human Resource Utilization Cost Analysis			
	Current State	**Future State**	**Savings**
People hours per unit of production			
Gains from improvement in talent utilization			
Management Costs			
Net			

Improving Revenue and Growth

In managing any organization there are always two sides: costs and revenue. It is generally easier to project cost savings than it is to project gains in revenue. To predict gains in revenue you are basically predicting the future behavior of a customer, and that is always difficult. No company ever became a great company by cutting costs. Ultimately, you have to innovate, create new products and services, and build revenue. That is the game of business.

Your new design should improve customer satisfaction. In several cases with which this writer has been involved there have been dramatic gains in customer satisfaction. Ultimately, business is a result of customer satisfaction. You can directly link customer satisfaction, of cars or airlines or hotels, for example, with the price customers are willing to pay and their loyalty to the brand.

Is there a way that you can predict an increase in customer satisfaction, brand loyalty, and therefore revenue? Without knowing the specifics of your redesign, it is impossible to offer advice in the abstract. However, you should consider potential revenue growth as an economic benefit of your design.

Improving Return on Operating Assets

Go back and review the work you did when you assessed the financial capital as part of the discovery process. You will remember the discussion of the following matrix. It is important when you present your design to your steering team.

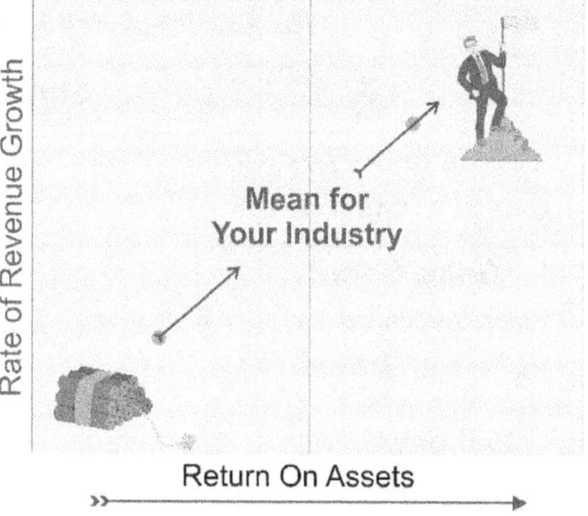

If you increase revenue or reduce expenses, or some combination, and you do not increase assets you will have increased the return-on-operating-assets. Operating assets are those assets that are actually used in operations.

This should be important to all senior managers because this is a primary determinant of valuation of companies. If you move the dot northeast on this matrix you are increasing shareholder value. That is the language of your senior executives and if you can speak their language you will have a listening ear.

They will be even more impressed if you can compare the rate of revenue growth and return-on-assets of competitive organizations with your own, and demonstrate how you can increase the rate of revenue growth and improve return-on-operating-assets.

In all these computations of financial benefits it will be very wise to involve and consult with your own financial professionals. Every company and every industry computes their finances in somewhat different ways, and it will be important to draw on their expertise.

Open-Book Management

Transparency in measurement and finance builds trust. *The Great Game of Business* [74] and other books on *Open Book Management* [75] advocate open accounting, sharing financial information with every team, even providing every work team with a weekly or monthly accounting statement, so that every team can play the "great game of business." Transparency, or open-book management, takes the practice of employee empowerment or teams to a new and more profound level.

It is common for executives to present financial results and financial goals to their employees. While this is good, it is far short of a genuine transparency in financial reporting. Break down the balance sheet and the profit and loss statement for employees. Give them credit for the ability to understand these financial statements. They are all available (for public companies) on the Internet anyway. Break them down by division and business unit. Explain which assets increased or decreased, and why that is desirable. Many employees (even many managers) don't understand that corporate assets are not like storing stuff in your basement or closet, which we always seem intent on filling up! Reducing assets is good, because it increases return-on-assets. Explain how a business unit succeeded in

---

[74] Stack, Jack. *The Great Game of Business*, New York, Doubleday, 1992.

[75] Schuster, John P; Carpenter Jill and Kane, Patricia M. *The Power of Open Book Management: Releasing the True Potential of People's Minds*, Hearts & Hands. New York. John C. Wiley & Sons, Inc.

increasing ROA by selling off some of its unneeded equipment, or sharing with another division. Explain the income statement and the reasons for the increase or decrease in different streams of income. Make all employees owners, through open information. This will create bonds of unity and energize them to contribute to financial results.

Should part of your architecture be a system of open-book management in which each work area receives a financial statement every week or month? Why not make them part of the great game of business? They can't play without the numbers.

Implementation Costs & Benefit Analysis

There are generally cost to implementation of the new design. It is important that the design team present a table of costs that will be associated with implementation. There are most likely one-time costs, and there may be on-going costs. It will be important to present these as two different tables, or two columns of a cost table, to analyze the one time investment, versus the on-going cost/benefit ratio of the new design.

Without knowing the specifics of the design it is impossible to recommend what should be included. But, think about all the technical changes and the costs associated with those changes. Then think about all the changes in people, training, recruiting, motivational programs, or any other costs. It is very important when you present to the steering team that these costs are presented realistically. Many senior managers have learned to be very skeptical about costs, and you can expect to be questioned about these. That is their job. It is your job to have the answers.

Hopefully you will have two sets of numbers to present to the senior team. First a list of all the financial benefits of the new design; second, the costs associated with that implementation. They can then weight the costs versus the benefits.

CHAPTER 18

DEPLOY AND DEVELOP THE DESIGN

A detailed implementation plan should be developed after the design team has presented their combined technical-social-economic design to the steering team and received their approval. Once the design team has developed an implementation plan, that plan should also be presented to the steering team for approval.

There are several key ideas behind implementation planning. The first is that implementation is still part of the development process. It is always the case that no matter how brilliant a job the design team has done, once you start implementing the design, you will learn important lessons that should result in modifications and improvement. That is why this stage is called *deploy* and *develop*, not just deploy. In a recent design implementation the design team had created a new job that did the scheduling of home health care providers. The previous job that was somewhat similar to this was considered a relatively low level job. However, in this new design, the "care coordinators" were integral to the team of care providers and their job largely determined the productivity of the team. The design team had underestimated the time required for training these individuals, and no one had understood how central these individuals

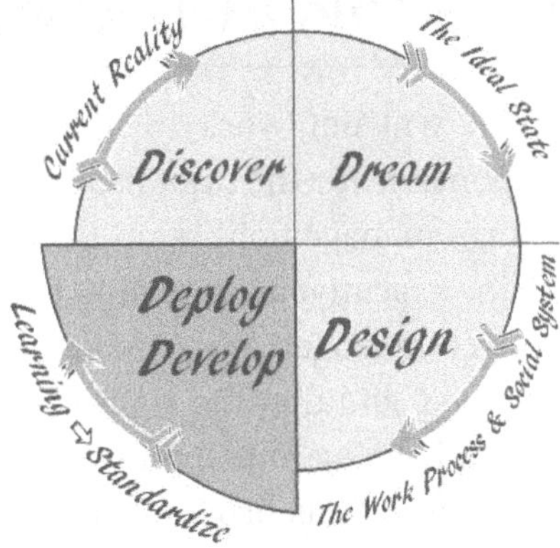

would be to the success of the entire organization. The time allocated for training and coaching these care coordinators needed to be increased in order to assure their success. This was a modification to the design, made quickly and without any feeling of failure. They had been taught to expect "discoveries", things that needed improvement as they implemented the design.

This type of modification happens in every design and the design team should expect it. What makes this a natural continuation of the design process is that the design team members are engaged in and critical actors in implementation process. Because the design team members are part of the implementation process they understand the thinking that went into the design and they feel free to make changes as needed improvements are identified. In the above health care case, the person who was doing the training of the new care coordinators had been on the design team and participated in the design of that training. She was quickly able to see that they had miscalculated the time required.

How You Change is the Change!

Remember our favorite slogan. It means that the change is not being driven from the top down, imposed in an autocratic or thoughtless manner. It is a process of co-creation, being designed and implemented by your own people. It means that there is constant learning and openness to change, and continual improvement. It means that if you build your own house and you feel ownership for it, you will make it work, and you will improve it. These are simple messages but they are powerful and make this change process different than changes that most people have experienced before.

Managing Implementation

It will not work to simply hand over the design to the line manager responsible for the organization that has been redesigned. There needs to be a change management team that includes the line manager, but also includes a senior executive responsible for the change process. It also needs to include a project manager who makes sure that the implementation plan is being followed, and that the right resources are in place at the right time. Often the design is being implemented in several locations at the same time. When this is the case it has proven very helpful to have a weekly design implementation meeting, probably held virtually, and using either simply the phone or a service like WebEx so documents can be displayed. In these meetings common problems are identified and solved together, and lessons learned in one location are shared with the other locations. This is extremely beneficial.

When developing your implementation plan it will be very helpful if you have Microsoft Project or some comparable software to develop and track activities and resources. Microsoft Project allows you to list the major tasks, sub tasks, and more detailed tasks; who will be responsible for each task; and, what date they are scheduled to start and end. It then displays a Gantt chart or Pert chart that makes the project implementation very visible. Everyone can look at the chart and see the tasks for which they are responsible, and when they are expected to start and end.

In the photo you can see a print out of a project plan. This, along with process maps, decision matrixes, and other work of the design team was on the wall and displayed when the steering team came into the room for the final meeting, before the steering team gave approval to move forward with the implementation of the design. The steering team members then walked around the room studying each of these displays. Seeing and studying this project plan gives the steering team confidence that the design team has carefully thought through the plan for implementation.

Communicating the Design

Like any new initiative that needs commitment and understanding from many people in the organization, the design needs a bit of good old fashion marketing. There is no possibility that the implementation of the new design will be a secret. You must be deliberate in sending the message you want people to hear. In the absence of clear communication it is not unusual for the worst possible interpretations to become rumor. Change creates anxiety and people tend to be comfortable with the current state, even though they may recognize that it needs to change.

It will be helpful to give a brief explanation of the 4D process stages. This will be easy for everyone to understand. It will also be a good idea to explain who is on the steering committee, and who is on the design and implementation teams. It will be good to explain some of the key features of the new design, and why you think this will be an improvement. Create the expectation that you will periodically inform them about the progress of the implementation, the lessons being learned, and the results being achieved. You can model a culture of continuous learning by how you communicate this progress. Make clear that the new design was done by your own people (facilitation by a consultant is OK, but don't give the consultant too much credit, give the credit to the members of the design team). This will help to create acceptance and commitment to the design.

In the communication of your design to the organization it will be helpful to give the customers perspective of both the current state and the desired future state. What does it feel like now to do business with your organization, and how will it feel in the future? Everyone understands that you must meet the needs of the customer, and it will help to understand the change from their perspective. It will also be helpful to share the increased responsibility that will be given to frontline employees, and how the teams are expected to function. This is generally a positive experience and will be viewed favorably by your employees.

In selling any product or service there is a well proven idea that you may wish to consider. It is the idea of *features and benefits.* In other words, if you are going to buy a new car and the salesman explains that it has a new six speed automatic transmission and then goes on to explain the next feature, this is not good salesmanship. However, if he explains that this new transmission results in an improved fuel economy of two miles per gallon and it is quieter and smoother when it shifts, now you know the benefits. People are persuaded to buy because of benefits, not features. Every feature should have a benefit.

In developing your communication plan to the organization think not only about the features of your new design, also think about the benefits. You could think in terms of a 2X2 matrix with features and benefits; and technical and social system changes. This could help organize your presentation.

Make a list of all the different categories of people who need to understand the new design, and when it will be implemented. Think both internally and externally, particularly about your customers.

- Who will be responsible for both developing and implementing the communication plan?
- For each group to whom communication must be delivered...
- What is the message?
- Who will deliver it?
- When will it be delivered?
- What role will the senior managers play in this communication?
- What roles will the design team play? A video presentation by the design team might be effective.

Components of the Implementation Plan

The following are elements of the implementation plan. Every implementation plan is different depending on exactly what has been redesigned. Moving equipment or buying new equipment might be part of the plan in one company and not in another. So, there is no one template. However, the following may at least prompt thinking by the design team laying out a proposed implementation plan.

1. Baseline Measurement

Part of the implementation should be the identification of four to eight key performance indicators that you expect to impact. There should be at least six months' worth of baseline data assembled and graphed. This data should serve both as a basis for evaluation of the implementation, and as the data that the teams in that organization should be monitoring daily, weekly or monthly. This data should be visually displayed so everyone working in that area can see it and see improvement.

- What are the key performance indicators?
- Who will gather the baseline data?
- Who will keep this data up-to-date?
- Where will it be displayed?

2. People Assignment and Preparation

Now it is time to assign specific people to specific positions. Typically, this will include naming the people to each team and their responsibilities on that team. It will also include naming team leaders and team coordinators if you have decided on those roles.

If you have designed different jobs in which different behavior is expected, you must be certain to provide training and coaching to help people adapt to those new jobs before implementation. If someone was a "supervisor" in the old system, and now she is to be a "team coordinator," for example, it is not rational to expect her to behave differently just because she has a new title. This job requires new skills and new behavior.

- Who is going to provide what training to prepare for the new jobs?
- The same question should be asked about the team members. Who will provide this training?
- Who will provide on-going coaching to these teams and team leaders?

3. Equipment and Technology Planning

Most redesigns include moving equipment, computers, new software, and a change in who will use of this technology. This is often one of the stumbling blocks in implementing a new design. Be sure that you have budgeted for buying or modifying any new equipment or software. Plan this well in advance because it has a tendency to show up late!

- What new or changed equipment is required?
- What new or different computers are required?
- What changes in software are required?
- Is new phone routing or numbers required?
- Which people will need to be trained in which technologies?
- Who will provide this training and when will this happen?
- Will you have a test run of the new technology before you "go live" with your new design?
- Is space planning required for office space changes in order to co-locate team members?

4. Symbols

If the design team has developed or changed symbols such as uniforms, names, hats, etc. how will these be implemented?

- List the different symbols that you have changed. What costs are associated with each?

- Have you received budget approval?
- Who will order them and distribute them? When?

5. Training Plan

In virtually every design there is a need for new or different skills on the part of everyone involved. Generally, these skills can be divided into those that are technical or functional, and those that are social or team skills. The design team needs to make a clear list of which skills need to be developed before "go live," and which ones can be on-going training after the implementation. You may have a matrix or table showing social and technical skills training; pre-implementation and post-implementation. This is an important consideration because if you go-live and people don't have the necessary skills you may experience unnecessary problems. [76]

- What technical skills are required before go-live?
- What social skills are required before go-live?
- What technical skills can/should be taught after go-live?
- What social skills are can/should be taught after go-live?
- Who will be responsible for providing each of the above?
- How will we know that the trainees are able to perform? How will we evaluate our training?

6. Human Resource Policy or Administration

In addition to training there are often other HR policies and practices that will need to change with redesign of the system. This can often be a problem to put in place before implementation. Too often the HR systems are viewed as fixed in stone, and HR professionals too often feel that they can veto changes. It must be made clear that the design team has, within its boundaries, the authority to redesign some HR practices as part of the "whole-system." It is wise to have an HR professional on the design team so they can both advise, but also understand the issues of alignment with the new principles and new design.

---

[76] This author's *Team Guide to Continuous Improvement* presents a complete training curriculum for both self-directed teams and management teams.

- What changes in titles have been made in the design, and who will make the appropriate changes in the HR database?
- What changes in compensation practices have been made, and who will institute those changes?
- Are there changes in how team members will be hired? Who is responsible for making those changes?
- Is job posting required for new positions? Who will do this and when?
- What changes in reward or recognition practices have been made and who will implement those?

7. Project Management

In addition to all of the above issues that should be on your project plan, you will want a plan for how you are going to manage the implementation, solve problems, and find improvement. It is very important that there be clear responsibility and effective teamwork during the implementation process. Teamwork between the operational area where the new design is being implemented and functions such as human resources, IT/IS and others is almost always essential. The implementation team should view this as a group learning project. Everyone will be learning and everyone is expert!

- Who will be on the Implementation Management Team?
- Who will be the site project manager and to whom will they report?
- When, where and how will the Implementation Management Team meet? Initially, they generally meet once a week, and then that can decrease in a few months after implementation.
- Who is the senior leader of the implementation process, and how will he or she report to the senior management team?
- Are all of the functional support areas represented on the Implementation Management Team?

All of the above tasks should be on your project plan and made visible to everyone involved. If you follow your project plan, if you consult well together as a team, and if you are prepared to solve problems and make improvements as they arise, you will be successful.

Congratulations!

Chapter 19

On Sustainability

In the introduction I briefly described the case of Merck's Cherokee Pharmaceutical plant where I had assisted in a whole-system design twenty years ago and the change has been sustained and improved over the years. I know of dozens of cases of significant and positive change that have been sustained. I also know of dozens of cases in which they have not been sustained. The reasons are not complicated.

Many leaders worry that their change efforts are not sustainable and they are too often right!

To understand sustainability we might look at larger changes in culture and ask why they are sustainable or not.

The American Revolutionary War transformed not only the system of governance; it also changed the culture of the former colonies. Our Civil War again changed the nature of our culture and system of governance. In neither case where those changes complete or final despite their significance. Yet, they were sustained. Why have those changes been sustained? In both cases there were changes on two levels. First, there was a change in sentiments, beliefs, leading to changes in personal behavior and leadership. This is the soft stuff. Second, there were significant changes in systems and structure that embedded the principles of the new culture in a practical process. This is the hard stuff. Both are necessary.

Before the Revolutionary War there was a process of dialogue among the colonists in which they debated the value of being loyal to the King of England versus the value of declaring independence. They openly discussed their grievances and pamphleteers, particularly Thomas Paine, argued the case and created a vision of a future country independent of England. But, once the war was engaged, pamphlets and sentiments were not enough. A Continental Congress had to be created and elections conducted. Following the war it became clear that the mandate of the Continental Congress was inadequate and a Constitutional Convention was formed to write a new Constitution that would define the new system of government.

I live in Annapolis, Maryland, where in 1786, twelve delegates from five states met to call for a Constitutional Convention. The formal title of the meeting was a *Meeting of Commissioners to Remedy Defects of the Federal Government.* The defects they sought to remedy were the trade barriers that limited and slowed commerce between the largely independent states.[77] In other words, they recognized that the silos of the organization structure of the states interrupted the flow of the commercial process through the newly formed nation. Sound familiar?

The Constitutional Convention was a design team, designing a structure that would balance the rights of individuals, states and a central government while eliminating barriers to commerce. They got it partly right, but it would be repeatedly modified with a Bill of Rights, and in the subsequent years, amendments giving full voting rights to women and ending slavery.

The ability of the government of the United States to be sustained was not based on trust in personalities, personal skills or sentiments. A new culture was embedded in the structure and systems, the process and principles of government. In both the early days and the final days of a culture personalities tend to dominate over principles and process. In maturity, principles and process take precedent over personalities. Reliance on personalities is never sustainable.

Examining large sustainable systems, as well as our experience changing the culture of organizations, what are the key lessons that we have learned for sustainable change management?

1. Don't Leave the *System* out of Toyota Production System:

Roland Sullivan, one of the original thought leaders of organization development, recently commented that too many OD professionals have left

---

[77] Richard B. Morris, *The Forging of the Union, 1781-1789* (1988) p. 255.

out the *organization* from *Organization Development.*[78] Similarly, too many lean or Toyota Production System consultants and writers have left out the *system* part of Toyota Production System. Too many lean change agents are comfortable with the tools such as 5S, the PDCA cycle, and process mapping, but have not understood the impact and importance of the structure and systems that embed the culture.

If you leave the old systems in place, such as how people are hired, trained, the definition of jobs, particularly management jobs, the information systems and organization structure, you will have left the old constitution and laws in place while trying to change behavior. The mechanisms of resistance to change are not simply the sentiments, skills or habits of people. The mechanism of resistance is the law – the Constitution, the formal systems that define decision-making, information flow and rewards. Change is not sustainable as long as this misalignment remains in place.

2. Allow for Amendments and Adaptation

Imagine what would have happened if there were no provisions for amending the Constitution. Women would still not have the right to vote, slavery would still be legal, and a President could be re-elected without end. Without a process of amendment it would have required a true revolution to make changes.

Some years ago my consultants did a whole-system design project in a Corning Fiber Optics plant. We always worked in partnership with an internal change agent. Five years after the original design the internal change agent came to one of our monthly consultant team meetings and gave a presentation on what had transpired in the five years after the initial design. He described how they had reformed the design team twice to make changes and improvements to the design. When I recently worked with Merck we formed a design team to recommended changes to their system. At HomeCare, the Implementation Steering Team, which meets regularly to assure implementation of their design, has made a number of small changes to the original design.

All living things are sustainable to the degree that they can adapt to changes in the external landscape and incorporate internal learning. The

---

[78] See LinkIn Whole-system Transformation discussion forum.

failure to adapt, to amend the system, will result in rigidity and rejection, and ultimately rebellion.

3. Leadership Continuity is Critical

If you have read the Harvard Business Review article by Steven J. Spears[79] on how Toyota develops leaders it will be clear that Bob Dallis (a fictional name used in the article) will not assume his job as plant manager and impose *His Way* on the organization. He has been thoroughly indoctrinated in the *Toyota Way* and he will be responsible for implementing that culture and that system while seeking continuous improvement.

Perhaps the single most common reason for the failure to sustain change is a lack of leadership continuity and the dominance of ego over the establishment of a system.

When I was working at the New Jersey refinery of one of the major oil companies it was explained to me how the management development process worked. There were two classes of people: those on the management fast track and the permanent residents of the refinery. The fast track managers were on two year assignments. They had to demonstrate some substantial change during their two years and then they would move on to a different location. They cared little about improvements that came before them. They had to stamp their name on some change. The permanent residents understood the process very well. They knew they had to nod their heads in approval and act like they were implementing the change. However, they kept on doing their work as they always had, knowing their manager would disappear before he realized he had accomplished nothing. This was their survival strategy. The game went on and everyone played their roles. The young fast-track managers never stayed long enough to experience the lasting consequences of their changes.

In many large companies, plant managers or similar mid-level leaders, have a typical two to five year period in their job. They are strongly motivated to demonstrate how they have personally made change, rather than reinforcing a company culture and company system. The changes at the Merck plant sustained for twenty years, not simply because of the five plant managers that rotated through during that period, but because the system had

---

[79] Spears, Steven J. *Learning to Lead at Toyota*. Harvard Business Review, May, 2004.

been embedded in the union contract, it had been designed by the people in the plant, and it was continuously improved. The ego of any manager was subordinate to the system.

4. Every System is a Sub-System of a Larger System

I began my career working in North Carolina prisons where I established the first free economy behind prison walls. It was an experiment. We created a luxury, quality, standard and efficiency dorm and the inmates had to pay rent accordingly. They were paid a salary, by check, for the work they did in the work areas. The check was for "points" not real money. Their pay was determined by the skill level of the job they did. It worked. We nearly doubled production in the work area. It was working like a real economy. Good behavior resulted in good consequences and they were learning to earn.

All my inmates were in the 16 to 21 year-old range. I ran the system for three years and there was a plan for them to earn their way out of this medium security prison to a minimum security prison and then on to parole, all based on their demonstrated performance. That was the plan. However, one day I showed up at the prison and my entire population was being sent to other prison units while this one was being populated with 50+ year old convicts. It blew up my entire plan! A new Governor appointed a new Commissioner of Corrections and he knew nothing about what we were doing and decided to re-allocate the prison population.

The prison, like a corporate facility, was a sub-system of a larger system. The entire correctional system was a sub-system of a larger socio-political system. My experiment, as worthwhile as it may have been, was not sustainable without creating change in the larger system of governance.

Far too often this exact same story is played out in our corporations. Worthy experiments producing positive results are overwhelmed by the larger corporate system. It is not true that small and successful experiments will then be adopted by the larger system. We wish that were so, but I can provide dozens of examples that prove the opposite.

A well-known author of books on lean management recently explained to me that his system of change was to take a model work cell on a line and implement the PDCA cycle and demonstrate results, hoping that this would be recognized and then lead to further adoption. My experience is that this will not work. Every manufacturing plant or facility is a village, a culturally cohesive unit. The village culture will most often overwhelm cultural deviations within the village. For a very long time I have refused to implement "experiments" within a village. Change the whole village together! The larger the system in which you can create change, the more likely that change will be sustained. Do not under estimate the force of cultural cohesion.

5. Develop and Reward the Habits of Continuous Improvement

Much of this blog and my books are focused on designing the systems of the organization, but that should not diminish the importance of developing the skills and habits, the *Kata*, [80] of continuous improvement.

In addition to redesigning systems, it will be important to train every team in the new organization to work as a team, engage in daily problem-solving, track and understand their data, and become experts in eliminating waste and variances from their process. I have outlined a complete process of team development in order to develop these habits in two workbooks.[81] These workbooks present learning modules that are each paired with DELIVERABLES, actions, that themselves are the source of learning. This is an action-learning model and has proven successful in the development of hundreds of teams.

The following is an accountability or progress reporting diagram that indicates where a team is in their progress toward becoming a high performance team. With every team in the organization developing the same skills and practices, the culture will change and those habits will become the norm. But the leaders must both practice these skills themselves, and they must reinforce these behaviors in others.

---

[80] Rother, Mike, *Toyota Kata.* New York, 2010, McGraw-Hill, New York.

[81] *HealthCare Lean – The Team Guide to Continuous Improvement,* Miller Management Press, LLC, 2012. *The Team Guide to Continuous Improvement,* Miller Management Press, LLC, 2013.

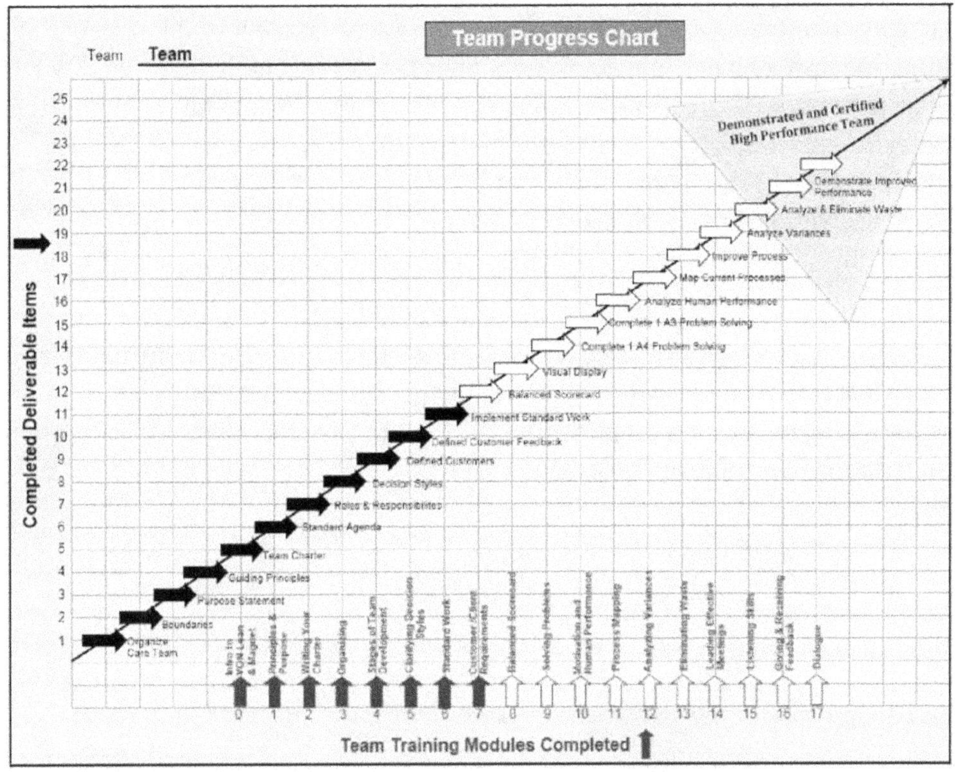

6. Build Internal Change Leadership Competence:

Having been in the consulting "game" for forty years now (I'm ashamed to say!), it is very clear to me that the major consulting firms structure their business to perpetuate additional contracts, rather than to build internal competence and independence on the part of their clients. As a business strategy, this is perfectly understandable.

I am not anti-consultant. After all, I are one! However, I feel that the goal should be to partner with clients in a way that builds their internal competence in managing change.

The longer a client is dependent on a consultant the less likely it is that the consultant is transferring his or her competence to the client organization and building capacity within the client firm. The less internal change management competence is developed, the less sustainable will be change efforts.

I recently completed an assignment at a manufacturing plant where seventy one teams are implementing lean practices in every department and function and at every level of the organization. Everyone is involved. My role was to work with the senior team of the plant and to train and coach fourteen internal coaches, both salaried and hourly, who serve as coaches to all of the other teams. Who learns the most in this scheme? Of course, the internal coaches who have to turn around and train all of the other teams. They now have the capacity to carry on the process indefinitely. As a team of coaches they meet and learn from each other. This is building internal capacity.

I am sure that there are other keys to sustainability. But in my experience the most important key is to align the formal systems with the landscape and create internal system alignment; and then, to provide for modification and adaptation over time. It works!

Appendix

The following articles are included because they each offer examples of redesigned or alternative organizations that may provide some inspiration or insight for your own work, or they represent a particular method employed in whole-system architecture.

1. Case Study: The Conference Method of Redesign.
2. Case Study: The Honda Way
3. Case Study: Reconciling STS and Lean
4. To Centralize Or Decentralize; And, To Standardize Or Customize.

A CASE STUDY

THE CONFERENCE METHOD OF REDESIGN

BY ALAN WILGUS[82]

It had been a long day, and the fifty-six participants had worked hard. But there was electricity in the large conference room.

As they stood around the back wall, they focused on six pieces of flipchart paper. Each flipchart reflected the thinking of a different subgroup on the ideal organizational structure. As they reported out each group's ideas, it became clear that there was great similarity in their thinking.

Based on the criteria given for forming teams, eliminating redundant and non-value-adding work, and their collective vision of the future, they had eliminated two of the five levels of management while organizing teams around products rather than function. No one agonized about how management would receive this because the entire group (including the plant manager) participated in its design.

Although frightened by the day's implications, the participants left that afternoon feeling satisfied that they had made the best choice for ensuring the future success of their plant, and closeness to one another they had rarely experienced in their work life. This closeness was the result not of some structured team building activity, but of a realization that whether a manager, supervisor, or employee they shared a common future. Despite the differences which had separated them for years, there was tremendous similarity in what they aspired to become as members of a manufacturing plant and as individuals.

---

[82] Alan Wilgus was one of my excellent consultants at my former Miller-Howard Consulting Group.

The twelve-person design team hung around afterward and within sixty minutes had reconciled the differences in the six subgroup proposals. The organization had accomplished in one day what normally takes weeks (if not months) using a traditional design team process! Not only had they saved time, they had created a critical mass of support for the new structure by involving almost one-third of the total organization in its design.

How did they do it? They employed a Conference Method for redesigning organizations, whose potential is just now being explored. Compared to traditional socio-technical or reengineering efforts it saves time and money, while increasing buy-in to the change effort without sacrificing quality of design. Sound to good to be true? Well it is true. This article reviews the evolution of the Conference Method of Redesign (CMR), its application in two similar manufacturing facilities, and lessons learned.

The Origins Of The Conference Method Of Redesign

Modern thinking about organizational redesign in large part originated with work conducted by two social scientists, Fred Emery and Eric Trist. Their fieldwork in the English coal mines in 1949 formed the basis for what developed as a theory for organizational design. Trist referred to this as socio-technical systems (STS). Many important contributions have been made over the years in expanding this body of knowledge to its current form.

Stated simply, any organization can be viewed as an open system consisting of work processes, tools, and techniques (the technical system) around which people interact and are organized for a common purpose (the social system). The effectiveness of any organization is related to the choices made in the design of these two systems. These choices are dictated by economic, technical, political, and social influences externally and human values internally. Effectively designed social systems typically provide teamwork, affiliation, connection to customers, knowledge of performance, control over the process and quality of one's work, and an opportunity for growth and learning. This is in sharp contrast to the teachings of Frederick Taylor, whose concepts of specialization, simple tasks, and highly-engineered jobs often reduced people to mere extensions of the technology.

Based on STS theory, organizational design efforts today frequently take the form of a cross-functional design team who have been chartered by a steering committee (normally the senior leaders) to design a more effective organization. Within this charter is an analysis of external influences and how the organization must change in response to these influences, a customer analysis, a vision of what the company aspires to become in the future, and the guiding principles or values which will guide behavior. The steering committee develops this charter and presents it to the design team and the organization. The design team then meets over a period of six to twelve months (usually with a consultant's help) and completes a redesign proposal for approval by the steering committee. The design effort consists of two parts, as you might expect: social and technical.

The technical portion includes an analysis of current state work processes, key variances, and a process cycle-time analysis. Relationship maps or flow charts are constructed which reflect each step in the process and are highly effective in highlighting redundancies, waste, delays, and other non-value-adding work.

The social analysis consists of an examination of structure, responsibilities, decision-making, skills, human support systems (e.g. hiring, training, discipline, recognition, compensation, etc.), symbols, and style. Based on the charter, the design team redesigns the organization to align the systems. Upon approval, the new design is communicated to the rest of the organization and the implementation phase begins.

In 1960 Emery and Trist pioneered an organizational planning process which they labeled the "Future Search Conference." It consisted of a multi-day conference gathering large groups of stakeholders together, often representing conflicting interests or adversarial positions. The participants' objectives were to explore and understand their similarities and differences, dwelling not on the differences but using their similarities as the basis for creating their common future. This was accomplished through a series of structured activities focusing on environmental influences, organizational responses, and reactions to both. Emery carried this initial work forward and has since refined the conference methodology. The process has been applied in many different ways since and popularized by Marvin Weisbord in his books *Productive Workplaces* (1987) and *Discovering Common Ground* (1992).

What is particularly intriguing about Future Search is the technique for involving large groups of people in planning their future rather than using a few managers, consultants, or even a twelve-person design team. Our experience has taught us that some of the best designs are never implemented due to lack of buy-in by the organization. The other fascinating aspect of this technique is speed. Many a design process has been thrown into chaos during its nine month existence due to a change in corporate direction or a take over.

What if you applied the search conference methodology to the process of socio-technical design? A few people, like consultant Dick Axelrod, were piloting the approach, but little information was available when we began our process. Of particular interest to us was our ability to incorporate the technique into the Miller design process, Whole-system architecture. These questions were being explored about the time an opportunity to try this new approach presented itself.

Client Background

We had been working with a major textile company for almost two years. A leader in the textile industry, their Grey Division manufactures cloth used for making sheets and pillowcases. The Division consists of fourteen plants spread over North and South Carolina. Each plant was similar in that it transformed cotton and polyester into cloth; however, they were different in the type of fabric, technology used, physical plant, and size.

The company attributes much of its success to a visionary leadership style which has continually challenged the organization to improve. On the heels of a massive technical modernization project, they committed to redesigning their plants from traditionally managed to a team-based culture and organization. Most plants consisted of approximately three hundred employees, although a few had as many as eight hundred.

The Miller Consulting Group was hired to help the company redesign their plants and began with a traditional approach that we have successfully applied over the last ten years. Using a cross-functional design team we completed the pilot plant after nine months. The Division steering committee was impressed with the results and gave the green light to begin work in three other plants. Over the next few months the design efforts progressed well. However, there were issues that became quite troubling, such as:

1. How can we avoid "re-inventing the wheel" by utilizing ideas from the initial plant redesign efforts? Given the similarities between plants, must we start each new design with a blank sheet of paper?

2. Future designs will become increasingly constrained as the Division steering committee approves design team recommendations applicable to all plants across the Division. For example, based on the recommendation of the

initial design effort, a gainsharing program and elimination of individual incentives was approved. This redesigned compensation system would apply across the Division, meaning that future design teams would not even consider this area.

3. Given these issues, how do we ensure that plants continue to experience ownership and commitment to their design?

4. How do we accelerate the process while at the same time reducing costs? Even by redesigning three plants at a time it would take at least two more years at our current pace. Clearly our current redesign process must change if we are to adequately address our client's concerns.

What emerged in a series of planning meetings over the next few months was a means of redesigning the remaining ten plants using the Future Search methodology. We proposed that subsequent plant designs consist of a series of three conferences involving fifty to eighty plant personnel. Participants would include the entire group of managers and supervisors, customers and suppliers, and a representative number of associates from each functional area. The manager/supervisor group would attend all three conferences, as would a design team, but participation by other employees would rotate to involve as many different people as possible. Conferences consisted of a series of design tasks completed by subgroups of eight to twelve people.

A ten-person design team was designated and trained; however, their role was different than a traditional design effort. The design team's job was to gather, edit, and compile data from flip charts generated during each conference; reconcile differences; present conference results to those not participating and seek their input; serve as subject matter experts during each conference; assist their subgroup in understanding the design process and design tools employed; actively participate in subgroup activities (not necessarily as the facilitator); and review the design proposal for alignment prior to presenting to the steering committee. Select members would serve on the implementation team following the design phase.

Managing a conference of this size required ground rules. Ours were:

1. All participants have an equal voice.

2. The focus is not on solving problems as much as sharing perceptions and increasing understanding.

3. Challenge assumptions.

4. Avoid defensiveness.

5. Accept responsibility for conference results.

Subgroups were self-managed in the sense that they provided their own leadership, facilitation, and time management. We proposed to pilot this method simultaneously in two plants. Part of our strategy also included working ourselves out of a job. The company was looking for an alternative to using Miller consultants for future redesigns and incurring the associated costs. Our solution was to train two Division people to be conference managers. They would watch me conduct the pilot in the first plant and then co-facilitate the same conference a week later in the second pilot plant (I was there if they needed me). Conceptually, what we proposed made sense, but would we get the results we wanted? We were about to find out.

The Vision Conference

Although it is patterned after a Future Search conference, the Vision Conference differs significantly. Under normal circumstances this conference would concern itself with reviewing past history, scanning the present environment, and creating a desired future state. The vision that emerges then becomes design criteria for the two subsequent conferences. This work had already been accomplished by the Division steering committee, and what resulted was a comprehensive mission statement. A copy hung somewhere in each of the fourteen plants. However, no one really knew what it meant since they had not been involved in its creation. Each plant needed to examine the existing mission statement and translate it into something meaningful to them -- into a plant vision.

The conference was divided into three parts. The first focused on the future. In mixed subgroups (cross-functional and cross-hierarchical), participants reviewed the Division mission statement and identified the top six organizational values. Examples of organizational values include customer focus, mutual trust, share responsibility, etc. The groups reported out and quickly came to consensus. Next, they reconfigured into groups reflecting organizational levels (e.g. plant leadership team, supervisors, salaried support staff, and front line worker) where each group was asked to describe specific behaviors they would demonstrate if they were acting in accordance with each value. They then described what they would expect to see behaviorally from the other groups.

As each group reported their findings, what was most striking was the similarities. Senior leaders believed they should behave in ways that were identical to the expectations of the other groups. These similarities were reflected between the other levels as well. The day ended with the table groups selecting different organizational values and doing a short role play of their applications in the plant. This was fun for the group and helped further define their vision of the future.

The second day began by focusing on the past and present. Taking a page out of the Future Search process, mixed subgroups identified those things they were proudest of and sorriest for in their relationship with the company. The purpose was to acknowledge those things about the company that were good and that they wanted to bring into the future and to admit what practices should be left behind. Again, the similarity was striking as groups presented their work. Managers openly admitted that in the past they were often insensitive to employee needs and turned a deaf ear to their ideas and suggestions. Employees talked about just "doing their eight and hitting the gate" while ignoring quality problems. Those practices left behind, or sorries, often represented the loss of something valued in some way. We discussed as a group the stages of loss and actually had a brief ceremony during which the sorries were eulogized and laid to rest. This was an important step in letting go and moving forward.

During the Vision Conference, key customers and suppliers participated in each activity either as a member of the leadership team subgroup or as a member of a mixed group. Their perspective was valuable in creating a plant vision and identifying opportunities to improve service and relationships. While they were identifying current and future requirements, the rest of the groups were identifying potential obstacles which might prevent them from realizing their vision and actions they could take to prevent those obstacles from happening. By the end of the Vision Conference, participants, perhaps for the first time, recognized that there was far more that brought them together than separated them.

Between Conference Activities

At the conclusion of each conference the design team sprang into action, gathering flipcharts and consolidating information produced during the conference. They conducted employee presentations and asked for additional input from those employees not in attendance. This not only kept the rest of the organization informed but provided a forum for their reaction and ideas. The output of each of the first two conferences became input to the next. For example, the Vision Conference provided design criteria for the Technical and Social Conferences. The Technical Conference output was necessary for redesigning the social system.

Preparations began immediately for the next conference. Workbooks were assembled, reference materials were gathered, and examples of what others had done were collected. Just the logistics to support the effort required detailed coordination from all parties involved.

THE TECHNICAL CONFERENCE

Approximately three weeks after the Vision Conference ends the Technical Conference begins. In terms of amount of work involved, the Technical Conference is the hardest. Again, the key to a successful conference lies in detailed preparation. To allow for both self-management within subgroups as well as successful task completion, all involved need clearly defined tasks, examples, and supporting worksheet materials.

To prepare for this conference we enlisted the help of each of the plant industrial engineers, who provided two items which expedited the technical analysis: a cycle-time analysis reflecting the entire manufacturing flow from inputs to outputs, and a plant floor plan depicting the facility design, equipment layout, and material flow. In addition, examples of work completed by earlier design teams were made available to the Technical Conference attendees, not for the purpose of asking them to "rubber stamp" it but to use it as a point of departure. (At the outset we feared the subgroups might think we were manipulating the direction of their thinking through use of the examples. However, as similar as their technology might be, the steps in their processes were often radically different. It never became an issue in either pilot plant.)

The Technical Conference was divided into two parts:

1. Analysis of the current state technical system, and

2. Redesign or creation of the ideal state.

The first day was spent analyzing the current state. Subgroups were configured based on functional area with management personnel equally distributed. As a large group, we reviewed the state changes within their manufacturing process (how the material is transformed at each step from input to output). This focused them on the core process rather than on what people do (which may or may not be related). After a brief explanation and demonstration of process mapping, each subgroup began to identify the steps in their part of the process and prepare a "relationship map," which traces the flow of activity and also identifies delays, transportation steps, decisions, and inspections. Using this tool, subgroups quickly identified opportunities for improvement. For example, if routine manufacturing decisions had to be elevated two levels, it became obvious that work cycle time would be reduced by placing decision-making in the hands of those closest to the process.

Once process maps were prepared, the subgroups reviewed the plant layout and material flow. The purpose here was to identify wasted movement. The groups quickly began to identify improvement opportunities and recorded them on flipcharts. Groups in both plants completed this portion of the analysis in two and a half hours!

The afternoon was spent analyzing key variances and cycle times. The last part of the day was spent reporting out to the large group each subgroup analysis. Beginning with the introduction of raw materials, each subgroup took its turn in sharing their findings. This resulted in tremendous learning. In a traditional organization, few people (managers included) actually understand their entire work process. At the end of the day, although tired, all involved were excited by the learning that had taken place and by realizing opportunities to improve.

Day two shifted from current state to the future. We began with a review of the Vision Conference and identified design criteria applicable to our technical system. In an effort to break people out of their "current state" mind-set and free their minds for creative thought, we brought in a member of the corporate R&D department who presented examples of state-of-the-art textile manufacturing facilities from around the world, many of which were fully automated. There were also examples of applications of the principles of "just-In-time" manufacturing techniques. This presentation not only expanded the participants' thinking, it scared the heck out of them! After the R&D representative left we spent a few minutes as a large group sharing our fears. We took a minute and reached back to one of the "obstacles to success" we identified during the Vision Conference, and guess what it was ? "Fear of change." We acknowledged that it was all right to experience fear of change as long as it didn't paralyze us and prevent us from thinking creatively.

The first subgroup activity was to generate an environment for breakthrough thinking. In mixed groups they brainstormed "wild ideas" that represented not just improvements to the current system, but ideas that would propel them far beyond their competition. This turned out to be not only productive but energizing and fun. After they reported to the group, the subgroups reconfigured into functional groups to create the ideal technical design for their plant. The redesign was a synthesis of:

1. "Wild ideas" applicable to their area;

2. Opportunities for improvement recorded during the current state analysis;

3. Observations based on a review of the plant layout and material flow;

4. Ideas about how to eliminate key variances or at least control them as close to the source as possible;

5. Customer requirements;

6. Design criteria gleaned from the plants vision; and finally

7. We introduced ideal state designs from one of the initial design team efforts. (We waited until now so their creativity would not be stifled.)

As subgroups began their work, it became obvious that as functional areas they could not redesign in a vacuum. Not only did new thinking about how work was conducted break down functional walls, but a decision one group makes often has severe downstream consequences. We encouraged them to coordinate their efforts and interact with each other to ensure alignment of recommendations. To the casual observer this probably looked like chaos, but it was beautiful to watch in action.

By the next day the groups presented an ideal state process map, reconfigured plant layouts and material flows, and a list of technical improvements and the benefits of each. The most touching experience I had was with a yarn department subgroup who asked for my advice. They looked concerned and appeared to be struggling with a tough issue. An hourly spokesperson for the group looked up at me and stated that after much analysis, they had discovered a way to modify the production process in a way that would eliminate a part of their function as well as their current jobs. It seemed the sensible thing to them, but they weren't sure they could make that type of recommendation. Such courage, commitment, and trust does not just happen. I attribute much of it to the cohesive team spirit created during the conference process.

THE SOCIAL CONFERENCE

The social system of an organization has the greatest impact on human creativity, teamwork, and motivation, and yet many reengineering efforts fail to address this important dimension. Unique to our approach is a separate conference developed to specifically address social system design. Our model is based on the five S's: structure, skills, style, symbols and human systems. Each element is impacted by changes in the environment and must be aligned with the vision, values, and technical system.

The third and final conference designs the ideal social system. This conference is tough because the issues hit close to home, such as "Will I have a job?" "What is my new role?" "Will I lose the management perks I worked so hard to earn?" At this point in traditional redesign, design teams feel a tremendous pressure not to "sell their buddies down the river." They will agonize for days as to whether they are making the correct recommendations and will often rebel against the facilitator when pressed for a decision.

In a conference setting, the design team is under no such pressure. What emerges is a practical consensus based on sharing across all levels in the organization. Whether the ideas are the plant manager's or an hourly employee's, they must be supported logically and be consistent with the plant vision. This open forum builds understanding and agreements. We used an opening exercise where participants shared characteristics of their "best" job. This demonstrated that regardless of level, employees are motivated and obtain job satisfaction in the same way. Through this exercise they identified additional criteria by which to evaluate their redesign.

As with the Technical Conference, there was an attempt to cause people to think differently about the possible choices in organizing around their work. Through the use of video and case study examples the participants were presented with alternatives to their current social system. This was the most lecture-intensive day of any of the conferences (about two and a half hours). The first task was for mixed subgroups to design an ideal team structure. Care was taken to set up this task through discussions about how to draw team boundaries from the bottom-up. Subgroups designed the team structure and determined each team's responsibilities and decision-making authority. The six groups shared their ideas and similarities were noted. It was understood that the design team would reconcile the differences.

Day two began with the same subgroups brainstorming "symbols." Symbols exist in every culture as a means of communicating values. It is the message rather than the symbol that is meaningful. For example, neckties themselves have little meaning. We all might wear them from time to time (to weddings, church, dinner, etc.). However, when worn in the workplace by senior management they may be a symbol that communicates the wearers are different (somehow better) than others, distinguish decision-makers from doers, people in charge from those not in charge, and serve to divide people rather than bring them together. The subgroups examined symbols in their plant and determined the intent of the symbol; the common perception of its meaning; and whether it was divisive or in support of their key concepts/values. They then recommended to either keep it, eliminate it, or change it and suggested any new symbols they felt were necessary.

As the final activity, we distributed a different redesign task to each of the six subgroups. For example, one group redesigned the hiring, orientation, and transfer process. Another group worked on recognition and safety. The goal was to align human support systems with the plant's key concepts or values through identifying minimum critical specifications for each. Again, the use of examples from other designs expedited this task by providing a point of departure from which the groups freely moved.

Conference evaluations during both pilots were unanimously positive. The only criticism was that the whole organization of three hundred employees could not attend each conference. Both plant managers were highly satisfied with the results and shared the same sense of camaraderie and commitment as the other participants.

Lessons Learned

The entire effort was completed for both plants in two and a half months. After this rather hectic period, we evaluated our efforts and some key learning's were noted:

1. The design process (or more specifically, the whole-system architecture design process) lends itself to the conference methodology. Given clear instructions, carefully structured tasks, examples, and support materials even a relatively unsophisticated audience can quickly learn and practically apply analytical design tools such as relationship mapping and structural design.

2. Our fear that we would sacrifice quality for speed was never realized. In fact, the opposite occurred. Given the number of participants providing input and the synergy created, the quality was actually better.

3. There continues to be a need for a design team. Although their role is much different than described earlier, consensus is difficult if not impossible to achieve with a group of sixty to eighty participants. By focusing on similarities, a consensus emerges naturally during each conference. And where it doesn't, participants who have had the opportunity to voice their opinion feel free to defer to a cross-functional design team.

4. Creating a forum for personal sharing leads to a recognition of a common fate and similar aspirations and values. This brings people together in extremely powerful ways. (I had not anticipated just how much.)

5. It is impossible to facilitate a design process for sixty plus people. Don't try. Participants are capable of self-management when given clear, concise guidance. Detailed planning is the key to success.

6. Each of the three conferences is uniquely different in how people are engaged. During the Vision Conference, people are dealing from the heart. Discussions are lofty and future-focused, and consensus is easy. The Technical Conference requires a lot of mental work. Participants spend most of their time in objective analysis or creative brainstorming. And the Social Conference hits people in the gut because it is no longer something way off in the future or to be objectively examined, it now impacts them personally. In each successive conference the issues draw closer. The same feelings and emotion experienced by a design team working six or nine months is compressed into three conferences.

The Conference Method of Redesign offers many advantages over traditional methods. But is it always the answer? Probably not. When a complex, non-linear work process is the subject of redesign, a Technical Conference may not be sufficient. In this case, a design team might conduct a current state technical analysis and then convene a conference to create the ideal state. As with any design effort, one size rarely fits all.

Does this method represent input to a design team or a way to do design itself? I see it as both: a process of "co-design" between the team and each conference. The participants ask little from the design team, but need them to act as the "honest broker" for change where consensus fails to emerge. Generally, consensus does emerge and agreements are reached in a way that creates a critical mass for change. As the pace of change increases and resources shrink, organizations can ill afford to spend six to twelve months on a design process that merely sits on a shelf for lack of buy-in and commitment. I believe the Conference Method of Redesign will become the standard for redesign in the future.

A Case Study
The Honda Way

I wrote the following case study in 1989. Many of the details may be out of date. However, the important lessons of building and aligning a culture will never be out of date.

As you read this you may wish to consider your own culture and how it has been designed to maximize human performance, quality and customer satisfaction. The following graphic is one way to describe the influences, internal and external, on the culture of any organization. I organized my observations as I visited Honda's plant according to this model.

During the early days of Honda America Manufacturing's operations in Marysville, Ohio, they used my book American Spirit as a management development text. This resulted in several invitations to visit and present to the Honda management group and supplier groups. I wrote the following after my first two day visit to the Marysville plants.

I spent two days touring the plants, speaking with managers and production associates, sitting in on meetings, and asking lots of questions. Why is Honda so good? The answer is both simple and complex. It is a combination of technical, or work process design; and, their unique culture.

There is nothing that stands out as their single secret to quality. The secret is - they do everything -and they do it as a team!

I find that in every healthy corporate culture there is a common understanding of philosophy, the values and visions upon which decisions and practices are based. The management practices, the structure, systems, skills, style, and symbols are consistent with the philosophy. At Honda there is clearly a "Team" culture.

Before entering the building the philosophy was evident. As we drove toward the plant I noticed lines of newly planted trees. I was told that they were planted by newly hired associates. Each new associate plants a tree "so they can grow with the company." All associates (the term used for all employees) know the company philosophy. They hear it consistently from their leaders. There are no contradictions.

The president of Honda of America is Shoichiro Irimajiri, known as Mr. Iri by the associates. Earlier in his career, Mr. Iri was responsible for managing Honda's successful racing efforts, designing engines and managing production facilities in Japan. He frequently speaks of the "Racing Spirit." The Racing Spirit includes five principles:

1. ***Seek the challenger.***
2. ***Be ready on time.***
3. ***Teamwork.***
4. ***Quick Response.***
5. ***Winner Takes All!***

Perhaps more instructive of the Honda philosophy is his story of one of his early racing efforts.

It was in 1965 when Mr. Iri was working on the Formula One racing engines. In the British Grand Prix of that year, the engine failed and it was torn down and examined by Mr. Honda himself.

Examining the failed piston he turned to Shoichiro Irimajiri and demanded, "Who designed this piston?" "I did," he acknowledged. After examining the engineering drawing Mr. Honda roared out, 'You! Stupid! No wonder the piston gets burned. You have changed the thickness here."

After the young Irimajiri attempted to defend his design change with some data from previous engines, Mr. Honda roared again: "I hate college graduates! They use only their heads. Do you really think you can use such obsolete data obtained from old, low-performance engines? I have been making and designing pistons for several years. I am fully aware how critical half a millimeter is here. A company does not need people like you who use only their heads. Before you laid out this design, why didn't you listen to opinions of those experienced people in the shop? If you think academic study in college is everything, you are totally wrong. You will be useless in Honda unless you spend more time on-the-spot for many years to come."

"You will go to the machining shop," Mr. Honda ordered the young engineer, "and you will apologize to every person there, for you have wasted their efforts." Mr. Honda followed him down the hall to make sure he did as directed. Mr. Iri recalls that he was only glad that he had no ambition of becoming president of the company. He was not even sure he would succeed as an engineer. He learned his lesson. He not only succeeded as an engineer, designing several successful racing engines, but he became the president of Honda of America, the first Japanese company to export cars back to Japan. Shoichiro Irimajiri still listens to those experienced people in the shop and he is not wasting their time.

The Honda philosophy stresses to be on-the-spot in the plant and see the problem, touch the part, and gain experience in the actual job, in order to effectively solve a problem. Engineers and management spend most of their time in the factory, in touch with their associates, the product, and the process. The Honda philosophy is manifested in all of the management practices. In the symbols, structure, systems, skills, and style , the philosophy can be seen and experienced every day, by every employee, every hour.

SYMBOLS:

When I arrived at the Marysville plant I was given a uniform to wear in the plant. I was told that this wasn't given to all guests, only "honored guests." To cover my tie with the white smock with the Honda name, to look the same as every other associate, was an honor. I can assure you that by the time my visit was finished it felt like an honor. To be part of a proud group of people, to share their symbol of equality, caused me to feel a part, invested, in their shared goals.

All associates, from president to newest hired associate, eat in the same cafeteria, park in the same undesignated parking spaces, and managers sit at the same metal desks in open office areas. Most of the desks are arranged in blocks of six, often with paired Japanese and American managers sitting across from one another. All of the managers of the motorcycle plant sit at one block of six identical desks, the Japanese vice-president and the American plant manager sitting across from each other.

As I walked through the plant, the cleanest non-food manufacturing plant out of several hundred I have been in, I observed a vice-president stop and pick up a misplaced object on the floor. There is nothing on the floor. There are also no maintenance people to clean up! Everyone, every associate and manager, cleans his or her own work area.

To many, these symbols will seem trivial. They would be if they stood alone, at odds with the behavior and attitudes of the people, or if the structure and systems stood in contradiction. However, they are one part of a total system, like a well-engineered engine with all components balanced and moving in unison. Symbols, structure, systems, skills and style are all aligned.

STRUCTURE:

Everyone is a member of a team. The team is the first level of organization. At 6:30 AM each day, every associate meets with his team and team leader. The day's work is discussed and feedback on the previous day's quality is given. Any problems, changes, or concerns are shared during this meeting.

A team is comprised of 15 to 20 associates who work in a common area. As I toured both the auto and motorcycle plant, I stood and watched the assembly line in operation. I asked which person was the team leader and which was the production coordinator, the second-level manager. It was very hard to find them or distinguish them. I watched as there was an apparent problem on the motorcycle line.

One employee, having difficulty getting a frame over an engine assembly, had stopped the line. He and another associate worked frantically to get the frame in place. It took about twenty seconds for the line to move again. I asked where the team leader was. The other associate, helping to form the frame, was the team leader. The production coordinator was at the next station on the assembly line helping another associate catch up on the placement of electrical wire assemblies. I watched for about fifteen minutes as the team leader and production coordinator (equivalent of first-line supervisor and department manager) worked on the line, smiling, joking, and working hard and fast with their associates.

Nowhere is there a private office for team leaders or production coordinators. They do not remove themselves from the work. They are on-the-spot, seeing and touching the product, gaining experience and solving problems. They are part of the working team.

All managers are organized into teams and solve problems together. The structure of the organization, as well as the physical arrangement of desks and offices, makes group problem-solving a natural and constant occurrence.

Participation in the continuous improvement process is also structured through Quality Circles. NH Circles (NH stands for "Now Honda, New Honda, Next Honda") are similar to quality circles in many other companies.

However, at Honda they are one component of a total involvement process which they call of VIP (Voluntary Involvement Program).

VIP includes a suggestion system, quality awards, and safety awards. Twenty percent of all associates participate in circles. The rate of suggestion adoption is 59.4 percent, and 60 percent participate in some component of the VIP process. In speaking with several NH Circle members, I was impressed that they felt the responsibility to see that accepted recommendations for improvement were implemented. They also felt that their circles were different from those in other companies in that they are constantly looking for any improvement in the production process, large or small, and even small improvements are highly valued. They said that the success of Honda was the result of constantly finding small improvements, not just looking for major ones.

SYSTEM:

I expected to find systems of employee involvement at Marysville. However, I was somewhat surprised to see the amount of thought put into the positive reinforcement systems. Honda of America practices performance management, or as I used to call it "behavior management." They have found ways to provide constant feedback, recognition, and tangible positive reinforcement for almost every form of desirable performance.

The NH Circle program, suggestion system, quality awards, and safety awards are all tied together with a point system. Every associate earns points by participating in any of these improvement processes. Awards include award certificates, gift certificates, Department Manager's Award, Plant Manager's Award, and President's Award. These also result in points accumulating over your career, and these points can earn a Honda Civic (that's for 2,500 points) and an Accord (5,000 points), plus two weeks off with pay and airplane tickets to anywhere in the world with spending money.

In addition to hourly or salaried compensation, all associates participate in profit sharing. This profit sharing is an innovation of Honda of America and is not part of the system in Japan. Ten percent of the gross profit generated by Honda Motor Company is shared with associates based on their relative compensation. Good attendance results in another bonus. The average bonus check for attendance in 1986 was $832. The average profit sharing check was $2,688.

Performance analysis and feedback is an important part of any total performance management system. In each of the open office areas and in each of the many conference rooms, all of the walls are literally covered with charts and graphs representing different quality and productivity performance variables. The graphs are of every possible variety, some employing Statistical Process Control methods and some simply reflecting historical data with means, trends, and goal lines. Frequently, along with the charts on the wall are lists of causes or solutions to problems. Diagrams of auto parts or production machinery with arrows pointing to sources of problems are also frequent. It is obvious that all of the managers at Honda are in touch with plant performance data.

Another system worthy of mention is the discipline system. There are some fairly traditional and sound procedures for gradual counseling and discipline. However, the unique part of the discipline process is the peer review provided for associates who are dismissed for poor conduct. If an associate wishes to appeal a termination, a peer review panel is formed by randomly selecting six or eight production associates. One senior manager also serves on the panel with equal vote. The panel hears both sides of the case and then decides to overturn or accept the management decision. Nine out of ten times the decisions are upheld by the associates.

SKILLS:

The measure of skills is found in the work product. There is no question Honda has highly skilled engineering and quality personnel. Most engineers are Japanese. Hiring and training more Americans is a goal for coming years. Honda is an engineering company. Most of the Japanese senior managers have served as design engineers for engines, including racing engines, or other components.

Having worked at other auto companies, it soon became obvious to me that at Honda the most valued personnel are those with engineering and technical competence. At many other companies, it is the financial managers and management professionals who are most valued. Honda is in the business of making excellent cars. Many other companies are in the business of making money, and, only secondarily, making cars. Honda makes money and does not need layers of bureaucratic managers because they are passionately dedicated to their technology and products.

On the assembly line, there is a process of continual skill development. Associates are rotated from one position to another to broaden their skills and increase their flexibility. Even when applicants are interviewed for employment at Honda, they are asked questions to determine their flexibility. Flexibility and the development of broad-based skills is a central principle.

At Honda, it is assumed the production associates are intelligent, skilled, and dedicated. They can, therefore, be trusted to manage the quality process. Every associate is a quality control inspector. The assembly process at Honda is based on just-in-time (JIT) inventory and assumption of 100 percent quality parts. Each associate knows it is his or her job to inspect each part to assure conformance to requirements. Any associate can reject a part. If a manager wants the part used after the associate has rejected it, the burden is on the manager to explain to the associate why it should be used. There is a quality assurance department with a team of associates who will call the suppliers regarding any and every bad part. Every vendor is assigned to one associate, who knows exactly who to call, including home telephones, to provide immediate feedback on any deviation from quality requirements.

STYLE:

As I interviewed managers, I repeatedly asked them how they felt working for, or with, Japanese managers. I wanted to know if there was any resentment toward the Japanese. I could find absolutely none. I could only find the most sincere respect and friendship. There was no feeling of "us Americans" working for "them." The reason for this mutual respect became clear the next morning.

Every morning the 10 or 12 managers of the motorcycle plant meet to review performance, solve problems, and make plans for the day. The Japanese vice-president responsible for the motorcycle operations sat at the end of the table. The meeting was led by a manager who was two levels down. There was a lively discussion about the handling of an "almost-in-time" inventory situation that had almost halted production the previous day. There were three or four Japanese managers and about eight Americans in the meeting. One of the Japanese managers was very vocal about how confusing the situation was and how it should have been handled better. Several others discussed what happened and how it was being resolved today. The vice-president sat quietly through a half hour of discussion, never saying anything until the meeting was coming to a conclusion. Only then did he speak out. He had two points. First, he wanted to thank everyone for their efforts yesterday, rising to meet the challenge presented by their problem. Second, he wanted to stress how important it was to meet another challenge that was coming up within the next week. His tone was calm and reassuring.

These incidents, and dozens of others like them, proved to me that the integration of cultures is working in Marysville. The Americans have adopted the Japanese patience and view things from a long-term perspective. The Japanese have adopted, or at least accepted, the American fun-loving familiarity and creativity.

The style at Honda is different than at other Japanese companies and this may be central to their success and initiative in manufacturing in the United States. The traditional Japanese company places a high value on age and seniority. Honda does not. Mr. Irimajiri is a young man excited by winning races and building racing engines. Mr. Honda has retired because he believes the company should be run by young men. The first principle of Honda management policy is: "Proceed always with ambition and youthfulness." The second is: "Respect sound theory, develop fresh ideas and make the most effective use of time." The third is: "Enjoy your work, and always brighten your working atmosphere."

Honda now employs 6,000 youthful-minded and creative Buckeye associates in Marysville. That number will be raised to over 8,000 as the second auto assembly plant is built nearby. The U.S.-manufactured content of the Honda Accord is now about 60 percent and will be increased to 75 percent. The Accord is more American than some GM, Ford, or Chrysler nameplates with higher imported content.

As I left Marysville, I didn't leave with the feeling that I had visited a "foreign" manufacturer. Rather, I had the feeling that I had visited something new. I had visited a world-embracing company, with a world-embracing philosophy, as much American as Japanese, perhaps the best of both world. I could also think of nothing that Honda was doing, no secret in either principle or practice, which could not be adopted by any company - if its senior managers were knowledgeable, committed, and would "proceed always with youthfulness."

Reconciling Top-Down and Bottom-Up Lean Implementation

by Mr. Jean Fuller,
Work Design, Montreal, Canada

This case study demonstrates how Lean and STS methodologies were both utilized in a plant that built light aircraft. The aim of the change project was to improve downstream on time delivery, product quality, cost effectiveness and employee engagement vis-à-vis their products. After more than seven years, this redesign is still in use. Business objectives and employee engagement goals were more than achieved.

Plant management had initiated an approach to implementing lean/Six Sigma practices using a team model. This was driven top-down. The goal was to certify teams in their utilization of lean tools and concepts as well as implementing team management practices. The project described below provided bottom-up involvement and ownership to designate the milestones with which team management practices would be incorporated into the lean team certification process for all units in this plant.

The contributions of Lean and STS methodologies to this effort can be described as follows:

Characteristics of the STS designed Product Teams that were deployed:

- Accountable for on-time delivery of parts to downstream work teams using direct interface with these teams to determine parts and quality needs
- Daily work plan developed by the team to meet downstream customer needs
- Contribution to the transformation and delivery of parts both within and outside their functional areas of work – multi-skilling for parts quality and delivery

- Contribution to the cost reduction efforts (as per benchmarking/competitiveness needs)
- Regular assessment of employee motivation for intrinsic and extrinsic needs

Contributions of Lean/Six Sigma methodology within this change project:

- Statistical process control of all parts being manufactured
- Identification of parts that have poor performance
- Support and guidance of improvement efforts/projects for designated parts

Background

The organization is a Canadian manufacturing and assembly plant of light aircraft that was built in an economically depressed area in the early 1980's. With government assistance, this plant became very successful and profitable. During its creation, it developed a culture of employee participation as part of the preparation for an STS, team based organisation model that was developed at that time by another consultant. That model was not implemented in1986 because of changes to the aircraft models that were to be produced. However, the dialogue that had been created with employees and managers of all levels was maintained and explains a good part of the plant's success. It achieved production and safety records and has a history of on time delivery that is among the best in the business.

At the time this project took place, this facility employed 2100 employees and produced a variety of commercial models; heavy duty for mining, oil and construction industries as well as a variety of small and medium size aircraft for private owners, surveillance aircraft for police corps, commercial transport and ambulance, to name just a few. Its customers were from all parts of the world. It was renowned for the quality of its products.

This organization was ISO certified with high quality and safety industry standards. Yet it was loosely structured, relying on dialogue with employees through a variety of committees to manage manpower scheduling, training, compensation, employee relations, etc.

The plant was structured around "mini-business units", each with its own support staff - engineering, logistics, scheduling, quality control, etc. This structure had been defined by local managers and it was still in its initial implementation phases at the time this project took place. The centralized support functions were design engineering, IT, Finance, Maintenance, HR and Six-Sigma.

This case study describes a redesign in one of these business units - the composite parts' business unit.

The parent company, owner of this plant, introduced a Six-Sigma Program at the turn of the 21st century.

The Six Sigma program was managed in a top down mode with management and staff employees volunteering to carry out improvement projects in an area of the plant they had selected so as to become "Green or Black Belts." Their project was approved by local and corporate management.

Phase One – Discovery

The manager of the composite materials' business unit understood something was wrong with the structure of his organisation. Efficiencies were tightly managed. The time it took to make parts, the quality issues related to these parts and, naturally, the costs were the main concerns in the management processes being used since his arrival a year prior. His business unit had good performance insofar as these indicators were concerned.

However, he and his management team, which acted as a steering team, constantly struggled with "on time delivery" of parts to downstream customers that used these to build, assemble and test the light aircraft this plant made. On time delivery was only 48%. He and his staff spent countless hours trying to make sense of what was really being produced so as to give accurate dates to downstream customers. Also, they realized that the parts being made spent 90% of their time on shelves (work in progress), waiting to be processed and delivered. Something was very wrong.

At another level, management staff was not utilizing its expertise to the fullest. They were spending too much time, as a team and individually, scheduling and second guessing which parts could be delivered. Also, they were spending a significant amount of their time "chasing" down parts that were on the verge of work stoppages for their downstream customers.

When examining the way a supervisor would personally take responsibility for a part that was a "show stopper" for a downstream customer, they realized that one of the main causes for poor on time delivery was a lack of accountability within their organization for what was being produced. People were accountable for the time and the quality of the parts they made but not for their delivery. But how could they do this given the complexity of the unit's transformation process? Making parts out of composite materials is not a simple task. It requires specialized, costly materials and equipment as well as a high level of expertise from specialists at every step in the process. To minimize this expertise would result in poor quality and an increase in production time and costs. The following is a map of the production process being used as well as downstream customers.

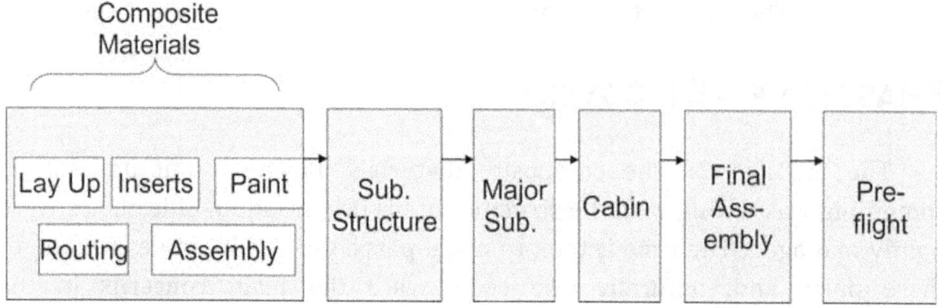

It is at this time that the idea of creating "product teams" began to take shape in the business unit's manager's mind and in dialogue with his steering/management team.

Outside help was then involved. The consultant hired to provide assistance was already working with plant management. He raised the issue that yes, this was a plant where there existed a strong "employee involvement" culture but, he pointed out that this involvement process was mostly focused on topics related to human resource management. At this company, employees had a significant say in establishing and applying policies relative to all issues in the realm of human resources. Only in rare occasions did management have to make a unilateral decision, even in situations where temporary layoffs had to be made. Participation in other areas was more arbitrary and not systematic.

PHASE TWO – THE DREAM: PRODUCT TEAMS

Involvement of employees in developing the dream of teams built around and taking responsibility for the process became the necessary next step. The management team was well aware that the management culture of the business unit was based on efficiencies. People were proud of this despite the fact that product delivery dates and quality were not meeting customer expectations. It became important to take on a different perspective.

Prior to the beginning of this project, the plant management team, including the business unit managers, developed a "future state" vision of employees' and managers' involvement in day-to-day decision making. Using Stafford Beer's "Viable Systems Model", it defined deliverables for employee, staff and management personnel. Beer defines management as being made up of five interdependent systems. For the sake of this project, these five systems were defined as being the processing of pertinent information for decision-making in five different systems:

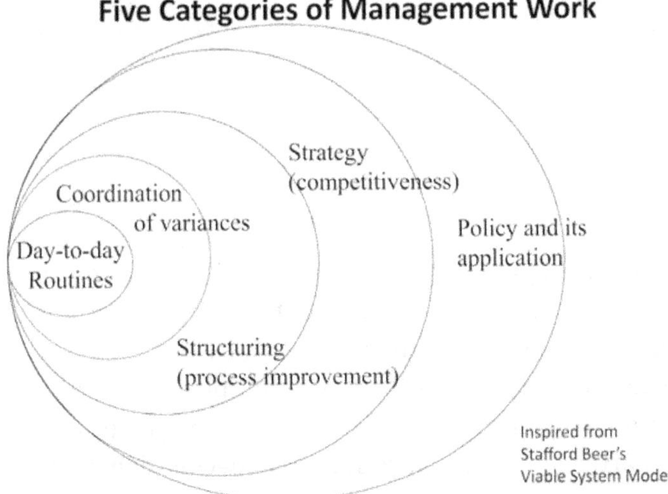

- System one: the execution of day-to-day tasks required by the unit's (team, department, etc.) mission
- System two: the resolution of recurring problems (variances) related to the execution of day-to-day tasks required by the unit's mission
- System three: the structuring of processes (business, transformation, management or otherwise) and roles/contributions of the people involved, concerned or impacted
- System four: the formulation and review of business strategy

- System five: the formulation and application of policy to make these systems work

The Composite Materials' Business Unit management/steering team used this future state vision to create a draft of how product teams could work. It would later ask the pilot/design team to see if this was a relevant idea to implement. This work was carried out by members of the business unit management team. Within this framework, employee participation took on another meaning since it was not limited to human resource management. Within this framework, employees' were recognized for their knowledge the business as it relates to the execution of day-to-day tasks.

Draft Contribution Matrix

	Employees	Supervisors	Manager	Support Team	Six Sigma specialist
Day-to-day execution for deliverables					
Coordination Processes					
Structuring roles and processes					
Strategy formulation and review					
Policy and its application					

The management team, in its steering committee role, decided to involve employees in the "discovery" process. It set up a series of meetings during which they shared the results of their business case as well as their thinking as to the creation of product teams. Given the plant's priorities for aircraft delivery, the product team to be the focus of the experiment was mandated to focus on one particular set of parts for two specific downstream customer teams.

The management team received support from employees' for this new level of thinking as demonstrated by the number of them who volunteered to be part of the pilot project.

The management team created a charter for a pilot team made up of 22 people from five areas of the business unit (assemblers, dispatch, technologist, QC inspector and one supervisor). Three other areas within the business unit were designated as service centres since they contributed to all composite parts made. The pilot team's initial mandate was to put together a team design that would improve on time delivery to at least 75% within three months without reducing quality and nor increasing costs. Members of the pilot team were to remain in the functional areas except for those tasks related to the delivery of their team's parts.

Phase Three – Design

Once recruited, the members of the pilot product team, acting as a design team, went through start up and design activities that included the following:

1. A work system simulation to highlight the differences between a classical organisational model resting on functional silos and on specialized functional jobs (scientific management approach) versus a work system that uses multi-skilled teams.
2. The application of these ideas to the product team they were to experiment. The team developed a matrix model in which they remained in their functional areas but to only work on the parts that were part of the Product Team's charter. In addition, team members were to take on tasks related to product delivery, helping out colleagues in their transformation process, quality checks and the training of Product Team members for multi-skilling.
3. The definition of performance indicators to measure customer satisfaction, quality, costs and employee engagement.
4. The definition of management processes to apply the product team approach – daily, weekly and monthly reviews as well as the progression of employees in their engagement towards team goals and multi-skilling.
5. The multi-skilling needs of their team to reach their goals while ensuring that functional expertise was not diminished.
6. The design team asked the Six Sigma person to support them in the problem areas they identified that were inhibiting on time product delivery, quality and costs.

The design team also defined a plan to meet its pilot project goals within the three month timeframe it was given. This plan included a communication strategy to inform the people impacted of their mandate and of their progress.

PHASE 4 – DEPLOY/DEVELOP

Reaction to the implementation was very positive since it was unusual to see assemblers meeting their downstream customers to discuss their needs. Under the plant's structure, these communications were usually carried out by supervisors or by support team members. The peer to peer relationships introduced by the Pilot Product Team generated a lot of excitement as well as collaboration and encouragement for the members of the Product Team.

The major challenges they encountered were:

- Becoming skilled in an area other than the one the person normally worked in – took more time than expected. Visual instructions were eventually introduced to facilitate the acquisition of new skills.
- Quality inspection became a bottleneck since too few persons were qualified in the three month period
- People complained there were too many meetings and not enough work was being done
- The supervisor's work load was significant at the beginning until team members also took on some the reporting tasks
- Some of the service teams within the business units were not always eager to modify their schedule to meet the pilot product team's needs

It only took a few weeks to reach the 75% on time delivery target. At the end of the 3 month period, the team was achieving more than 80% on time delivery, quality was improved as well as costs reduced.

There was no hesitation to introduce the Product Team concept across the Composite Materials' Business Unit. Downstream customers' needs were the basis for the creation and implementation of other product teams. Over a period of 15 months, the conversion to product teams was made across the Composite Materials Business Unit, including its service teams. On time delivery of parts to downstream customers was no longer a lingering issue to deal with.

And, yes, management staff time chasing parts was greatly reduced.

Centralize or Decentralize; Standardize or Customize

I have placed this discussion in the Appendix because it will only come up in some WSA projects. It is not likely to be relevant to a single manufacturing plant or facility, but it will be highly relevant for any organization that is dispersed, has multiple locations and centralized functions.

The issue is the location of functions, centralized or decentralized; and, whether or not those functions should be customized to local needs or standardized across the organization. For example, should the function of scheduling office visits, home care visits, or laboratory tests for a health care organization that covers a large georgraphic area be centralized in one location or should that be done in local offices? Should the process of scheduling be standardized or should that process be left to the discretion of the local clinics? The answer to these questions will have large ramifications for both the design of work process and for the design of the organization and its social system.

These are not easy questions to answer and they may become among the most important. They may determine both systems and structure. How are these questions decided?

First, let's consider the nature of these questions. They are different ideas and should not be confused, although they are related.

- *Centralization* is doing something, gathering people and tools, in the same place. *Decentralization* is doing those things in different and diverse places.
- *Standardization* is arriving at a best way of doing something and gaining the advantage of that *method*, knowledge, tools, etc., regardless of where it is done. *Customization* is doing things differently based on diverse needs or desires.

To illustrate the distinction you can consider McDonald's. No organization in the world is more decentralized in the activity of preparing the product for the customer and serving the product to the customer. It is done in tens of thousands of small locations worldwide. But, there are some centralized activities. There is a centralized corporate finance system; a centralized corporate training and development process; and centralized quality control and product development. There must be some criteria by which McDonald's decided certain activities were to be centralized and others decentralized.

Now, consider the different topic of standardization versus customization. McDonald's has a relatively standardized menu. You can get the same Big Mac and Egg McMuffin in every location worldwide. They also have a global supply contract with Coca-Cola and other suppliers. Those are standardized. On the other hand, if you go to a McDonald's in China or Japan you will find some local items on the menu that would not sell in Chicago or Atlanta. So, there is some customization of the menu. Also, you can ask them to "hold the pickle and mustard." But, you cannot tell them that you want three beef patties in your Big Mac. So, there is some customization, yet there are clear boundaries on that customization. How was this decided, and does this have anything to do with the design of the architecture of your organization?

What are the Advantages of Each?

	Decentralized	Centralized
Standardized	• Easier to manage things done the same way • Less training cost • When best way found, develop consistency in delivery • Brand recognition and trust in the market • Economies of research and marketing • Leverage investment in software (Example: All fast food, most chain stores, UPS delivery)	• Economies of scale • When large capital investment is required in plant and equipment. • Quick knowledge transfer • Build each one the same for brand reliability (All auto assembly plants, airline hubs, Expedia, Airline Reservations)
Customized	• Give the customer exactly what they want. • Personalized, intimate, customer relationship with customers or clients. • Immediate response to the customer • Quick response to local, diverse, realities. • Better response to complexity. (Local grocer, Build-A-Bear, most small businesses, your doctor, lawyer, etc.)	• Mass customization • Utilizes technology to deliver exactly what the customer wants. • Leverages brand • Economies of scale in contracts, purchasing (Your I-Tunes store, Pandora, Amazon preferences, Facebook, LinkedIn, Match.com)

If you look at the above table you can see that a process may be standardized and centralized; or standardized and decentralized, etc. Each has its advantages and disadvantages. And, you can easily see that one is well suited to certain types of processes. For example, the auto assembly plant requires a huge investment in stamping processes and other equipment. If you tried to decentralize auto assembly to each auto dealer, the price of a car would rise incredibly. Some things are now centralized due to technology. Facebook or I-Tunes are amazingly centralized and customized. The design of the software, the database, and the management of the database are all centralized and standardized. But, the use of the software is in the hands of every user or subscriber who customizes his or her own music library or Facebook page.

A good understanding of the value of each of these four quadrants can lead to significant innovation in business models. Build-A-Bear is an interesting case. If you haven't taken your child or grandchild to Build-A-Bear you have missed an interesting experience. The idea is that the child picks out their own bear (or Hello Kitty), they stuff the insides, pick out and put in a heart, give it a name, get a birth certificate, dress it, etc. You can spend a lot of money accessorizing that little new born! The interesting thing about this model is that it is all based on customer intimacy. What can be more intimate than giving birth to your own child? The child picks out everything. So, there is high customization, and it is decentralized in shopping malls; it is also a centrally planned and managed process. Training, purchasing, pricing, and information systems are all centralized. They have created a very workable mix of the four quadrants.

What are the criteria that should drive decisions about centralization and decentralization; and customization and standardization? Here are a few, and you may think of others that are relevant to your business.

- Customer intimacy: is the process able to respond to the immediate needs of the customer?
- Customer familiarity: a customer may wish to personally know a provider of service that he or she returns to repeatedly.
- Economies of scale: is the cost of equipment required in the process such that it can be duplicated locally or does that argue for centralization?
- Product diversity: does the nature of customer choice require a high diversity of responses? Is customization or "mass-customization" possible to meet that need?

- Brand value and management: In order to build a brand you have to build trust. Does that require standardization, such as standard practices to clean rest rooms in a fast food chain, or standardized coffee?
- Flexible technologies: The Internet has changed many businesses because of the flexibility that allows one to design your own running shoes on the New Balance website, for example. Is there opportunity to employ technology to allow for economical and high levels of customization?

Steps in Hotel Reservations

A good example that combines some elements of each of the four quadrants can be seen in hotel reservations. Here is a simple process map and the steps in the process?

1. Customer decides to call Hilton Hotels for a reservation
2. There is an available and accurate schedule of available rooms at different prices and accommodations.
3. Reservation clerk responds to customer call with statement of availability.
4. Customer agrees to book type and location of room.
5. Reservation is entered in computer.
6. Customer arrives on-site and checks in and requests to be on 1st floor, sunny side, etc.
7. Customer is assigned a specific room.
8. Customer goes to room and doesn't like the odor.
9. Customer requests a change of room.
10. Front desk changes room and customer is happy.
11. Customer spends night in room
12. Customer checks out and clerk offers to make another reservation.
13. Customer agrees to another reservation.
14. Clerk enters next reservation.

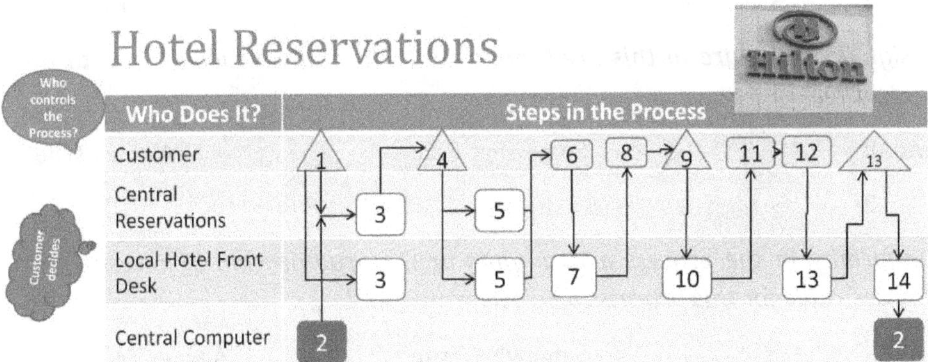

Looking at this process, how are the needs for customer intimacy met? How are economies of scale gained by the hotel chain? Which steps represent standardization and which represent customization?

The following is a survey that asks questions that may determine that a process will be centralized within a corporation, or may be decentralized to business units or locations of that corporation.

When you score this, the higher the score the more it argues for centralization of the process, the lower score argues for decentralization. You will see how this could apply to financial processes, regulatory control, or human resource functions. Designing these always involves decisions and which activities will be centralized and which will be decentralized.

Decision Criteria for Centralization-Decentralization

A. Audit and Regulatory Control: Those accounting and legal functions that represent significant risk or risk avoidance will be centralized. Most chief executives will not, or cannot, fail to provide a significant level of control over the processes of financial management and accounting. Since Sarbanes-Oxley this concern has been heightened by additional legal responsibility on the part of the CEO. When evaluating a process on this criterion it is useful to literally ask "who will go to jail if there is a failure?"

1. For this process, the President or other senior executives will be held accountable by law for a significant failure:

Not At All | Somewhat True | Always True

1 2 3 4 5 6 7 8 9 10

2. A significant failure in this area may result in significant legal costs to the organization.

Not At All Somewhat True Always True

1 2 3 4 5 6 7 8 9 10

3. Uniformity in the process across units of the organization is necessary or highly desirable for this process to be performed well.

Not At All Somewhat True Always True

1 2 3 4 5 6 7 8 9 10

B. Process Integration: Process integration creates shared resources across groups. Process integration may integrate the work processes of different business units. For example, the process of designing a new car integrates work of the chassis, body, engine and other divisions or work units. No one of these units can "own" the design process.

4. Operating units have common customers for this process whose needs may be met concurrently or consecutively.

Not At All Somewhat True Always True

1 2 3 4 5 6 7 8 9 10

5. There are common core technical competencies or methods employed across business units.

Not At All Somewhat True Always True

1 2 3 4 5 6 7 8 9 10

6. Information gathered by one business unit may be used and represent an advantage to another business unit.

Not At All Somewhat True Always True

1 2 3 4 5 6 7 8 9 10

C. Economies of Scale: By combining business units under a corporate umbrella and by the mere increase in volume of production, there may be lower costs if economies of scale are exploited through a shared process. These costs include purchasing supplies but also research and marketing.

7. This process involves the purchase of large quantities of incoming materials that can be purchased for more than one division at the same time gaining price advantage.

Not At All				Somewhat True				Always True	
1	2	3	4	5	6	7	8	9	10

8. The cost of expertise and time spent developing the process (such as research or marketing) can be leveraged across more than one division through a central process.

Not At All				Somewhat True				Always True	
1	2	3	4	5	6	7	8	9	10

9. This process involves high capital costs that can be leveraged, or employed, across organization units.

Not At All				Somewhat True				Always True	
1	2	3	4	5	6	7	8	9	10

D. Shared Human Capital: Organizations may centralize functions or a process based on the desirability of sharing and developing managerial or technical competence. Competence may be either technical or managerial. Either technical or managerial competence may be sufficiently important that the process of developing competence and allocating or assigning that competence across units represents a significant advantage. Managerial competence may be better developed across divisions so that managers have an opportunity to share experience, tools, models, and people. General Electric, for example, has worked very hard at the development, sharing, and leveraging of managerial competence.

10. This process requires human competencies that are not required full time within a business unit, but which may be employed across units.

Not At All				Somewhat True				Always True	
1	2	3	4	5	6	7	8	9	10

11. The competence required for this process is not required for the core work processes that serve the customers of business units. (For example, the core work process of an academic department is teaching and research in the academic field. The skill of administering health care benefits to faculty members is not related to the core work of the department.)

Not At All Somewhat True Always True

1 2 3 4 5 6 7 8 9 10

12. The development of individuals with these competencies can benefit all or many of the business units and their development will be enhanced by merging them within one unit where they may share practices and skills.

Not At All Somewhat True Always True

1 2 3 4 5 6 7 8 9 10

E. Speed and Responsiveness of Decision-making: A primary reason for the decentralization of a decision process is the need to serve customers in unique ways and to respond quickly to customer demands. The most extreme example of this may be the emergency room of a hospital where you would not centralize the decision to use x-rays, for example, because that decision must be made within minutes or seconds to save a patient's life, and requires on-site expertise. Regional retail stores in a chain will have decentralized authority to display items that may have regional appeal. (Please note that the scale is reversed in the following three questions. Unlike the prior items, the higher the number, the less true the statement.)

13. This process directly impacts customers of the core work of the individual operating units who require that decisions be made rapidly.

Always True Somewhat True Not At All

1 2 3 4 5 6 7 8 9 10

14. The customers of this process have very different needs or preferences that can only be determined at the lowest organizational level.

Always True Somewhat True Not At All

1 2 3 4 5 6 7 8 9 10

15. The expertise required to make effective decisions must be very close to the end use customer.

Always True Somewhat True Not At All

1 2 3 4 5 6 7 8 9 10

Add the scores for each criterion. Now discuss with your team how these scores argue for either centralizing or decentralizing that process. Discuss the implications for both the design of the work process and the social system.

GLOSSARY

- **5S:** 5S is a common tool and component of a lean workplace. The Five S program focuses on having visual order, organization, cleanliness and standardization. The results you can expect from a Five S program are: improved profitability, efficiency, service and safety. The 5S's are Sort, Set in order, Shine, Standardize, and Sustain.
- **5 Why's:** The 5 Why's is a simple problem-solving technique that helps you to get to the root of a problem quickly. Made popular in the 1970s by the Toyota Production System, the 5 Whys strategy involves looking at any problem and asking: "Why?" and "What caused this problem?"
- **A3:** An A3 is literally a size of paper (297 × 420 mm). However, it has become popular in lean management as a simple and structured form of problem-solving that can fit on or be displayed on one A3 sized paper.
- **A4:** An A4 is again a size of paper. However, it has become known for an even simpler problem-solving process than an A3. It is a one sheet PDCA cycle problem-solving tool. (see PDCA)
- **A-B-C Model:** This is a model for changing behavior, whether at work or in any setting. It stands for Antecedents, Behavior and Consequences. Doing an ABC analysis is a way of analyzing why someone may be behaving in a given way and what can be done to change that behavior.
- **Action Planning**: After deciding on a solution to a problem, a team should develop an action plan that clearly states what steps are going to be taken to implement a solution; who is going to do them; and, when are they going to be done by. Action plans are generally reviewed at each team meeting.
- **Affinity Diagram:** An affinity diagram is a component of brainstorming in which participants write ideas down on Post-it-Notes, then put them on a wall, and then silently organize them into like blocks of notes.
- **Antecedents:** A stimulus that precedes a behavior and acts as a stimulus or cue for that behavior to occur.

- **Balanced Scorecard:** A team or management scorecard that includes four types of measures: Financial, learning and development, customer satisfaction and process measures. This concept was developed and promoted in a book by Kaplan and Norton.
- **Behavior Analysis:** The application of behavioral psychology to behavior in a natural setting. Also referred to as *behavior management* or *performance management.*
- **Behavior Management:** A term used to describe the application of behavior analysis or behavior modification in the work place. It generally involves seeking to employ positive reinforcement to increase the strength and learning of desired behavior.
- **Behavioral psychology:** That school of psychology developed by B.F. Skinner and others that states that behavior is learned a function of the contingencies of reinforcement in the environment. Behavioral psychology is based on scientific or the experimental analysis of behavior in which antecedent stimuli and consequences to behavior are controlled and modified and the resulting changes in rate of behavior are monitored.
- **Brainstorming:** Brainstorming is one component of both problem-solving and group decision-making. It is a way to bring out the creativity of the group by focusing on generating ideas while not judging them. There are many methods of brainstorming but they all include the element of suspending judgment, allowing, even encouraging, wild and crazy ideas so that each idea may stimulate another.
- **Cause and Effect:** A cause and effect diagram is also known as a fishbone diagram because it looks something like the skeleton of a fish. At the backbone of the diagram is the definition of a problem. Then each of the major parts of the skeleton are labeled (and this is only one way of many) People, Process, Materials, Equipment, Information. Then you use this to brainstorm possible causes under each of these categories.
- **CEDAC:** Cause and Effect Diagrams with the Addition of Cards. This is simply a very large cause and effect diagram placed on a wall in a prominent place, such as a hallway where employees pass by, and there are two color cards, one for problems and the other for solutions. Employees are encouraged to add problem or solution cards as they think of them. This creates an on-going brainstorming process.

- **Command Decisions:** Command decisions are those made by one individual. This is generally considered most efficient when time is a priority and/or the one individual has superior expertise. Command decision is considered the traditional military model of decision-making and battlefield conditions are the environment where this is most appropriate.
- **Consensus Decisions:** Consensus decisions are those decisions that are owned by an entire group and the entire group agrees on a decision after giving everyone an opportunity to speak and be heard respectfully. Consensus decision-making assumes that the formal leader is willing to delegate the decision authority to the group. Consensus decisions are more time consuming but result in greater commitment from the group.
- **Consultative Decisions:** Consultative decisions are those in which one individual owns and controls the decision, but does not make it alone. Rather the individual consults with those who have knowledge, who care, or who must act to implement the decision.
- **Continuous Improvement:** Continuous improvement is one of the fundamental ideas of lean management. It is based on the simple idea that every process can always be improved in some increment. It is a process in which all employees engaged in the work are encouraged to participate in thinking about better ways to do things, conducting experiments, and agreeing on improved standard work.
- **Cycle Time:** A cycle time is the time from the beginning to the end of a work process. There are generally two types of cycle time: CT = The actual Cycle Time from beginning to end, and VCT=Value-adding Cycle Time. In other words, if you look at your daily work process, that may be eight hours, how much of that time is actually adding value to your customers? It is usually a fraction of the actual time. In lean terms, the remaining time is considered "waste."
- **Debate:** Debate is a form of conversation in which two or more parties have predetermined positions on a matter and are attempting to convince others that they are correct and the others are wrong. The participants are not willing to learn from each other or change their positions.
- **Deliberations:** Most knowledge work involves a pattern of communication between knowledgeable individuals who consider diverse points of view on a matter and jointly arrive at a conclusion or decision.

- **Deliberation Analysis:** The analysis of the pattern of communication that leads to a deliberate conclusion and usually involves examining both the participation and the quality of contributions to the deliberations.
- **Design Team:** A team appointed by a steering team and given the responsibility to analyze the current state of the technical, social and economic system and redesign those systems consistent with the guidance in the charter. Design teams typically include both frontline workers, managers and functional staff who support the area being redesigned.
- **Dialogue:** Dialogue is the art of thinking together rather than thinking alone. It is often considered the opposite of debate, a conversation in which all parties are seeking to learn, to discover truth together.
- **DIMPABAC:** This is an acronym representing one problem-solving model. ***Define*** the problem to be solved; ***Inquire*** with all those who have facts regarding the problem to gain different understanding and insight; ***Measure*** actual performance on the problem; ***Principles*** should be defined that are important to understanding this problem and its solution; ***Analyze*** the data and causes of the problem; ***Brainstorm*** solutions to the problem; Agree to ***Act*** on a solution; ***Control*** and standardize the process and evaluate results.
- **Empathy:** Empathy is the capacity to recognize and, to some extent, share feelings (such as sadness or happiness) that are being experienced by another. Empathy is one of the effective listening skills that enables another person to express their thoughts and feelings.
- **Facilitation:** Facilitation is the skill or art of helping others participate in group problem-solving or decision-making. There are a set of skills that are components of effective facilitation and these include clarifying topics, active listening, conflict resolution, and helping a group reach and clarify a decision.
- **Feedback:** Feedback is information on performance that is "fed back" to the group or individual in control of that performance. Feedback is not necessarily positive or negative, but may simply be information on performance. Feedback is the most essential element of all systems of human performance.
- **Fishbone Diagrams:** See cause and effect diagrams.

- **Four-to-One:** The practice of recognizing four desirable behaviors to every one negative. Based on the research of Dr. Ogden Lindsley who found that the optimum rate of positive to negative in classrooms was 3.57 to 1.
- **Gemba:** Gemba is a Japanese word meaning "the real place where work gets done." It refers to the place where value is created in a work system. Being "on-the-spot" is another term meaning being where the work gets done. This is an important concept in lean management and it expresses the value of managers "going and seeing" what is really happening where the work is being done.
- **Gemba Walk:** The Gemba walk is simply that act of managers talking a walk around the work place and observing, learning, from those doing the work. In manufacturing it is recommended that plant managers take frequent Gemba walks to be in touch with the real work.
- **Kaizen:** Kaizen is the Japanese word for continuous improvement. It is one of the core philosophies and practices of lean management. Kaizen is intended to be practiced by all employees, at every level, engaged in every work process in the organization.
- **Kaizen Event:** A kaizen event is an intensified and short effort to make a major improvement in a process. It generally involves a cross-functional team of employees who work for a period, such as a week, studying a process to solve a problem and make a recommendation at the end of that period.
- **Knowledge Work:** Work that does not involve producing a tangible product.
- **Leader Standard Work:** Leader standard work (LSW) is a process by which standard work, activities that are to be done daily, weekly or monthly, are defined by or for a manager. LSW involves the regular review of the completion and lessons learned from these activities by the manager at the next level above.
- **Lean Management:** Lean management is the set of management and work practices derived from the Toyota Production System (TPS). These include the elimination of waste, continuous improvement, and involvement of all employees in improvement activities. Lean and TPS are not a static set of practices, but are continually evolving as lessons are learned from application in different settings such as health care.

- **Lean Process:** A lean process is one in which every step adds value, speed through the process is optimized, there are no interruptions or re-work, and those who work in the process seek continuous improvement.
- **Muda:** The Japanese term for waste. See 7 forms of waste.
- **PDCA Cycle:** The PDCA (Plan, Do, Check and Act) cycle of problem-solving is also known as the Schewhart Cycle after Walter Schewhart a pioneer in the quality field. During the quality movement it was adopted as a common problem-solving model at many companies. The PDCA cycle is best used for relatively simple problems, although you can place many different methods or steps within these four major steps.
- **PDSA:** This is essentially the same as the PDCA cycle of problem-solving: Plan, Do, Study, Act. This is the term used at ThedaCare.
- **Performance Analysis:** A model of problem-solving human behavior. It is based on the work of Robert Mager and Peter Pipe who suggested that we ask "Is the problem *a can't* do, or a *won't do* problem." In other words, does the individual have the required skill or knowledge, or is it a motivation problem.
- **Performance Management:** This term has two different usages. One is another term to describe behavior management or applied behavior analysis in the work setting. A second describes the process of individual performance appraisal and the development of periodic personal improvement plans, generally negotiated between an employee and his or her manager.
- **Positive Reinforcement:** In behavioral psychology or applied behavior analysis positive reinforcement is the presentation of a stimulus following a behavior that results in a subsequent increase in the rate of that behavior.
- **Process:** A process is a set of related activities that together produce a desired outcome. All processes have both input and output. The process transforms input to a value-adding output. Teams are generally organized around, and take responsibility for, a defined process.
- **Process Management Teams:** A team that owns and takes responsibility for the continuous improvement of a defined process.
- **Process Maps:** A visual display of a process that illustrates each step in a process and their chronological relationship to one another. It describes

the flow of the process. Process mapping allows a team to define cycle times, identify waste and variances in the process.

- **Process Measures:** Measures of process performance. These measures may be derived from within the process or at the end of a process. For example, if you are cooking a turkey dinner (a process) you may take a measure of the temperature of the meat while it is cooking (a measure within the process), and you may measure the satisfaction of the guests when they are finished eating the turkey (end of process measure).
- **Reflective Listening:** Also known as rephrasing or active listening. Reflective listening is somewhat like holding up a mirror, a reflection, of what you think another person meant to say. For example, "In other words I hear you saying that you enjoy doing that job." This gives the other person the opportunity to say "Well, no, that isn't really what I meant." Or, "Yes, that's right." The other person may clarify and will feel that he or she has genuinely been heard.
- **Relationship Maps:** A process or value-stream map that has horizontal lines indicating the activities of each player in the process. It demonstrates who does what, in what sequence, indicating the relationships between people in regard to that work process.
- **Scorecards**: A score card is an agreed upon set of metrics that reflect the performance of a team. See "balanced scorecard." Scorecards are best visually displayed and reviewed regularly.
- **Self-Directed Teams:** Also known as autonomous or semi-autonomous teams, self-directed teams take responsibility for managing a process and continuously improving that process. While no team is ultimately "self-managed," the process of self-directed teams seeks to maximize the responsibility and maturity of a team to manage performance. Continuous Improvement is a self-directed team process.
- **Shaping Behavior:** Shaping is a concept of behavior analysis. Shaping is the successive reinforcement of approximations to a terminal goal set of responses or skill. In other words, when your child is first learning to play the piano, you praise (reinforce) small improvements and effort, rather than waiting for the ultimate performance.
- **SIPOC:** An acronym that stands for Supplier, Input, Process, Output and Customer. This describes the process flow through a team or organization and is a fundamental tool of lean and process improvement.

- **Six-Sigma:** An improvement process first developed at Motorola and an extension of the total quality movement. It relies heavily on statistical methods and has been used predominantly in manufacturing. A six sigma process is one in which 99.99966% of the products manufactured are statistically expected to be free of defects (3.4 defects per million).
- **SMED:** Single Minute Exchange of Dies. This is a component of lean manufacturing and was one of the early efforts to eliminate waste from the core work process in automotive or other metal manufacturing.
- **Socio-Technical Systems (STS):** A process developed, originally at the Tavistock Institute in Great Britain by Fred Emery and Eric Trist to improve both the productivity of the work system while at the same time improving the social system. The theory of STS is that there is one whole-system, comprised of both social and technical components that are interdependent. Failing to change one element sub-optimizes any change effort.
- **Special Cause:** Dr. W. Edwards Deming described the statistical evidence of a process *in control* in which all of the causes of variation are within three standard deviations of the mean. The cause of variation is common to the system and can only be improved by changing the system itself.
- **Standard Work:** A set of activities that have been agreed to be the best way to perform any work activity. Standard work is the best way we know now to perform a work process. However, continuous improvement will find better ways that will then become standard work.
- **Statistical Variation:** A set of statistical recording of performance that define a mean of that set and the variations around that mean.
- **Steering Team:** The team that has the authority to appoint a design team and approve its design. This is typically the senior management team of the organization that is being designed or redesigned.
- **Subject Matter Experts**: (SME's) May be permanent or temporary members of a team who are assigned or recognized to possess expertise in some function or knowledge area that contributes to the performance of the team.
- **Team Charter:** A document that defines a team's purpose, its processes, its customers and the principles by which it will function.
- **TQM:** Total Quality Management, a set of practices that involves a focus on the requirements of customers (or customers), the use of statistical

measures of quality performance, teams improving quality and customer service at every level of the organization.

- **Value Stream Mapping:** Mapping the work flow, or processes, in a manner that identifies the points where value is added and non-value-adding activities, or waste.
- **Variances or Variation:** A variance may be described statistically, or it may simply be something that deviates or varies from how things should be done in order to meet customer requirements. A variance is a problem.
- **Waste:** Any activity that does not directly add value to the product or service delivered to a customer. Waste (*Muda* in Japanese) is the use of any material or resource beyond what the customer requires and is willing to pay for. Shigeo Shingo identified "Seven" forms of waste (Plus one – The eighth waste, under-utilization of people) These 7 forms of waste are 1) Over production, 2) Inventory, 3) Motion, 4) Waiting, 5) Transportation, 6) Over-processing, 7) Scrap or rework.
- **Whole-System Architecture (WSA):** Another term used for socio-technical systems design in which all elements of an organization's systems are examined together to assess how they enhance or reduce the quality of product or service to customers or customers.

INDEX

About the Author

For the past forty years Lawrence M. Miller has worked to improve the performance of organizations and the skills of their leaders. His expertise is derived from hands on experience creating change in the culture of many dozens of organizations.

He began his work in North Carolina prisons after recognizing that the system in the organization had exactly the opposite of its intended effect - increasing, rather than decreasing, dysfunctional behavior. For four years he worked to redesign the prison system by establishing the first free-economy behind prison walls, where each inmate had to pay rent, maintain a checking account, and pay for everything he desired. This was one of the first applications of *behavior analys*is in the correctional setting.

He has been consulting, writing and speaking about business organization and culture since 1973. He and his firm were one of the early proponents of team-based management and worked with many customers from the senior executive team to include every level and every employee in the organization. Mr. Miller personally coaches the senior management team of many of his customers.

Among his consulting customers have been Allina Health Systems, HomeCare, 3M, Corning, Shell Oil Company, Amoco and Texaco, Shell Chemicals, Bacardi, Air Canada, Eastman Chemicals, Xerox, Harris Corporation, McDonald's, Merck and Upjohn Pharmaceuticals, United Technologies, American Express, and Metropolitan Life.

His website is www.ManagementMeditations.com. His email is LMMiller@lmmiller.com.

Other Current Publications

- *Barbarians to Bureaucrats: Corporate Life Cycle Strategies;* Clarkson Potter (Crown Books), 1989.
- *Lean Culture – The Leader's Guide; L. M. Miller Consulting, 2011*
- *HealthCare Lean – The Team Guide to Continuous Improvement,* Miller Management Press, LLC, 2012.

- *The Team Guide to Continuous Improvement,* Miller Management Press, LLC, 2013.

While *Getting to Lean* is about transformational change, the two team guides are guides to continuous improvement. They cover the same material - one for healthcare organizations and the other for all organizations -

SERVICES

CONSULTING

Mr. Miller works with his clients on sustainable culture change and lean implementation. He assists with both more systemic change, Whole-System Architecture, and with continuous improvement. He works with internal coaches or change agents to prepare and assist them as they coach teams throughout the organization. He also directly coaches the senior leadership teams of his customers.

EXECUTIVE COACHING

Senior managers often can benefit most from one-on-one private coaching and feedback. Mr. Miller has coached senior executives at major corporations such as Honeywell, American Express, Shell and others. This coaching is most often a component of a larger effort to improve the culture of the organization.

Training and Training Materials

Mr. Miller provides seminars on Transformational Change Management for regional groups or associations and to internal company groups. He also provides training to internal coaches and senior managers in the process of *Continuous Improvement* and Lean Culture. His Continuous Improvement workbook is accompanied by a complete set of PowerPoint presentation and teaching notes.

Speaking Engagements & Workshops

Mr. Miller has been a popular speaker at hundreds of company and association conferences. He speaks on lean culture, change management and corporate life-cycles and leadership based on his Barbarians to Bureaucrats book. He also leads leadership workshops to initiate lean culture change.

www.ingramcontent.com/pod-product-compliance
Lightning Source LLC
Chambersburg PA
CBHW080713220326
41598CB00033B/5409